WHERE AMERICA STANDS 1996

WHERE AMERICA STANDS 1996

MICHAEL GOLAY
AND
CARL ROLLYSON

FOREWORD BY EVERETT CARLL LADD, PRESIDENT, THE ROPER CENTER
FOR PUBLIC OPINION RESEARCH, UNIVERSITY OF CONNECTICUT

INTRODUCTION BY FRANK NEWPORT,
EDITOR-IN-CHIEF, THE GALLUP POLL

A NEW ENGLAND PUBLISHING
ASSOCIATES BOOK

John Wiley & Sons, Inc.
New York • Chichester • Brisbane • Toronto • Singapore

NEW ENGLAND
PUBLISHING
ASSOCIATES

Produced by New England Publishing Associates, Inc.
Editor: Edward W. Knappman
Illustration and Design: Phanyada Sriranpong
Copyediting: Toni Rachiele
Indexing: Roberta Buland
Editorial Administration: David Voytek

Library of Congress Cataloging-in-Publication Data

Golay, Michael
    Where America Stands 1996 / Michael Golay and Carl Rollyson ;
foreword by Everett Carll Ladd : introduction by Frank Newport.
        p. cm.
    "A New England Publishing Associates book."
    Includes index.
    ISBN 0-471-14526-2 (pbk. : alk. paper)
    1. Public opinion—United States.   I. Rollyson, Carl.   II. Title.
HN90.P8G63   1996
303.3'8'0973—dc20   96-5486

Printed in the United States of America

10 9 8 7 6 5 4 3 2 1

CONTENTS

CONTENTS

FOREWORD

by Everett Carll Ladd
President, the Roper Center for
Public Opinion Research
University of Connecticut

Where *America Stands 1996* should be on the bookshelf or on the coffee table of every politically interested citizen this election year. Authors Michael Golay and Carl Rollyson, together with Frank Newport and his colleagues at Gallup, have given us a readable and informative guide to the issues of the 1996 campaign.

Democratic theory builds on two key assumptions. The first holds that the populace at large has the capability to act as citizens—that is, as a public that decides or sets direction for the nation on the big questions of the day. No question is bigger than the question of which individuals and political party will occupy the White House and hold a majority in Congress. The second key assumption is that those charged with formal governmental responsibilities should and will pay close and respectful attention to what the people are saying they want done. This doesn't mean that presidents, governors, and legislators should do no more than raise moistened fingers into the air of public opinion and then follow the prevailing breeze. It does mean that our democratic idea requires

FOREWORD

that the populace really be sovereign. *Its* wishes, not those of office holders or interest groups, must be controlling.

George H. Gallup, who founded the Gallup Organization in 1935, believed deeply that the American public was up to the tasks democratic theory set for it. Though it is not omnicompetent—able to handle everything in the governing process—it is mature and responsible and fully able to chart the nation's course. Throughout thirty years of study of what the people are saying and how they are saying it, I've stayed with the same conclusion. The public's voice is loud and clear and coherent. The Gallup poll data brought together in this volume provide policymakers and individual citizens alike with a reliable summary of what citizens at large have been saying on key issues, from the proper role of the federal government to crime and gun control.

This insight into the public's thinking and priorities is especially timely, because over the past two decades or so Americans have been signaling a big change in national direction. This "philosophical" realignment is now very far advanced, and its outlines are clear. We see them boldly outlined in the Gallup poll findings.

Storrs, Connecticut
February 1996

How We Know
Where America Stands

by
Frank Newport
Editor-in-Chief, The Gallup Poll

here America Stands views the major issues in America through the wide-angle lens of public opinion within a traditional, "events of the year" context. The writers and editors of this book have used Gallup public opinion polls to go "outside the Beltway" to understand what issues are important to the American people, where they stand on those issues, and what they want our elected leaders to do about them.

The availability of national polls to use in this fashion is a relatively recent phenomenon. It was only in the mid-1930s that George Gallup and others institutionalized the idea of using random-sample polling to create a direct link between the citizens of a democracy and its policymakers. Newly developed random-sampling techniques provided the functional

equivalent of interviewing every adult resident of the country. The polls established the basis for a true direct democracy, with the voices of the people being heard on a continuous basis. Thus the dream of a democracy run directly by its people had come closer to reality.

At the same time, as polls have increased in both number and accuracy, they have become an exceptionally rich and useful mine of historical information that helps us understand and interpret events that have already occurred. As journalists and historians look back on a year or an epoch and try to interpret what happened, they have traditionally relied on official documents, laws, public pronouncements, public rallies, events, and other so-called public occurrences. Polling provides a view of history from the ground up, through the minds of the individuals who—taken together—constitute the entire society. The immense power of public opinion polling lies in our ability to identify and interview a cross section of the population that very precisely mirrors the demographic and ideological composition of the whole country, permitting the pollster to know that within a small margin of error the same pattern of opinion would have resulted had he or she traveled to every home, farm, apartment, and nook and cranny of America and interviewed each and every one of its citizens.

In short, public opinion polling in theory provides a systematic and comprehensive mechanism for assessing how the totality of a society's people feel about issues, policies, and their lives.

The use of polls to assess the political climate—as is done in this book—combines the reportorial talents of a huge number of people who are figuratively deputized as "quasi journalists." When pollsters do their jobs correctly, they pick up on and collectively put together the observations of a large number of observers of society—observers who are living in every type of setting and are peeking into every aspect of American society.

Thus, for example, when Gallup asks a question about how satisfied respondents are with the way things are going in the United States, the answers do not simply reflect the views of a journalist who sits in Washington or who tours the country interviewing people in gas stations and diners. Rather, collected together and tabulated, the responses reflect the perceptions of over a thousand Americans sprinkled across the country, who are taking in what they see from their own unique but representative vantage points.

Polls measure perceptions, and when it comes to human behavior, particularly political behavior, perceptions can be in a sense more real than facts. Take, for example, the issue of crime,

which is explored in Chapter 6 of this book. Various state and federal agencies may report—after systematically collecting data on crimes, arrests, and convictions—that, *factually* the crime rate has declined. But if polling shows that most Americans perceive that crime is on the rise, that perception too is a *fact*. Indeed, it is *reality* for the public, and that reality can be a more important fact to politicians than reams of statistics collected by a government agency "proving" that crime rates are down. Americans' views on their perceived safety and the perceived effectiveness of the criminal justice system remain the best predictors of the public's ultimate awareness of crime and its willingness to do something about it.

Not everyone agrees with the proliferation of the use of polls, of course. As marvelous a tool as public opinion polls can be, they have always been subject to criticism. Some observers, beginning with the editors of the *Literary Digest* in the 1930s, have refused to believe that as few as a thousand interviews could represent the attitudes and opinions of hundreds of millions of people. Others question not so much the accuracy of the polling itself as the wisdom of relying on the attitudes of the common people. These critics say that the opinions of all of the people in a country, even if it is possible to measure them or represent them with polls, do not matter or are not useful be-

cause many of these people are "rationally ig-
norant": they do not follow national events, do
not think about the issues of the day, and in general do not have much to say about the world
around them. Still other critics focus on more
"micro" faults of polling—the influence that the
wording of questions and the order of questions
can have on responses, the sometimes conflicting results of independent polls on the same top-
ics, and the occasional failure of a poll or polls
to predict an election outcome accurately.

All these concerns, while raising important and complex issues, have been addressed
and responded to. Polling certainly has its limi-
tations, to some degree based on the inability of
people to always be able to accurately assess
their own behavior or motivations. But when
polling is used correctly in as scientific a method
as possible, it opens up intriguing, fascinating,
and deeply illuminating ways of understand-
ing human social and political behavior.

As will be seen in the pages that follow,
the country entered the 1996 election year focused on a wide variety of issues, from the battle
over a balanced budget in Washington and intervention by U.S. government troops in the
Bosnian situation to school prayer and the racial divide underscored by the murder trial of
O.J. Simpson. The review of Gallup polling in
Where America Stands reveals a finely textured
view of these issues and events. Polling data

show that the public almost immediately felt that O.J. Simpson was not telling the truth and was in fact guilty of the murders of which he was accused and that blacks and whites had significant differences over the issue of Simpson's guilt. The polls found a very wary public on the topic of United States involvement in Bosnia and the prospect of casualties, but also a public willing to go along with the use of U.S. troops if it was emphasized that we were contributing troops to an international peacekeeping force and that the president had the power to commit our armed forces as commander-in-chief. The polling showed that—despite initial support for the Republican idea of reducing the size of the federal government and for a constitutional amendment that would ensure a balancing of the budget—the public became sensitive to the implications of deep cuts in popular programs, and in particular, soured on the public persona of House Majority Leader Newt Gingrich and projected reductions in the rate of growth of Medicare. In all of these instances, the polling showed how these events played out in the minds of Mr. and Ms. America and ultimately provided a leading indicator of the impact of the events on the nation's long-term social and political structure.

This book is a very useful start toward a merger of traditional reporting with reporting based on the perspective of the people as mea-

sured in polls. The factual background—legislation, election results, and government statistics—for each of the issues covered has been
provided to give context for how these issues
and events were perceived by the country's citizens. In this year's election, the *perceived* reality
will shape the campaigns and determine the outcome far more than the background facts. In
both the long and the short term, it is the public
perception of events and issues that steers the
democratic ship of state into the future.

The 1996 Election-Year Campaign: Background and Prognostication

by
Frank Newport, David W. Moore,
and Lydia Saad
Editors, The Gallup Poll

The 1994 congressional election may well have signaled a major turning point in American political history, as significant and pervasive in its impact as was the New Deal six decades earlier. It is not just that Republicans won both houses of Congress for the first time since the Eisenhower administration, in the 1950s, but also that the new Congress brought with it an agenda to curtail the role of government in major areas of domestic policy, an agenda that—at least in the short run—has dominated national politics.

The *rhetoric* of downsizing government has been with us at least since Ronald Reagan's

Favorability Toward Parties

Values represent the percentage of respondents who rated each party favorably.

	December 1993		November 1994		Net Swing to Republican
	Republican	**Democrat**	**Republican**	**Democrat**	
Total	72	68	70	55	+11
Gender					
Male	74	67	71	53	+11
Female	70	68	69	56	+11
Race					
White	73	65	73	50	+15
Nonwhite	67	88	48	80	−11
Age					
18–29	82	70	70	60	− 2
30–49	75	67	72	51	+13
50–64	67	66	66	54	+11
65+	60	68	67	58	+17
Region					
East	69	74	68	58	+16
Midwest	72	66	69	60	+ 3
South	75	67	69	50	+11
West	73	63	72	52	+10
Party					
Republican	93	43	97	27	+20
Independent	71	65	68	59	+ 3
Democrat	55	92	37	84	−10
Ideology					
Conservative	80	57	81	35	+23
Moderate	68	75	69	63	+13
Liberal	65	78	45	80	−22

Source: The Gallup Poll

presidency, a period that many people at the time characterized as the "Reagan Revolution," but in reality the size of government continued to increase and the federal budget deficits grew at even faster rates than before. Portraying himself as a "new" Democrat in the 1992 presidential election campaign, candidate Bill Clinton also promised a downsized government, with a middle-class tax cut and significant reductions in the budget deficit. His first major budget effort did, in fact, result in reducing the size of the deficit (although the promised tax cut was not included), but even he acknowledged the deficit would resume its climb unless health care costs were contained. And for the major part of 1994, the national debate was over a new health care program that would have *expanded*, not contracted, the role of government. Because of the popularity of the health care reform effort, even most congressional Republicans at that time felt obligated to pay lip service to some kind of health care reform, although one that would have involved far less government intervention.

Then came the historic 1994 congressional election, with Republicans capturing both the House and the Senate. The Republicans had won a majority of the Senate in 1980 and retained control for the next six years, but not since the early 1950s had the Republicans controlled the House. It had seemed as though Democrats had a "lock" on the House that could not be broken—

despite the success of Republicans in occupying the presidency for twenty of the past twenty-eight years. But in 1994, under the leadership of then House Minority Whip Newt Gingrich, many of the Republicans running for the House loosely coordinated their campaign message under the rubric of the Contract with America, a statement of goals and specific legislative items they promised to enact if elected. The polls showed that few Americans had explicitly heard of the Contract, but the central message of Republicans—that they would cut back on government programs—did seem to resonate with the voters. In a relatively low-turnout election, where less than four in ten eligible voters showed up at the polls, those who did participate were decidedly more in tune with the Republican agenda for a downsized government than were those who did not vote.

Once in control of Congress, the Republican leadership used the Contract with America as an operational guide for their legislative agenda. Suddenly, the debate in Washington had shifted one hundred eighty degrees—from *expansion* of government (in considering Clinton's new health care program) to *reduction* of government. Until the Republican congressional victory, President Clinton had not presented Congress with a plan that would lead to a balanced budget, but under pressure from congressional Republicans, he eventually did present such a plan, and along with it major cuts in entitlement programs and the most significant curtailment of the welfare program since the New Deal.

The public reacted to the Republican victory with some degree of skepticism. Most Americans supported the major items of the Contract with America and initially indicated greater confidence in the newly elected Republicans in Congress than in the president. But they were somewhat divided on whether the Republicans could accomplish what they promised, and even when major changes were being made, the public did not always acknowledge it. Within six months, the "honeymoon" period was over. Although the Republicans were still viewed more favorably than before the election, they had lost their favorable edge over Clinton and the Democrats. By the end of the year, the debate over how much to cut the budget initially seemed to be hurting the Republicans more than the Democrats, but then in January—after the extended partial shutdown of the federal government—voters seemed upset as much with Clinton and the Democrats as with the Republicans. As the 1996 election year began, it was anybody's guess as to which party the voters would eventually choose to provide them a president and a majority in Congress.

To understand where public opinion was at the beginning of 1996, it is useful to examine four areas:

1. President Clinton's approval rating over the term of his presidency, to see how it compares with that of other presidents at comparable points in their presidencies;

2. Public opinion just before and after the Republican election victory of 1994, to see not only how much opinion affected the election but also how the election in turn affected opinion;

3. The public's level of support for the Contract with America, and the shift in public opinion during the budget confrontation between the Congress and the President; and

4. The standoff between the two parties as the 1996 election year began.

The Popularity of the President

After his first year in office, President Clinton was widely perceived as one of the most unpopular presidents in recent times. There is some truth to that perception, but some distortion as well. Whatever his standing among the public after the first year, by the beginning of the 1996 election year Clinton's popularity was about in the middle range among recent presidents.

One way to measure popularity is the size of the president's electoral victory. With just 43 percent of the popular vote, Clinton would indeed have to be categorized as the least popular president in recent times. Not since Richard

Nixon's razor-thin victory over Hubert Humphrey in 1968 had a candidate won the presidency with such a small percentage of the popular vote. But both Nixon and Clinton faced significant opposition from an independent or third-party candidate as well as from the candidate of the other major party. George Wallace drew substantial support in 1968 (more than 13 percent of the vote), as did Ross Perot in 1992 (19 percent of the vote), leaving the victor with a plurality—not a majority—of the final vote. Those examples illustrate the general rule that the more major candidates there are in an election, the lower the winning vote total will be. The percentage of the popular vote received by a president against two other candidates does not tell us what percentage he would have received with only one other candidate. With three major candidates in an election, it is difficult for even a popular candidate to win a majority of the vote.

Another measure of a president's popularity is based on a polling question first asked of the general public by George Gallup over five decades ago: Whether people approve or disapprove of the way the president is handling his job. The trend shown by approval ratings can be compared with those of previous presidents. Clinton's first rating, taken shortly after he assumed office, was 58 percent approval—higher than the two most recent presidents,

George Bush and Ronald Reagan, both of whom were initially approved by just 51 percent of Americans. Jimmy Carter and Gerald Ford both received higher initial ratings—Carter 66 percent and Ford 71 percent—but Richard Nixon received about the same rating (59 percent). Initially, then, Clinton did moderately well compared with other recent presidents.

Five months into his presidency, however, Clinton's approval dropped to the lowest level that any president had received at a comparable point in his presidency since the 1940s, the beginning of scientific polling. This period was marked by controversy over how to deal with gays in the military and Clinton's difficulty in selecting an attorney general, among other issues. By the beginning of June 1993, only 37 percent of the American public approved of Clinton's job performance, down 22 points from January—the lowest number he has yet (as of January 1996) received.

By the end of 1993, Clinton had rebounded and was receiving ratings roughly comparable to those received by both Reagan and Carter at the end of the first year of their presidencies. This occurred at a time when Clinton's budget plan had passed the Congress by one vote, when the North American Free Trade Agreement (Nafta) had been approved, and when it appeared that Clinton was making progress on his legislative proposals. At the

Presidential Approval Rating by Quarter

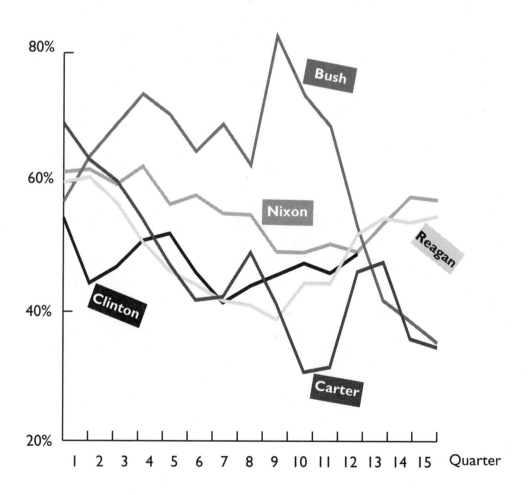

Source: The Gallup Poll

end of the summer of 1993, his approval rating had climbed to the mid-forties, and after his health care speech in September, his rating climbed to 56 percent, just 2 points lower than his initial rating. But two weeks later, approval dropped back to the 50 percent level, where it languished for the next three months.

In his January 1994 State of the Union speech, Clinton outlined his budget priorities and once again emphasized his health care proposals. The generally positive news coverage following this speech prompted a new surge in his approval rating, to 58 percent. Over the next several months, however, the Democratically controlled Congress considered—and finally rejected—all of Clinton's health care proposals. During this period of great controversy, approval of the president showed a steady decline, and at the end of the summer it had fallen once again below the 40 percent level.

During the fall congressional campaign, House Minority Whip Newt Gingrich led an effort to nationalize the election, to give Republican House candidates across the country a common campaign platform reflecting conservative views on the role of government, by advocating a Contract with America. Although the Gallup poll, along with other major polls, showed that few voters had explicitly heard of the Contract, the fact that it existed and was signed by so many candidates did encourage a consistent campaign theme by Republican candidates. And the GOP seemed remarkably successful in winning voters to their side: the Gallup polls showed that for the first time in many years, support for Republican and Democratic candidates for the House was about even among the public at large (rather than greater for the Democrats) and significantly greater for Republicans among those most likely to vote. Still, as the campaign neared its end, Clinton's approval rating actually improved, rising almost to the 50 percent mark.

Once the Republicans had won a majority in Congress, however, that fact itself influenced public opinion: President Clinton's rating dropped 8 points, from 48 percent approval just before the election to 40 percent by the end of December. (As discussed later in this essay, the GOP congressional victory was also followed by an improvement in the public's perceptions of the Republican party in general.) It was a short-lived drop for Clinton personally, as his approval surged to 49 percent by the beginning of February—in part, it would seem, a reflection of Clinton's well-received State of the Union address and in part a result of the general optimism and cooperation that Clinton and the Republican leaders in Congress expressed at the beginning of the new term.

Over the remainder of 1995, despite controversies over the budget and the presence of

American troops in Haiti and Bosnia, among other issues, Clinton's approval rating fluctuated within a fairly narrow range—from the mid-forties to the low fifties. In mid-December, his final rating of the year showed a 51 percent approval rating, remarkably close to the four previous full-term presidents at the same time juncture: Nixon (50 percent), Carter (54 percent), Reagan (54 percent), and Bush (50 percent). Despite a rocky start, and the lowest approval rating of any president in his first six months of office, Clinton began the fourth year of his presidency as popular with the American public as any of the recent presidents. Two had gone on to win reelection in landslide proportions (Nixon and Reagan), and two had been defeated (Carter and Bush). Clearly, presidential popularity at the end of the third year shows little predictive power for what will happen in November of the fourth year.

The Republican Victory in Congress

During the first two years of Clinton's presidency, the Democrats controlled both the House and the Senate—the House by 256 to 178, the Senate by 56 to 44. Typically, in non-presidential years the party that holds the White House loses seats in the Congress, and no exception to this rule was expected in the congressional elections of 1994.

Do you generally favor or oppose the proposals contained in the Contract with America?

	Favor	Oppose	Split/Mixed	No opinion
Total	56%	23%	7%	14%
Gender				
Men	62	20	7	11
Women	44	27	9	20
Age				
18–29	48	28	1	23
30–49	58	21	9	12
50–64	55	26	5	14
65+	58	17	11	14
Race				
White	57	21	7	15
Nonwhite	43	35	16	6
Income				
Under $20K	35	27	15	23
$20K–$30K	52	24	5	19
$30K–$50K	53	26	7	14
Over $50K	68	16	6	10
Party				
Republican	78	5	3	14
Democrat	31	45	11	13
Independent	47	28	10	15
Ideology				
Conservative	79	7	4	10
Moderate	46	26	9	19
Liberal	22	56	9	13
1992 Vote				
Clinton	27	46	11	16
Bush	80	4	5	11
Perot	63	18	5	14
Region				
East	57	24	5	14
Midwest	58	17	9	16
South	58	16	10	16
West	51	35	5	9

Source: The Gallup Poll, November 28–29, 1994

One explanation for this predictable pattern is that people are more likely to turn out to vote when they are dissatisfied with the course of politics than when they are satisfied —especially in elections that receive relatively little media attention. (This is not to say that all voters in nonpresidential elections are dissatisfied, but just that such voters turn out in disproportionately larger numbers.) And dissatisfied voters tend to blame the president's party for whatever ills they perceive. Thus, in off-year elections, when the president is not up for election and media coverage of House races is relatively light, the "protest" vote almost always results in the president's party in Congress losing seats in the House and Senate. (The only exception in the House was in 1934, in the midst of the Depression, when Franklin Roosevelt had been in office just two years and the Democrats actually gained seats.)

As the country approached the 1994 elections, most political observers therefore expected the Democrats to lose seats in both the House and Senate, but there was substantial disagreement over the number. In the Senate, where only a third of the Senators are elected every two years, twenty-one Democrats were up for reelection, compared with just thirteen Republicans. Thus, just on the basis of these numbers alone, Democrats were seen as more vulnerable to losing seats, and most predictions were for a loss of anywhere from three to six seats. A loss of seven seats would give Republicans majority control for the first time since 1986. Many observers felt there was a reasonable chance of a Republican victory in the Senate; even those who disagreed thought the Democrats could at best win a narrow victory.

The House was a different story. Most political observers expected Democrats to lose seats but not to lose the majority control that the Democratic party had retained for forty years. With 435 seats in the House, a party needs 218 to win majority control. The average number of seats won by the Democrats in the previous twenty elections was 261, with a low of 232 (in 1954) and a high of 295 (in the landslide election of Lyndon Johnson in 1964). In 1992, Democrats had won 256 seats—five short of the average but still a comfortable majority. Given the past pattern of Democratic victories, along with the state of the economy (sluggish but still growing) and Clinton's standing in the polls (not good, but not really bad), several mathematical models predicted the Democrats would lose under twenty seats in the House. Many political observers, using a district-by-district analysis, made similar predictions.

As it turned out, the 1994 congressional election was unusual in several ways. Perhaps the most unusual was the Contract with America. The conventional wisdom at the time, supported by much actual experience, was that "all politics is local." Loosely translated, that meant that the candidates from each congressional district would run on local issues, not national ones—that voters in the First District in New Hampshire, for example, had little in common with voters in the Fourteenth District in California. But Gingrich wanted to transcend local politics and instead focus on the national issues, and to do that he proposed a Contract with America that all Republican House candidates would sign. It primarily promised to cut spending and taxes, balance the budget, and enact term limits for members of Congress.

Gallup polls showed that only about a quarter of the voters had actually heard of the Contract before the election, but the effect of the Contract seemed to go well beyond just the numbers who had heard of it. Most Republican candidates did sign it in a ceremony on the Capitol steps, and many used it in their campaign. More important, it provided perhaps the most coherent and sustained political message of the campaign. Voters did not need to know explicitly that the Contract existed to know that most Republicans were intent on cutting government, cutting taxes, and balancing the budget.

Election Year 1994 was unusual, too, in the national focus on a major domestic issue. With the efforts of the Clinton administration

Do you favor or oppose these proposals in the Contract with America that the Republicans pledged to bring to a vote in the House of Representatives within the first 100 days of 1995?

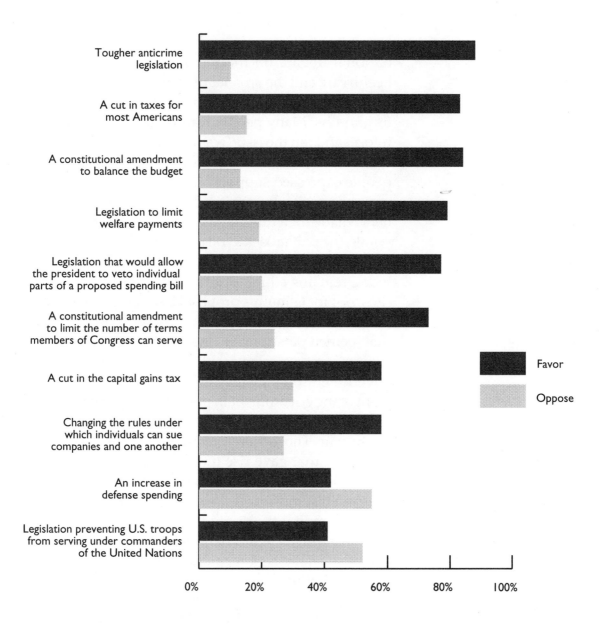

Source: The Gallup Poll, November 28–29, 1994

to enact some kind of health care reform, the national debate on the narrow question of health care and the broader question of the role of government dominated political coverage for months. Many people wanted health care reform and felt the issue was an important one that needed to be addressed. Initially these people expressed support for Clinton's health care proposals. But during the year, as opponents made their arguments against these proposals, the public backed off of its support—not for health care reform in general, which even today remains a high priority among Americans, but for Clinton's proposals. And some of the major arguments against those proposals that seemed persuasive to the public were that Clinton's reform plan would entail too much government bureaucracy, too much involvement of the government in people's daily lives, and therefore a less efficient and lower-quality system. Those were precisely the types of argument that gave rise to the Contract with America, and with the defeat of all health care reform bills, those arguments were given additional credibility.

The effect of this national debate on the congressional election can be seen in the results of Gallup's "generic ballot," a question designed to measure people's congressional vote. (With 435 different districts, it is not practical to mention the specific names of the candidates who are running in each respondent's district. Instead, people are asked which party's candidate they intend to vote for, an approach that provides valid estimates of the total popular vote received by each party.) In the spring and summer of 1994, the Democrats led Republicans in this generic ballot by 8 to 9 percentage points. In the late summer and fall, however, as the Clinton administration was losing the battle to get its health care proposals enacted, Republicans gained in support, and by election time they had tied the Democrats among registered voters and actually led Democrats by 7 percentage points among those most likely to turn out and vote. The final tally of all votes for the House cast nationwide was precisely a 7-point win by Republicans, resulting in a 52-seat gain and majority control.

If all registered voters had turned out to vote, it is likely the Republicans would have gained between 25 and 30 seats in the House—their best showing in four decades but not quite enough for majority control. But all registered voters did not vote. Those who did were more conservative and more Republican than those who stayed at home, and also much more likely to agree that the role of government should be curtailed. Thus, instead of just eroding the Democrats' power in the House, the Republicans took majority control themselves.

In the Senate, the Republicans achieved the most optimistic preelection estimates, beating two incumbent Democrats and winning the 6 open seats. In addition, two Democratic Senators changed party, thus giving the Republicans a substantial 54-to-46 majority.

The Republican victory in the House and Senate was followed by a major, albeit perhaps temporary, shift in public opinion toward the Republican party. There was an increase in the number who identified with the Republican party, who felt that Republicans could do a better job than Democrats in handling several public policy problems, and who thought the Republicans did a better job than the Democrats in representing the public's values. The change in party identification was perhaps most striking: just before the election, the number who identified as Democrats (47 percent) was greater than the number identifying as Republicans (43 percent). But after the election, Republicans led Democrats in party identification by 12 points, 53 percent to 41 percent—a net swing of 16 points.

Flushed with their stunning congressional victory, the Republicans in Congress began 1995 determined to fulfill their promises in the Contract with America. Only the House members had agreed to the provisions of the Contract, but its influence extended to the Senate as well. If the Republicans were to be successful, both branches of Congress would have to work together.

The Contract with America and the Budget Confrontation

The Contract included numerous legislative proposals that were generally popular with the public, proposals receiving clear majority support: tougher anticrime legislation, a tax cut for most Americans, a constitutional amendment to force the president and Congress to balance the budget, another constitutional amendment to limit the number of terms members of Congress could serve, cuts in welfare, a line-item veto for the president, and a change in the rules under which individuals could sue businesses. Two Contract items not so popular with the public included an increase in defense spending and prohibiting U.S. troops from serving under United Nations' commanders—both of which were opposed by a majority of Americans.

The Republicans in the House passed most of the Contract provisions within the first hundred days (although they had promised only to bring them to a vote within that time period), but the Senate acted far more slowly on these matters. Ultimately, the Senate did not support the House in passing the constitutional amendment to balance the budget (failing to reach the required two-thirds majority by one vote), and neither legislative branch passed the constitutional amendment to impose term limits.

As the year progressed, the crucial legislative debate eventually focused on the budget. If Republicans could not get a constitutional amendment passed that would require a balanced budget, they could at least try to force a balanced budget through legislative means. Under the leadership of Speaker Newt Gingrich and Majority Leader Dick Armey, the House Republicans produced a seven-year plan to do just that. With some adjustments in the plan, the Senate Republicans joined forces with their House colleagues in an overall approach that would significantly curtail the growth of federal programs, primarily Medicare and Medicaid, and at the same time provide a major reduction in income taxes—all leading to a balanced budget within seven years.

President Clinton responded by saying that he, too, supported a balanced budget, but he strongly criticized the seven-year plan as too draconian, requiring—he argued—too many cuts in the growth of Medicare and Medicaid and providing too large a tax cut that would mostly benefit the wealthy. Republicans, on the other hand, argued that Clinton's plan to balance the budget did not even attempt to do so within seven years and relied on numbers that were too optimistic. The Republicans demanded that the president agree to a seven-year plan using what they called "real numbers," economic estimates provided by the Congressional Budget Office, rather than those provided by the Office of Management and Budget within the Executive Branch.

The budget controversy, and the Republicans' efforts to cut the size of government, quickly ran into public resistance. Shortly after the 1994 congressional victory, just 19 percent of Americans felt that Republican proposals to cut spending went too far; three months later, that number had doubled, to 39 percent. And by November 1995, just a year after the historic Republican victory, a majority (57 percent) felt the proposals went too far, three times as great as the year before.

In mid-November 1995, Clinton vetoed the Republican budget plan, and the Republicans refused to pass another bill until the president would agree to a seven-year time frame for eliminating the deficit. Without funds, the federal government was forced to shut down all nonessential services—the "train wreck" that had been predicted by journalists and political observers. Clinton eventually agreed to the Republican demands to work toward a balanced budget within seven years, and the government was reopened while the president and Republican leaders in Congress resumed negotiations. Again, in December, Clinton vetoed the Republican budget plan, and again the government was shut down—this time for almost three weeks, the longest shutdown in America's history.

The public did not react well to this conflict between the president and the Congress. Despite the arguments from both sides that they were involved in a serious struggle over principles and the future direction of government, only about a third of Americans (37 percent) saw the conflict in these terms, while a majority (52 percent) felt the controversy was mostly an attempt by both sides to gain political advantage before the 1996 election. A Gallup poll two months earlier had foreseen this reaction, when six of ten Americans (60 percent) said they preferred to see the leaders of both sides compromise on the issues; only a third (35 percent) wanted their leaders to hold out for their principles even if that meant shutting down the government.

Initially, the standoff between Clinton and the Republican leaders in Congress seemed to be helping the president. By the end of the first shutdown in November, Clinton's approval rating had risen to its highest level in almost two years (53 percent), and his lead over Dole in the presidential race had expanded to 16 points. But the second shutdown was a different story: it dragged on through the Christmas and New Year holidays, and by the time it was over, Americans were just as upset with Clinton as they were with the Republicans. Clinton had agreed to a seven-year plan to balance the budget and to using estimates from the Congressional Budget Office, but among other reservations, he wanted a smaller tax cut and smaller cuts in the growth of Medicare and Medicaid than what Republicans included in their plan. Finally, on January 5, the Republican leaders agreed to a resolution that would reopen the government until the end of the month. By then, Clinton's approval rating had dropped 11 points, the presidential race was back to a dead heat, and the Democratic advantage in the congressional "generic ballot" measure had disappeared.

As debate over the budget extended into the new year, public opinion seemed likely to continue fluctuating between the two sides, and the controversy itself seemed destined to have a dominant influence on the presidential and congressional elections in November 1996.

The 1996 Presidential and Congressional Campaign

Whatever the outcome of the budget standoff, the Republican Congress had profoundly changed the debate in Washington. But that did not necessarily mean the GOP would benefit at the polls. The stereotypical image of Democrats is that they are "tax-and-spenders," while that of Republicans is that they represent the wealthy more than the middle class. Even in the flush of the 1994 congressional victory, Republicans were viewed by most Americans (69 percent) as proposing spending cuts that would "unfairly favor some groups over others," while only 21 percent felt those cuts would "fairly apply to all groups in society." And President Clinton echoed that sentiment in his charges that the Republican budget plan included major tax cuts for the wealthy that were funded by unnecessarily large cuts in programs for the elderly and poor.

On the other hand, Americans strongly support efforts to reduce the budget deficit and could ultimately give Republicans—more than Democrats—credit for these efforts. In a January 1996 poll, only 44 percent of Americans felt Democrats were seriously committed to reducing the deficit, while 63 percent felt Republicans were seriously committed to that goal. It seems likely that the debate in most congressional races will revolve around the size of government—how much and how quickly government programs should be cut. Which party benefits most from that debate greatly depends on the eventual outcome of the budget standoff.

The presidential race is also likely to be influenced by the budget controversy, but in such a highly visible contest, many other factors are likely to be important as well. In the January poll just mentioned, Americans

Are the following seriously committed to balancing the federal budget or not?

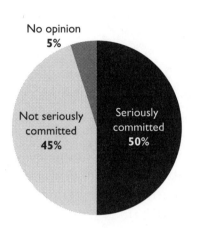

President Clinton

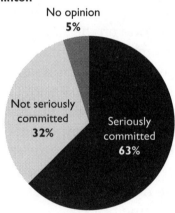

The Republicans in Congress

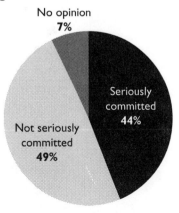

The Democrats in Congress

Source: The Gallup Poll, January 5–7, 1996

pointed to the issues of crime, the quality of education, the economy, the availability of good jobs, and health care as more important than the budget deficit. Of course, all of those items can be greatly influenced by how much government spends in addressing them, so some form of the budget debate is likely to prevail regardless of which issue is emphasized.

Typically, presidential reelection fortunes ride on the state of the economy—if the economy is good, the incumbent has a good chance of reelection; if not, he doesn't. That certainly was the case with George Bush in 1992, when the Clinton campaign's motto pointed to the single most important issue in the election: "The economy, stupid!" At the beginning of 1996, perceptions of the state of the economy were not as negative as they had been at the beginning of 1992.

In addition to policy issues, public perceptions of the candidates' personal characteristics play a role in the election. In the 1992 campaign, questions about Clinton's character—as reflected in the controversy over alleged marital infidelities and attempts to avoid the draft during the Vietnam War—were overshadowed by the public's concern about the economy. Questions about Bush's character were raised as well—especially late in the campaign, when the incumbent president's late surge faltered after new allegations surfaced about his role in the Iran–Contra controversy. In 1996, there are some nagging issues that could resurface and raise new questions about Clinton's character: the investigation of the role played by the Clintons in the Whitewater controversy, the First Lady's role in the firing of personnel in the White House travel office, and the court suit by Paula Jones alleging sexual harassment by Bill Clinton when he was governor. As of January 1996, these items were not major issues, but they lurked in the background as potential campaign problems for the incumbent president.

Questions of character had yet to be raised about the Republican presidential candidate. In early 1996, the strong favorite to win the Republican nomination was Bob Dole, who himself had been the target of criticism about his personal character in the 1976 presidential race (when he was President Ford's vice presidential running mate) and in the 1988 Republican primaries.

Typically, foreign policy is not a major determinant of voters' choices for president, but when the lives of American soldiers are at stake, the story can be different. Most Americans did not embrace sending U.S. troops on peacekeeping missions to Haiti and Bosnia, and if there should be a large number of American casualties in either country, public sentiment could turn strongly against the president. On the other hand, Clinton could gain some credit from the

Is there any candidate running this year that you think would make a good president?

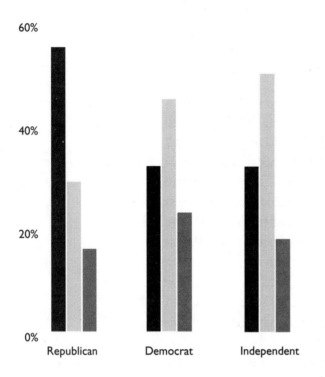

January 3–6, 1992

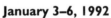

Yes

No

No opinion

Source: The Gallup Poll,
January 5–7, 1996

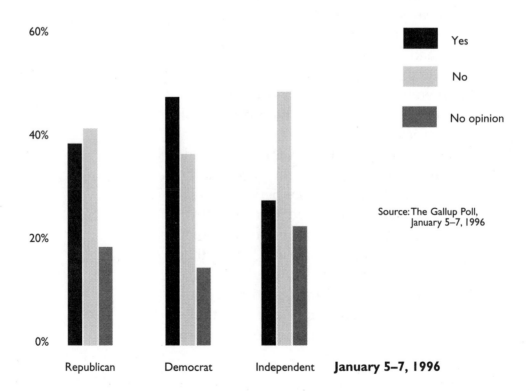

January 5–7, 1996

apparent success (as of this writing) of the peace-keeping mission in Haiti and from the peace-keeping mission in Bosnia as well, if that also is successful. In any case, these two foreign policy undertakings, along with any other sudden change in international politics, represent great uncertainty in the presidential campaign—not *likely* to be major factors but still capable of creating sudden changes in the political environment that could have major, unforeseen consequences for one candidate or the other.

A final important note: In years when an incumbent president is seeking reelection, the election is first and foremost a referendum on the incumbent. Most presidents who win reelection have job-approval ratings in the 50 percent range or higher going into the late spring or summer of their reelection years. This includes Presidents Eisenhower, Johnson, Nixon, and Reagan. The one exception was Harry S. Truman, who seemed quite vulnerable throughout 1948 but went on to surprise pollsters and pundits alike by winning the fall election against Republican Thomas Dewey. Truman's major target: the "do-nothing" Republican Congress. Almost a half century later, another Democratic president seems likely to run against a Republican Congress—not for doing nothing but for doing "too much." At this stage of the campaign, it is not at all clear whether history will once again side with the incumbent president or with the Congress.

The American People's Agenda

by
Michael Golay

What issues do Americans regard as important? And what do they expect their national leaders to do about them?

In opinion surveys during 1994 and 1995, the Gallup organization found people in a state of disquiet about the nation's course, skeptical of government's ability to solve problems, apprehensive about what many perceive as a degeneration of moral values, and doubtful of America's evolving role in Bosnia.

"In general," Gallup asked in July 1995, "are you satisfied or dissatisfied with the way things are going in the United States?" Nearly two-thirds (65 percent) said they were not satisfied. Only around a third (32 percent) thought things were going well.

In January 1996, Gallup found that only about a third of respondents, 31 percent, believed the United States would be in better shape in the year 2000 than it is today. Nearly two-thirds thought things would be about the same or worse at the millennium. Paradoxically, though, the polltakers also found a remarkably self-satisfied America. More than six of every ten respondents (62 percent) in a September 1995 poll described themselves as "very happy." Around a third said that, all things considered, they were "somewhat happy." Only 4 percent admitted they were "not too happy."

Americans may say they are contented in their private lives, but their views on public issues are far from complacent. The potential for disaster in Bosnia, the threat of violent crime, the rising costs of health care,

> « Americans may say they are contented in their private lives, but their views on public issues are far from complacent. »

the future of Medicare, and the old standbys of taxes, spending, and the federal deficit are among the matters that concern them most deeply.

In a September 1995 Gallup survey that might have been titled "America's Anxieties," respondents ranked violent crime as the most serious problem facing the nation. Drug abuse, "the moral values of society," the federal budget deficit, and the welfare system followed, in that order. Farther down the list on Gallup's "seriousness" scale were health care, public education, the economy, and jobs.

Crime is a relative newcomer at or even near the top of Gallup's issues chart. In a January 1993 poll, for example, only 9 percent of respondents rated it the nation's "most important" problem. Two years later, more than a quarter (27 percent) put crime at the head of the list. And in January 1996, it remained number one for 18 percent of those polled.

Thirteen percent identified the federal budget deficit as the top problem in January 1993. In January 1995, the ranking of the deficit had risen only a tick, to 14

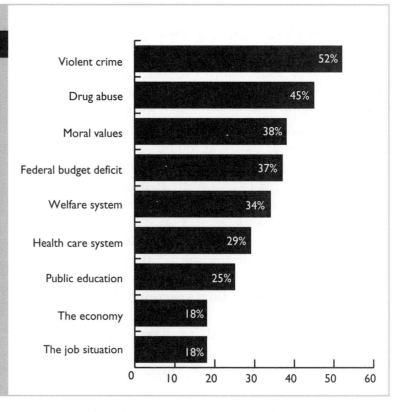

American Opinion

Gallup asked Americans to consider nine separate national issues and rate the seriousness of each on a 10-point scale, where a "10" is extremely serious and "zero" is not serious. On this scale, a majority of Americans give crime the highest scores of "10," and close to half give drugs this score. All other issues receive a significantly lower seriousness rating on this scale.

Source: The Gallup Poll,
September 14–17, 1995

Violent crime	52%
Drug abuse	45%
Moral values	38%
Federal budget deficit	37%
Welfare system	34%
Health care system	29%
Public education	25%
The economy	18%
The job situation	18%

percent. But in January 1996, after months of deadlock in Washington, 26 percent judged the federal government's inability to live within its means to be the nation's most important problem.

People express considerably less concern about the economy today than they did on the eve of the last presidential election. In March 1992, the "economy in general" was listed as the nation's most important problem by 42 percent of respondents. ("It's the economy, stupid," candidate Clinton's campaign advisers reiterated.) By January 1994, the proportion of those who saw the economy as the most urgent single issue had dropped to 17 percent. In January 1996, only 14 percent said they were more concerned about the economy than anything else.

Military Ventures Abroad

Americans historically have been reluctant to send the nation's military forces into harm's way. Support built slowly in 1990–91 for George Bush's Persian Gulf campaign. Opinion polling showed lukewarm backing for the 1994 U.S. intervention to restore democracy in Haiti. Gallup surveys suggested deep doubts about the U.S. commitment of 20,000 troops to join a NATO force in implementing the peace treaty of December 14, 1995, that sought to end forty-three months of civil war in Bosnia.

In making his case for the U.S. military presence, President Clinton argued that the U.S. had a moral obligation and a strategic interest in bringing a lasting peace to the Balkans. At the same time, he conceded the mission carried great risks, with the probability of death and wounds for Americans.

The polls suggest the public will be paying close attention to the casualty figures. In October 1995, Gallup found that two-thirds of respondents supported a U.S. military role in Bosnia on the assumption that no Americans would be killed. The level of support dropped sharply on the assumption of casualties. Only 31 percent said they supported the peacekeeping mission supposing twenty-five Americans would be killed.

« **Most politicians and opinionmakers endorsed the Bosnia venture, though in some cases very reluctantly.** »

Most politicians and opinionmakers endorsed the Bosnia venture, though in some cases very reluctantly. In a shaky vote of confidence, both the House and the Senate turned back attempts to deny funds for the mission.[1] Though he made few converts, some prominent editorial voices credited President Clinton with making an effective argument for the deployment. "We think Mr. Clinton has taken a strong position and articulated it well," *The Washington Post* said. "Finally in long-suffering Bosnia, there is an opportunity at least to ameliorate a horrific situation."[2]

Priorities at Home

For most of 1995, according to Gallup, domestic concerns absorbed policymakers, politicians, and their constituents. In all likelihood, the issues of crime; taxes, and spending; the social safety net, including Medicare; the environment; and related issues will be the focus of debate during the 1996 political season.

Gallup opinion surveys were a rough guide to Americans' developing views on these issues.

- Most people, white-haired or otherwise, broadly supported Medicare and opposed Republican attempts to "reform" it. In a May 1995 poll, 59 percent of respondents said Medicare should not be cut even if

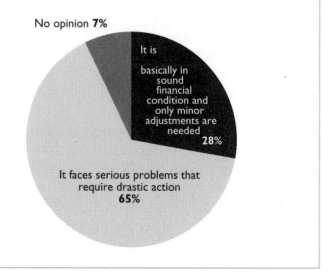

American Opinion

Which of these statements do you think best describes the financial condition of the Medicare system today?

No opinion **7%**

It is basically in sound financial condition and only minor adjustments are needed **28%**

It faces serious problems that require drastic action **65%**

Source: The Gallup Poll, May 11–14, 1995

protecting it means the budget deficit will rise. Four months later, Gallup reported that nearly two-thirds said the Republicans in Congress were pushing ahead too quickly with changes to Medicare.

- Most of those polled strongly supported protection of the environment and opposed congressional Republicans' efforts to modify environmental legislation. Support for America's mountains, forests, watercourses, and oceans cuts across some party and ideological lines, though self-described Democrats and independents tend to be more aggressively "green" than Republicans.

    In an April 1995 poll, nearly two-thirds of respondents (63 percent) described themselves as "environmentalists." Sixty-two percent said they would choose environmental protection over economic growth. And more than eight of every ten (83 percent) said the country should take "some additional actions" to safeguard the environment. Only 15 percent said existing efforts are sufficient.

    Despite these opinion findings, the Republican-dominated Congress approved two bills in 1995 that would reduce the government's ability to monitor and protect the environment. One makes cuts of up to 14 percent in spending for Environmental Protection Agency regulatory programs. The other

> «
> **Nearly two-thirds of respondents described themselves as environmentalists.**
> »

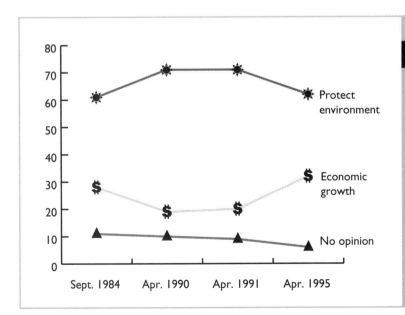

American Opinion

Which of these statements comes closer to your own point of view: Protection of the environment should be given priority, even at the risk of curbing economic growth, or, Economic growth should be given priority, even if the environment suffers to some extent?

Source: The Gallup Poll

eases restrictions on Alaska logging and extends a moratorium on adding new species to the endangered list. President Clinton threatened vetoes of both measures.[3]

«

The government reported sharp rises in juvenile violent crime in 1995.

»

- Americans are fearful of violent crime. During much of 1995, Gallup respondents listed crime as the nation's "most important problem" more often than any other. Statistically, crime actually decreased in 1994 (the last year for which figures were available); by the numbers, rates of violent crime were at their lowest levels since 1989. Yet there is reason for apprehension. The government reported sharp rises in juvenile violent crime in 1995. America's 40 million children age ten or younger form a vast reservoir of tomorrow's potential criminals. "The ominous increase in juvenile crime, coupled with population trends, portends future crime and violence at nearly unprecedented levels," FBI director Louis J. Freeh warned.[4]

- Drug abuse and drug-related mayhem trailed only violent crime in a December 1995 ranking of America's problems. In fact, 94 percent in the poll said drug abuse is a "crisis" or a "serious problem." In a September 1995 survey, more than half the respondents, 51 percent, felt so passionately about the issue that they favored the death penalty for anyone convicted of smuggling a large quantity of drugs into the United States.

  According to the December poll, people believe education and prevention to be the most effective of four strategies in the war against drugs. Forty-one percent listed education as the best approach, compared with 32 percent for reducing the supply of drugs, 23 percent for tougher punishments for drug offenders, and only 4 percent for improved treatment programs for drug users.

- Doubts about the system of welfare entitlement have risen steadily since 1994. In August 1994, only 3 percent of respondents rated welfare as the nation's most serious problem. In January 1996, it ranked at the top of the list for 9 percent of those polled.

Candidate Clinton ran for president in 1992 on a pledge to "end welfare as we know it," with time limits on benefits, strict work requirements, and aggressive collection of child support from absent fathers.

President Clinton delayed introducing his welfare legislation, and the Republicans appropriated the issue after they captured control of Congress in November 1994. The Republican welfare measure aimed to replace an array of federal antipoverty initiatives dating from the New Deal with limited lump-sum payments to the states, which would be given broad authority to manage their own programs.

Though people want to see welfare curtailed, many say they are reluctant to go too far with reforms. While Gallup found that 58 percent of poll respondents favored denying benefits to people who had not become self-sufficient after two years, 78 percent opposed striking the children of such people off the rolls. Opponents of Republican welfare reform have hammered away at its supposed impact on the young, citing a government study that claimed the measure would push another 1.2 million children into poverty. "This is a crucial

« **Though people want to see welfare curtailed, many say they are reluctant to go too far with reforms.** »

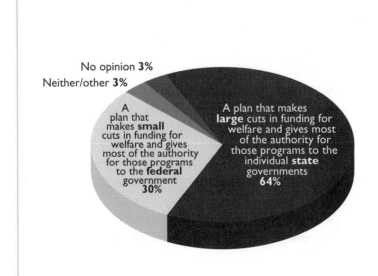

No opinion **3%**

Neither/other **3%**

A plan that makes **small** cuts in funding for welfare and gives most of the authority for those programs to the **federal** government **30%**

A plan that makes **large** cuts in funding for welfare and gives most of the authority for those programs to the individual **state** governments **64%**

American Opinion

Which of these proposals to deal with welfare do you prefer?

Source: The Gallup Poll, January 12–15, 1996

«

Supporters of affirmative action took a number of hits in 1995.

»

moral litmus test for this presidency and this nation," said Marian Wright Edelman, director of the Children's Defense Fund.[5] The president vetoed the Republican reform bill in January 1996.

- Most Americans strongly support existing gun-control laws, including the ban on assault weapons that so violently agitated the National Rifle Association in 1994 and 1995. Polling in 1995 showed little support outside the gun lobby for Republican efforts to repeal the assault-weapons ban.

- Most support the general goals of affirmative action, according to Gallup, though they see less need for such programs today and do not favor racial quotas as a corrective for decades of discrimination.

  Supporters of affirmative action took a number of hits in 1995. Federal court cases, administrative rulings, and legislative action combined to threaten three decades of preferential programs for dispossessed minorities and women. By year's end, though, the campaign against preference appeared to be losing momentum, and measures to roll back affirmative action had stalled in many states.

- Many Americans say the federal government has grown too big and too powerful. In an October 1995 poll, respondents singled out the Internal Revenue Service, the Central Intelligence Agency, and the Federal Bureau of Investigation as governmental agencies with too much power. At the same time, many people believe institutions of local government, including the municipal police, are not powerful enough.

- To nobody's surprise, the polltakers found that a lot of people think they pay too much in taxes. In December 1994, two-thirds of respondents told Gallup their federal income tax was too high. Fewer than a third (30 percent) said their tax bill seemed "about right." Who would say they should pay more? An eccentric fringe of 1 percent complained that their taxes were too low.

  Many people were dubious about Republican tax-cut proposals, however. In a May 1995 poll, 57 percent told Gallup they believed the cuts would benefit mostly the rich. Only around a third, 35 percent, thought everyone would benefit about the same. And respondents divided about evenly over the so-called flat tax, in which everyone would pay at the same rate regardless of income. In a January 1996 survey, 50 percent favored the flat tax, while 46 percent preferred the existing system, in which people with higher incomes pay a higher percentage of federal taxes.

Grumbling about the federal levy does not necessarily translate into overwhelming support for Republican efforts to reduce spending and taxes and balance the budget. In fact, in March 1995, only a slight majority, 52 percent, agreed that the Republicans' proposed spending cuts did not go too far. More than four in every ten (42 percent) thought the suggested cuts were too deep.

All the same, people believe the government ought to do something about the budget deficit. In September 1995, around a third (37 percent) of respondents graded the deficit as "very serious." Taxes, though, are another matter. In a July poll, only 5 percent cited taxes as one of the most important economic problems facing the country. In the same survey, a substantial majority rated social issues such as crime and welfare more important than

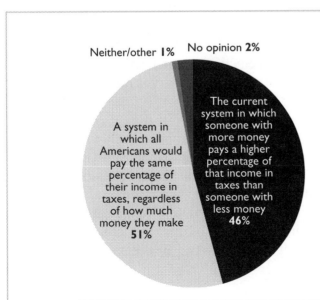

Neither/other 1%   No opinion 2%

A system in which all Americans would pay the same percentage of their income in taxes, regardless of how much money they make
51%

The current system in which someone with more money pays a higher percentage of that income in taxes than someone with less money
46%

American Opinion

Which federal income tax policy do you think would be better for the country?

Source: The Gallup Poll,
January 5–7, 1996

jobs, spending, taxes, the deficit, and other economic issues.

Can Government Help?

The great majority of Americans who told Gallup they were "very happy" or "somewhat happy" express at the same time a high degree of anxiety about the future and scant expectation that things will become better rather than worse. They also do not look to government to deliver improvements.

Results of an October 1994 poll revealed a deep strain of skepticism about the role of government. Gallup asked:

- Have federal government actions of the last twenty years made things better or worse? Only 18 percent answered better; 75 percent answered worse.

- Are there satisfactory opportunities for poor people to push ahead by working hard? Fewer than four in ten (38 percent) thought there were such opportunities; 59 percent thought there were not.

- Were respondents satisfied or dissatisfied with the way democracy is working? In October 1994, an even 50 percent were satisfied; nearly as many, 48 percent, were dissatisfied with the democratic system. By April 1995, though, nearly two-thirds, 64 percent, said they were satisfied; more than a quarter, 27 percent, remained disaffected. The improvement may have been the result of the 1994 congressional elections, which shifted party control in the House of Representatives for the first time in forty years.

All the same, Americans increasingly view the government not just with skepticism but with distrust and even fear. In 1958, during the second presidential term of Dwight D. Eisenhower, Gallup found that three-quarters of respondents trusted the government to do the right thing most of the time. In October 1995, only 23 percent felt that way. And in the same poll, nearly

«
Only 23 percent trusted the government to do the right thing most of the time.
»

four of every ten (39 percent) agreed that "the federal government has become so large and powerful that it poses an immediate threat to the rights and freedoms of ordinary citizens."

A Look Ahead

Presidential candidates sift through opinion polls in search of a guide to the future. Yet the president and his leading challengers, with their high visibility and instant access to the press and television, shape public opinion at least as much as they follow it. They have great power to focus the public's attention on an issue. Crime rose to the top of Gallup's list of "most important issues" in part because of the intense attention President Clinton, the Republicans in Congress, and the gun lobby paid to law enforcement, the courts, and gun control. As the White House and congressional Republicans debated welfare, public concerns on the issue began to build and were reflected in the polls.

(As it happens, Gallup polls have explored the question of who shapes public opinion. Around 40 percent of those surveyed in 1994 said news media commentators and reporters most influenced their views on the issues of the day. Ten percent said political leaders were most influential. Thirty percent were swayed more by family and friends than anyone else.)

Barring a debacle in Bosnia, the national election of 1996 is likely to be fought on home ground, along the lines laid down in 1994 and 1995. Some specific issues—welfare, Medicare, taxes, spending and the deficit, the size and scope of government, crime, and affirmative action—are examined in detail in the following chapters. The overarching issue is the function and future of the federal government. During 1995, the Democratic White House and the Republican Congress pursued contrasting visions of government's role. Voters will have a clear choice in November 1996. The result could set America's course well into the new century.

« **The national election of 1996 is likely to be fought on home ground.** »

Notes: The American People's Agenda

1. Katharine Q. Seelye, "Senate and House Won't Stop Funds on Bosnia Mission," *The New York Times*, December 14, 1995, 1.
2. "Bosnia Opportunity," editorial, *The Washington Post*, November 29, 1995.
3. John H. Cushman Jr., "Senate Backs Cuts in Environmental Spending," *The New York Times*, December 15, 1995, 35.
4. Fox Butterfield, "Crime Continues to Decline, but Experts Warn of Coming `Storm' of Juvenile Violence," *The New York Times*, November 19, 1995, 18.
5. Alison Mitchell, "On Welfare, Clinton Faces a Litmus Test," *The New York Times*, November 20, 1995, B9.

2 The Budget
Can We Learn to Live Within Our Means?

by
Michael Golay

Opinion surveys suggested that a lot of people questioned the politicians' motives during the great federal budget impasse of 1995. For all the posturing, though, and the all-too-obvious positioning for political advantage for the 1996 presidential campaign, real issues were in the balance. The dispute turned on more than numbers. The Democratic White House and the Republican-controlled Congress were joined in a battle over the future role of government in American life.

In a November 1995 poll, Gallup found that a majority of respondents, 52 percent, viewed the budget standoff as mostly political. Only around a third, 37 percent, thought the Clinton administration and Congress were involved in a struggle over principles.

Nevertheless, the two sides divided along clear ideological lines. On some matters, there seemed to be no middle way. Should a balanced federal budget be a goal or a requirement? Should the increases that have already been planned for Medicare, the popular and successful government health insurance program for the elderly, be trimmed at the edges or changed fundamentally? Should the eligibility standard for Medicaid, the health insurance program for the poor, be tightened to reduce the number of people who qualify

« **The Democratic White House and the Republican-controlled Congress were joined in a battle over the future role of government in American life.** »

« **The fogs of rhetoric and the numbing effect of numbers rising to the billions and even trillions tended to obscure the human element.** »

for government assistance? Should federal aid for education, training, and technology be expanded or cut back?

The Republicans were determined to bring the federal budget into balance within seven years and to shrink government and alter its priorities. They proposed tax cuts and sharp reductions in the growth of spending for the needy, for education and technology, and for environmental protection. The Democrats defended government's activist role. They tried to block Republican efforts to make structural changes in Medicare, Medicaid, and other long-standing social programs.

Politics is the art of compromise, so expectations were that Congress and the White House eventually would split the difference—after all, the dollar amounts at issue were not great in many cases—and reach an accord on the budget. But for a time, at least, ideology prevailed.

"One assumes when you engage in negotiations, the best interest of the country will prevail and both sides will give a little," said Leon Panetta, President Clinton's chief negotiator in the budget dispute. In 1995, though, the adversaries had "some significant differences—there are some fundamental divides," Panetta said.[1]

As the dispute lengthened, political manners became offhand, political language rougher. Protecting old people, schools, and Mother Nature from Republican "abuse"—"honoring the commitments that we all have and that keep our people together," in President Clinton's phrase—became the shorthand for Democratic fundamental principle.[2]

Republican sound bites envisioned a prosperous tomorrow for America's children who, in House Speaker Newt Gingrich's words, would be given "a chance to have a future in which they're not going to be crushed by debt and taxation and high interest rates"—but only if the president went along with Congress on the budget. Later, Gingrich suggested failure to reach an agreement on a balanced budget would cause the stock market to crash.[3]

The fogs of rhetoric and the numbing effect of numbers rising to the billions and even trillions tended to obscure the human element: decisions about government have real effects on real people. For some people who use food stamps, a 15 percent reduction in that federal program will mean less nourishment. Not every college student will be able to arrange alternative sources of funding if the federal student loan program has less money to lend or requires loans to be paid back sooner. If Medicaid is turned back to the states, some poor people in poorer states certainly will lose access to doctors and medicines.

The Deficit

In recent Gallup polling, the federal budget deficit rated fairly high on the list of important national issues. In July 1995, 11 percent of respondents ranked the deficit as the nation's most important problem. In September, the deficit registered a "10" on Gallup's 1-to-10 seriousness scale for more than one-third of those polled.

During the 1980s, public concern intensified as the federal deficit grew larger. The deficit did not register at all on Gallup's "most important" list in the late 1970s and early 1980s. From 1985 to 1987, during the Ronald

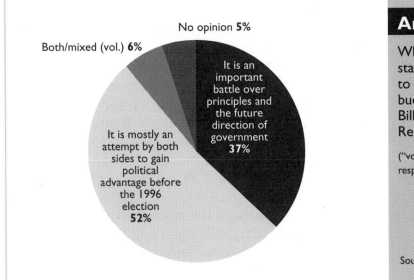

No opinion **5%**

Both/mixed (vol.) **6%**

It is an important battle over principles and the future direction of government **37%**

It is mostly an attempt by both sides to gain political advantage before the 1996 election **52%**

American Opinion

Which of the following statements comes closer to your view about the budget debate between Bill Clinton and the Republicans in Congress?

("vol." refers to a volunteered response)

Source: The Gallup Poll, November 17, 1995

« **Deficit spending has been the American way since the era of the Great Depression.** »

Reagan administration, it registered in double digits, with a peak of 16 percent in October 1985. In August 1992, 9 percent of those polled put the deficit at the top of the list.

In December 1994, eight of every ten respondents, 82 percent, said "significant" deficit reduction should be the top or a high priority for the new Republican-led Congress then preparing to take office. Around three-quarters thought a tax cut should be the top or a high priority. At the same time, three-quarters said Congress should cut *spending* before it cut *taxes.*

The Republicans ran in 1994 on a Contract with America that pledged to eliminate deficit spending within seven years. Initially, they intended to pass a constitutional amendment that would require a balanced budget. When this measure failed in the Senate (it lacked one vote of the necessary two-thirds majority), the Republicans decided to meet the objective through legislation.

The White House set a general goal of a balanced budget, though over a longer period, perhaps a decade. In fact, the first Clinton administration budget proposal of 1995 accepted deficits of around $200 billion a year for several years.

Deficit spending has been the American way since the era of the Great Depression. Only eight times since 1933 has the government taken in as much as it dealt out. President Truman balanced the budget four times. President Eisenhower managed it three times in the 1950s; President Johnson achieved one balanced budget, in fiscal year 1969.

Still, the deficits were generally modest until the Reagan years of the 1980s. For purposes of comparison, the Eisenhower administration ran a $3.3 billion deficit in fiscal 1961. From what was then a post–World War II record of $25.2 billion in fiscal 1968, the gap between intake and outgo increased to $200 billion in 1983. Annual deficits of $200 billion became the norm during the 1980s.[4]

Historically, Americans have seen a close connection between a balanced budget and a limited national government. To Thomas Jefferson, deficits were "a mortal cancer," and until the 1930s, most political leaders concurred. Deficits might be acceptable during periods of war or depression but not otherwise. Abraham Lincoln, whose administration ran up enormous debts during the Civil War, was one of the few dissenters. Lincoln in the 1860s took what in the mid-twentieth century would become the conventional view of liberal economists of the school of John Maynard Keynes: "Men readily perceive that they cannot be much oppressed by a debt which they owe to themselves," Lincoln said.[5]

Government's role and functions have greatly expanded since 1933. The New Deal of Franklin D. Roosevelt introduced a basic system of public welfare, and the Truman and Eisenhower administrations consolidated it. The Democratic Great Society of the 1960s substantially expanded the New Deal welfare state. At the same time, America assumed unprecedented global responsibilities. The costs of the Cold War of the late 1940s through the era of Reagan were astronomical—literally, it turned out, in the case of Reagan's fabulously expensive proposed space-based Strategic Defense Initiative missile defense system of the 1980s, dubbed "Star Wars."

From the New Deal on, governments increasingly used fiscal policy as an instrument of economic man-

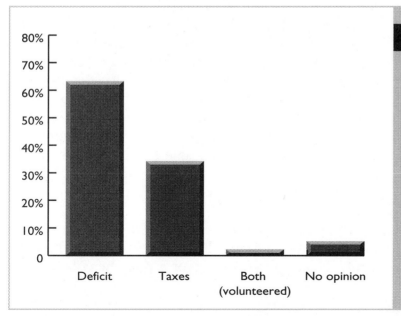

American Opinion

Between the two, which should receive higher priority—cutting taxes or cutting the deficit?

Source: The Gallup Poll, April 1995

agement. For Keynes and his Depression-era followers, government deficits could speed economic recovery. Government spending would boost demand—the consumption side of the economy—and therefore increase jobs and, eventually, revenue that could be used to pay down the debt. And in prosperous times, Keynsians favor government spending to develop the nation's physical and human resources: roads and bridges, education, training, and technology.

Conservative economists rely on tax cuts to stimulate economic growth. Supply-side theorists, influential during the early years of the Reagan administration, called for investment incentives that would increase the supply of goods and services. High taxes, supply-siders argued, were the chief cause of America's economic problems.

Reagan's economic advisers forecast that economic growth would gradually eliminate the deficit, so that no painful spending cuts would be necessary. As it turned out, an economic downturn coupled with the Reagan tax cuts led to a sharp fall in revenues in the early 1980s. Government spending continued to rise, especially for defense (the defense budget grew 25 percent in *real* terms from 1982 to 1985) and in the Social Security entitlement. Even with cuts in discretionary social programs, government expenditures increased 8.5 percent from the end of President Carter's term to the end of President Reagan's first term.[6]

As a result, the deficit shot upward, forcing Congress to take some preliminary steps to bring it under control. A Republican-controlled Senate approved a balanced-budget amendment in 1982. The Democratic House rejected it. The Democratic nominee for president in 1984 ran on a platform of progressive tax increases to reduce the deficit. The voters were not persuaded, and Fritz Mondale lost in a landslide. "I taught a whole generation of politicians how to handle the tax issue: to not mention it," Mondale remarked afterward.[7]

The Gramm-Rudman Act of 1985 sought to bring the deficit down gradually by capping debt. The debt limit was supposed to trigger automatic cuts in government spending. In fact, it was a slow trigger. The deficit did, however, come down a bit, to $153 billion in Reagan's last year, only to rise again dramatically during the Bush administration—to record levels approaching $300 billion in fiscal 1991 and 1992.[8]

Few economists would argue that an absolutely balanced budget year after year is essential to the nation's well-being. Most do, however, recognize the massive deficits of the 1980s and early 1990s as dangerous. Interest on the national debt became the fastest-growing component of the federal budget, rising from 10 percent of outlays in fiscal 1981 to 15 percent in fiscal 1989. At around $250 billion, the annual interest payment now exceeds the annual deficit.[9]

A slow-growth economy and the enormous national debt have hindered the development of new programs to address new or worsening problems: the AIDS epidemic, illegal drugs, crime and violence, substandard schools. The debt has major implications, too, for eco-

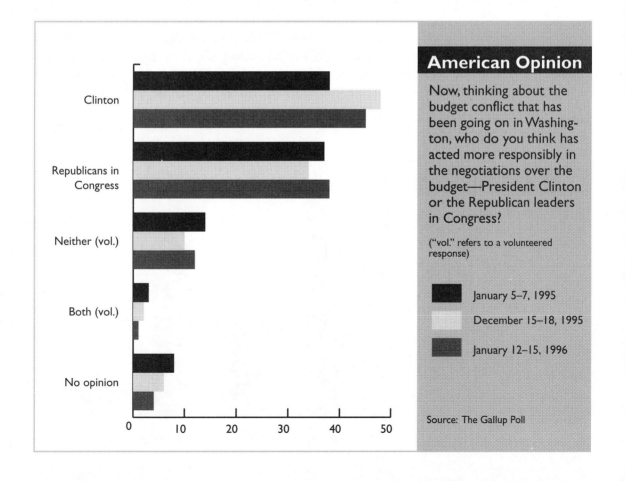

American Opinion

Now, thinking about the budget conflict that has been going on in Washington, who do you think has acted more responsibly in the negotiations over the budget—President Clinton or the Republican leaders in Congress?

("vol." refers to a volunteered response)

January 5–7, 1995

December 15–18, 1995

January 12–15, 1996

Source: The Gallup Poll

nomic growth, the standard of living, and even America's standing in the world. The Reagan deficits eroded the national savings, sent interest rates up, and helped create a gaping imbalance of trade.

In observing that debts owed to oneself are less onerous than those due others, Lincoln could not have foreseen the massive outflow of American financial resources during the 1980s. For various reasons, outsiders found investing in America increasingly attractive and profitable. Foreigners held as much as 15 to 20 percent of the national debt during the Reagan years, up from around 10 percent in 1960.

"A large national debt funded domestically simply redistributed income in favor of American citizens who purchased government bonds," remarks economic historian Iwan Morgan, "but payment of interest to foreigners required the transfer of national income out of the country."[10]

All these factors combined to impel Washington to act. In 1990, deficit-cutting pressure forced President Bush to break his "Read my lips: no new taxes" pledge of two years earlier. Not long afterward, and not coincidentally, Gallup recorded a historic high point of public concern about the deficit—21 percent of respondents put it at the head of the list of "most important problems."

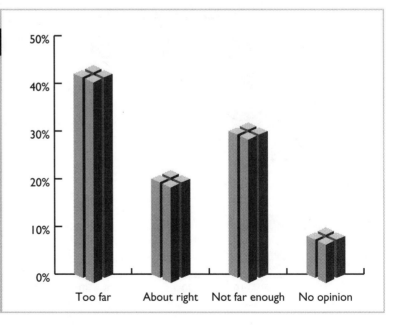

American Opinion

Are current Republican proposals to cut spending about right, or do they not go far enough?

Source: The Gallup Poll, July 7–9, 1995

Too far About right Not far enough No opinion

When he was running for president in 1992, Bill Clinton promised to balance the budget within five years, and he gave deficit reduction a high priority during his first year in office. But he barely managed to push his first budget—which called for a mix of tax increases and spending cuts totaling nearly $500 billion over five years—through a Democratic Congress. The Clinton package, coupled with economic recovery, helped bring down the fiscal 1993 deficit to $254 billion and the 1995 deficit to an estimated $176 billion—$100 billion below projections of just one year earlier.

Even so, it has been the Republicans, Reagan's heirs, who have insisted on an absolutely balanced budget, and to reduce taxes at the same time by making sharp reductions in spending.

Public opinion generally favors action on the deficit over tax cuts. In a March 1995 Gallup survey, nearly two-thirds of respondents said bringing down the deficit should take priority over easing the tax burden.

The Budget Standoff

The budget is a compilation of vast heft, filled with figures, facts, estimates, and projections. For most people, the document itself has all the narrative force

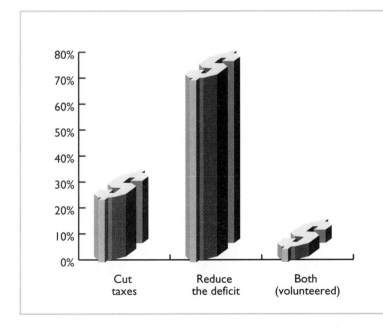

American Opinion

If Congress is able to cut federal spending, what do you think they should do with the savings?

Cut taxes

Reduce the deficit

Both (volunteered)

Source: The Gallup Poll, December 16–18, 1994

of a telephone directory. But in fact, it is the chief blueprint for the nation's social policy.

Lyndon B. Johnson put it this way: "The budget determines how many hungry children are going to be fed; how many poor people are going to be housed; how many sick people are going to be cared for; how many schoolchildren are going to receive federal aid for books; and how our entire population is going to be protected against a possible enemy attack."[11]

The federal budget consists of two component parts. The first is a package of thirteen appropriations bills, spending authority for various government departments and agencies. Seven of these, including the defense budget, were enacted without much trouble in 1995. President Clinton vetoed three for failing to provide sufficient funding for education, environmental protection, and other programs he favors. The Republicans in Congress failed to pass three others.

The second component of the annual budget is an omnibus measure known as the Reconciliation Bill. This was the focus of dispute in 1995. It contained the Republican scheme for balancing the budget, cutting taxes, reducing the planned growth of Medicare and Medicaid, and cutting welfare, food stamps, and other social programs.

As the dispute dragged on for weeks and then months beyond the September 30 end of the federal fiscal year, money to operate the government ran out. When Congress refused to grant temporary spending authority, the administration suspended nonessential operations, from staffing national parks to writing welfare and veterans' benefit checks.

To end the first government shutdown, Clinton agreed in principle to Republican demands for a balanced budget in seven years as calculated by the Congressional Budget Office (CBO), so long as the budget protected Medicare and Medicaid and allocated "adequate" funds for programs the Democrats favor.

Some liberal commentators thought the president had been outmaneuvered. "The moment Mr. Clinton agreed to a seven-year bloodletting, he guaranteed that any budget he signed would look almost as unforgiving as the one the Republicans have passed," *The New York Times* remarked. "He can fight hard to make it gentler at the margins. But [this] shows how much the GOP has already won."[12]

As the winter of 1996 advanced, though, the line between winners and losers began to blur. The government continued to operate on temporary authorizations, and the president and Congress remained deadlocked, with no budget agreement in sight.

Here is a summary of some of the specific areas of dispute:

- TAXES. The Republicans proposed lowering the capital gains tax (the levy on profits from the sale of investments) from 28 percent to 19.8 percent— the lowest level in four decades. They also offered a $500-per-child tax credit to families.

  Initially, the Republicans offered $245 billion in tax cuts over seven years. The Clinton administration proposed around $100 million in cuts.

- INSURANCE. Republicans sought an annual ceiling on Medicare, meaning old people would no longer be guaranteed all the medical services and treatment they wanted. They planned to turn Medicaid over to the states, which would decide how much to spend on health care for the poor and who would be eligible for benefits. (In recent years, costs

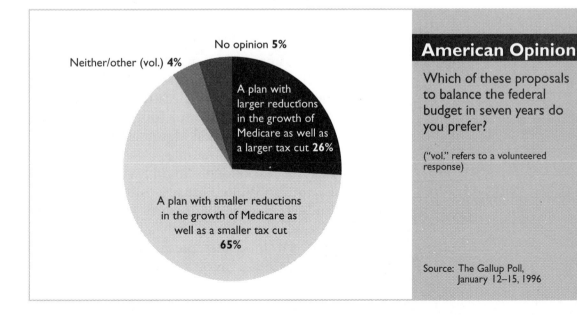

No opinion **5%**

Neither/other (vol.) **4%**

A plan with larger reductions in the growth of Medicare as well as a larger tax cut **26%**

A plan with smaller reductions in the growth of Medicare as well as a smaller tax cut **65%**

American Opinion

Which of these proposals to balance the federal budget in seven years do you prefer?

("vol." refers to a volunteered response)

Source: The Gallup Poll, January 12–15, 1996

for both programs had been rising at more than double the rate of health care paid for by private insurers.)

Clinton proposed smaller savings in projected Medicare and Medicaid expenditures and rejected structural changes in either program.

« **Nearly six of every ten respondents urged the president to veto the Republican budget.** »

- WELFARE. The Republicans moved to end the guarantee of aid to poor people with children, which had been in effect for sixty years. They also called for limits on benefits and cuts in projected spending on food stamps and other nutritional programs.

  Clinton supported a general toughening of welfare requirements and appeared ready to acquiesce in the withdrawal of the entitlement. He objected, however, to reductions in the growth of spending for food stamps and programs for children, and he ended up vetoing the Republican reform bill.

- EDUCATION. The Republicans in Congress proposed cuts in education spending of 15 percent over the next seven years. The White House wanted to increase education spending by 18 percent over the same period.

  Republicans called for cuts in the Federal Direct Student Loan Program, a 1993 Clinton administration initiative. Clinton hoped to protect that program, as well as Head Start and a program that aids school districts with large populations of poor children.

- THE ENVIRONMENT. The Republican budget called for greater access to public lands for loggers, miners, oil drillers, and ranchers. The Clinton administration opposed easing restrictions on exploitation of common lands and fought cutbacks in funding for environmental monitoring.

A majority of respondents to a November Gallup poll sided with the White House position on the Republican budget. Nearly six of every ten, 58 percent, urged the president to veto it. Only a third thought he should sign it as it stood. (Ten percent had no opinion.) On December 6, 1995, Clinton vetoed the budget bill.

"With this, the Republican budget is dead, the Contract with America is dead," Clinton senior adviser George Stephanopoulos said. "Now let's get to work."[13]

Stephanopoulos's bold victory claim doubtless owed something to opinion polls that showed steady gains for the White House during the early phase of the budget crisis.

In May 1995, Gallup respondents had divided about evenly when asked whether they preferred the Republican (44 percent) or the Democratic (43 percent) approach in balancing spending cuts with maintaining federal programs. By mid-November, 49 percent favored the Democratic approach; only 36 percent preferred the Republicans'.

Republicans were also graded low on fairness. In a December 1994 poll, nearly seven in every ten, 69 percent, thought Republican proposals for spending cuts applied unfairly to some groups. Only 21 percent thought they applied evenly to everyone.

Republicans took a larger share of criticism, too, for the government shutdowns. A quarter of respondents in a November 1995 poll blamed Clinton for the first shutdown, which temporarily idled 250,000 federal employees. But nearly half, 47 percent, held congressional Republicans responsible.

In the same poll, three-quarters of respondents thought Republican leaders in Congress should move

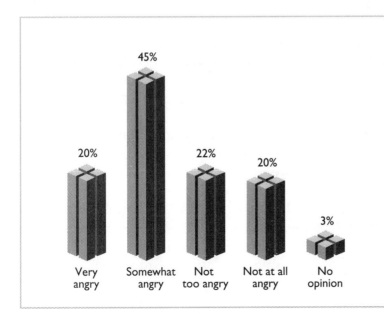

Very angry	Somewhat angry	Not too angry	Not at all angry	No opinion
20%	45%	22%	20%	3%

American Opinion

How do you feel about the budget confrontation between the president and Congress over the past few days? Do you feel very angry, somewhat angry, not too angry, or not at all angry?

Source: The Gallup Poll, November 14, 1995

«

Both parties understood the imperative to slow growth rates of Medicare and Medicaid.

»

closer to the Clinton administration's positions; only 17 percent said they should not yield ground to reach a budget agreement. Fifty-nine percent said the president should be more willing to compromise; 32 percent thought he ought to stand firm.

Polling in mid–January 1996 suggested Clinton had lost some of his advantage. Respondents divided about evenly when asked which budget-balancing plan they preferred, the president's (43 percent) or the congressional Republicans' (41 percent). Forty five percent said Clinton had acted more responsibly than the Republicans during the budget negotiations; 38 percent thought the Republicans had been more responsible.

Medicare and Medicaid

The White House seized on the presumed threat to Medicare and Medicaid to dramatize its differences with congressional Republicans over the budget. Hardly anyone, expert or otherwise, believes either health insurance program can be sustained at existing rates of growth. In a May 1995 survey, Gallup found that nearly two-thirds of respondents thought Medicare faced serious financial problems that required drastic action. With no changes, costs for both programs are projected to rise from $293 billion today, around 18 percent of the federal budget, to $664 billion by 2005—when they would reach 27 percent of all federal spending.[14]

So both camps understood the imperative to slow growth rates of Medicare and Medicaid. Both proposed substantial savings over the seven-year cycle. But the Republicans cut deeper. And they proposed premium increases and structural changes in both programs. The Democrats opposed any alterations that would reduce the scope of Medicare and favored heavier premium increases for well-to-do beneficiaries. And they defended the Medicaid entitlement.

The White House charged that Republican plans to cut projected expenditures by 14.4 percent over seven years would turn Medicare, which serves 37.5 million elderly and disabled Americans, into "a second-class

system," with profound consequences for beneficiaries.[15] Republicans countered that the Democrats ex-
aggerated the actual spending differences in the two
plans to scare elderly voters away from the GOP.

In fact, the two sides used different sets of figures,
making comparison difficult. Republicans relied on
Congressional Budget Office calculations, which generally are more cautious in predicting future costs and
revenues. The White House, which offered a savings
plan of its own that aimed to reduce planned Medicare spending by 6.6 percent over seven years, used
Office of Management and Budget estimates, which are
more optimistic about economic performance.

Both sides also proposed increases in Medicare premiums. Here the differences did not appear to be significant. The Republican plan would raise monthly
premiums from $46.10 today to $87.60 by 2002. Democratic projections show the premiums rising to $82.80 in
seven years—a difference of around $5.[16]

Established in 1965 as a centerpiece of Lyndon
Johnson's Great Society, Medicare is vital to the health
and well-being of millions of old people. Many Republicans opposed Medicare in 1965. And today the public
is skeptical about Republican plans to change it.

In September 1995, a Gallup survey reported a substantial minority of respondents, 23 percent, believed
Medicare to be in a state of crisis, with another 58 percent saying the system has serious problems. Yet in the
same poll, nearly two-thirds, 64 percent, said Republicans were trying to push reforms through too quickly.
Only 28 percent favored Republican plans to reform
Medicare.

President Clinton played on these doubts and fears
in a November 1995 radio address on the budget standoff that could foreshadow the tone and style of his reelection campaign: "Imagine the Republican Congress
as a banker and the United States as a family that has
to go to the bank for a short-term loan for a family
emergency," Clinton said. "The banker says to the family, 'I'll give you the loan, but only if you'll throw the
grandparents and the kids out of the house first.' Well,
speaking on behalf of the family, I say, no thanks."[17]

«
**Most people
recognize the
issue is more
complicated than
the president's
homily suggests.**
»

All the same, most people recognize the issue is more complicated than the president's homily suggests. Anne Henderson, sixty-six years old, of Montclair, New Jersey, suffered a serious illness in 1993. Her managed-care program paid medical bills totaling some $200,000. She now has Medicare. The $46.10 monthly premium is deducted from her Social Security check. Under the Republican plan, the premium would nearly double by 2002.

"We can't afford Medicare for everyone, and it should not continue to benefit the middle classes over others who need it," Ms. Henderson said.[18]

The White House and Congress are equally at odds over Medicaid, enacted as part of the same Great Society legislative package that created Medicare. The program serves 36.2 million poor people, half of them children. In 1995, the federal government spent $89 billion on Medicaid and the states $67 billion, with the federal share of costs larger (ranging up to 80 percent) in the poorer states. Overall, Medicaid costs have quadrupled in the past decade.[19]

The Republicans say several successful experimental programs in recent years suggest the states could manage Medicaid more efficiently than the federal government. Arizona and other states claim to have saved money and expanded coverage with shifts of Medicaid beneficiaries into managed-care programs and health-maintenance organizations.[20]

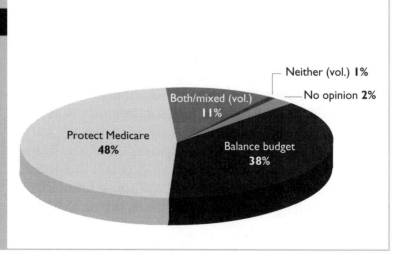

American Opinion

Which of the following goals do you think is more important—balancing the federal budget or protecting the Medicare system from major changes?

("vol." refers to a volunteered response)

Source: The Gallup Poll, November 14, 1995

Neither (vol.) 1%
No opinion 2%
Both/mixed (vol.) 11%
Protect Medicare 48%
Balance budget 38%

"States have proven that for less money you can provide better care," Haley Barbour, the Republican national chairman, asserted. "States that have had Medicaid reform like Arizona find patient satisfaction is up, and the quality of care is up."[21] The Democrats counter that the states cannot be trusted to provide adequate levels of coverage—anyway, not all of them. The powerful American Medical Association agrees. In calling on Congress to preserve the federal guarantee of coverage, the AMA argued that a rapid shift to managed care could seriously disrupt poor peoples' access to health care and erode the quality of care.[22]

As managed care has grown in recent years, the income of America's more than 660,000 doctors has declined. Employers demand lower insurance premiums. In turn, insurers demand that doctors cut costs. After climbing steadily for more than a decade, average physician earnings fell 3.8 percent in 1994 from the year before, from $156,000 to $150,000.[23]

A Look Ahead

Only the bravest or most foolhardy observer would have ventured to predict the outcome of the great budget fight as 1995 drew to a close. What did seem clear enough was that the White House and the Republican challengers had surveyed their political territory for 1996 and staked out the boundaries.

Clinton put up a stout defense of much of the safety net, as well as popular programs such as education aid and environmental protection. "That is his reelection campaign," an aide said, "and he is prepared to fight all winter on that line."[24] James Carville, Clinton's 1992 campaign manager and an adviser for the 1996 campaign, believes that well-defined differences between the White House and Congress are healthy for the political process. They are not so much divisive as clarifying. "Some people are going to say this is the politics of anger, the politics of fear, but the point is that all this can produce is a big election about a big thing," Carville said.[25] And the Democrats evidently like their chances in a "big" election. "Already now, people are being

« **'Some people are going to say this is the politics of anger, the politics of fear, but the point is that all this can produce is a big election about a big thing.'** »

« **'The fiscal future of the United States is on the line. Either the government starts getting entitlement spending under control now or it goes bankrupt later.'** »

confronted by what it means to balance a budget," Carville went on. "It is being brought home every day what this means. I think the Republicans are scared to run a campaign on this."[26]

In fact, the polls showed the Republicans taking hits on many of the budget issues. Conservative commentators conceded Republican political mistakes, such as allowing the White House a clear field of fire on Medicare and on the environment. But they insisted the objective is worth fighting for. Boston political consultant John Ellis argued that House Speaker Newt Gingrich and his supporters have "advanced the cause of good governance" with their stand on the budget deficit. "The fiscal future of the United States is on the line. Either the federal government starts getting entitlement spending under control now or it goes bankrupt later," Ellis said.

"No good deed goes unpunished," he added. "Gingrich has been savaged for his efforts."[27]

Liberal and conservative analysts alike see the possibility of 1996 as a critical election, fought out over the scope and role of government, that will shape American political alignments well into the new century.

"It may just be that we need one more election," Gingrich said. "It may literally be that the Clinton administration cannot agree to the kind of decentralization and lower spending and lower taxes we represent."[28]

Republicans claimed a mandate based on the November 1994 vote that gave them control of Congress. But a Gallup poll a month after the election showed that some 60 percent of the voters were unfamiliar with what the Contract with America proposed. That contrasts with the 80 percent who acknowledged familiarity with the Civil Rights Act of 1964, as well as with who supported and who opposed it, the defining issue of the 1964 election. President Johnson could legitimately claim a mandate to push ahead with the civil rights program after his landslide victory over Republican Barry Goldwater.

The issues that divide the Clinton White House and the Republicans in Congress—more taxes, a balanced budget, a tight rein on federal spending and services, the loosening of federal welfare guarantees—may be too great in any case for the political bargainers in Washington to settle among themselves.

"There is much to be said for thrashing it out in another election," political scientist Walter Dean Burnham of the University of Texas observed.[29]

Notes: The Budget Can We Learn to Live Within Our Means?

1. Alison Mitchell, "Budget Bargainer for Clinton Reaches a Defining Moment," *The New York Times*, December 2, 1995, 1.
2. Todd S. Purdum, "As Long Promised, President Vetoes the GOP Budget," *The New York Times*, December 7, 1995, 1.
3. Michael Kelly, "Grandma Versus the Kids," *The New Yorker*, December 4, 1995, 41; Michael Wines, "Such a Doable Deal," *The New York Times*, December 9, 1995, B15.
4. Iwan W. Morgan, *Deficit Government: Taxing and Spending in Modern America* (Chicago: Ivan R. Dee, 1995), 89; 155; 148.
5. Jefferson, Lincoln quotes are drawn from Morgan, *Deficit Government*, 8.
6. Morgan, *Deficit Government*, 155–61.
7. Morgan, *Deficit Government*, 165.
8. Morgan, *Deficit Government*, 167; 187.
9. Morgan, *Deficit Government*, 179; John Ellis, "Like Him or Not, Gingrich Is Doing the Right Thing on Deficit," Op-Ed, *The Boston Globe*, December 2, 1995.
10. Morgan, *Deficit Government*, 180.
11. Morgan, *Deficit Government*, 14.
12. "Mr. Clinton's Budget," Editorial, *The New York Times*, December 8, 1995.
13. Purdum, "As Long Promised, President Vetoes the GOP Budget."
14. David E. Rosenbaum, "Behind the Budget Deadlock," *The New York Times*, December 16, 1995, 16.
15. Robert Pear, "GOP Emphasizes Similar Estimates in Medicare Plans," *The New York Times*, December 11, 1995, 1.
16. Kelly, "Grandma Versus the Kids," 42.
17. Kelly, "Grandma Versus the Kids," 44.
18. "Hearts, Minds and Wallets: The Showdown over the Budget Will Define the Republican Party and Change Millions of Lives," *U.S. News & World Report*, November 20, 1995, 55.
19. Monica Borkowski, "Medicaid at a Glance," *The New York Times*, December 5, 1995, B9.
20. David S. Broder, "A Battle of Substance over Medicaid, Welfare Funding," Op-Ed in *The Boston Globe*, December 14, 1995.
21. Robert Pear, "Leaders of AMA Critical of Plan to Alter Medicaid," *The New York Times*, December 5, 1995, 1.
22. Pear, "Leaders of AMA Critical of Plan to Alter Medicaid."
23. Milt Freudenheim, "Doctors' Incomes Fall as Managed Care Grows," *The New York Times*, November 11, 1995, 1.
24. R.W. Apple, Jr., "A Fight in Which Polls Weigh All Moves," *The New York Times*, November 15, 1995, 1.
25. Kelly, "Grandma Versus the Kids," 41.
26. Kelly, "Grandma Versus the Kids," 42.
27. Ellis, "Like Him or Not, Gingrich is Doing the Right Thing."
28. Alison Mitchell, "Budget Foes See Fight Continuing Till the Election," *The New York Times*, January 11, 1996, 1.
29. Robin Toner, "Accord on Budget Won't End the Debate," *The New York Times*, The Week in Review, December 10, 1995, 3.

3 The Federal Government
The Cause of Our Problems or the Solution?

by
Michael Golay

Americans are ambivalent about their government. They are quick to say it is too big and too powerful, that it is clumsy, inept, unresponsive. Yet opinion surveys show that many Americans retain a stubborn faith in what government can deliver. They expect it to curb crime, alleviate poverty, create jobs, even put a college education within reach of everyone who wants one.

Two Gallup Organization polls taken nineteen months apart reflect Americans' conflicting, contradictory views of government's role. In March 1993, Gallup asked about government's use of its power to promote citizens' welfare. Does the government use about the right amount of power, the polltakers asked, not enough, or too much power? Fifty-eight percent of respondents thought the government exercised the right amount of power or should use more. Fewer than four in every ten—38 percent—thought government had become too powerful.

An October 1994 survey rephrased the question: Does the government try to do too many things that should be left to individuals or private organizations?

« **Americans retain a stubborn faith in what government can deliver.** »

« **On no other general philosophical issue do Republicans and Democrats stand so far apart as they do on government's role.** »

Fifty-seven percent thought the government tried to do too much. Only 37 percent said government ought to do more.

The debate over how much government is enough dominated American politics in 1995. Distrust of federal solutions to the nation's problems has been widespread in the 1990s. The conviction that the central government usually makes things worse fueled Ross Perot's strong showing as an independent presidential candidate in 1992. In a blaze of publicity in 1993, the Clinton administration launched its effort to "reinvent" government—to build a system that, in the administration's catchphrase, "works better and costs less." In 1995, the new Republican majority in Congress began reversing a half century of growth in federal programs for the general welfare.

Rhetorically, at least, on no other general philosophical issue do Republicans and Democrats stand so far apart as they do on government's role. Yet Gallup reported that a fair number of respondents found little difference in the approach of the two mainstream parties.

Slightly more than a quarter, 27 percent, of respondents said Republicans generally want government to do too much; nearly half, 46 percent, said this about Democrats. But roughly equal numbers said both parties had it "about right": 40 percent thought that way about the Republicans, 35 percent about the Democrats.

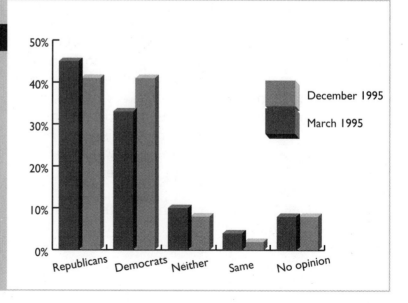

American Opinion

Do you think the country would be better off if the Republicans controlled Congress or if the Democrats controlled Congress?

December 1995

March 1995

Republicans   Democrats   Neither   Same   No opinion

Source: The Gallup Poll

Faith, Trust, and Expectation

As the federal government attempts to trim away the fat, the opinion polls turn up contradictory attitudes about what citizens expect of it.

"There is no government service that could not be delivered by nongovernmental organizations," wrote Professor Donald F. Kettl, a University of Wisconsin political scientist. "Because the private sector *can* do anything, there is less certainty about what government *ought* to do."[1]

Gallup at least found some agreement on the notion that the federal government should provide moral leadership. In a January 1996 survey, a majority of respondents, 59 percent, said government ought to lead the way in promoting "traditional values in our society." A strong minority of 36 percent thought government had no business endorsing values, traditional or otherwise; 5 percent had no opinion.

For all the battering it has taken in recent years, the federal government still inspires a fair amount of trust, Gallup reported. There is, however, a slight hedging of bets. According to a June 1994 Gallup poll, nearly three-quarters of respondents (73 percent) thought they could trust the government in Washington to do the right thing "some of the time"; only 14 percent had faith in government "most of the time." A fringe of 9 per-

«

'Because the private sector *can* do anything, there is less certainty about what government *ought* to do.'

»

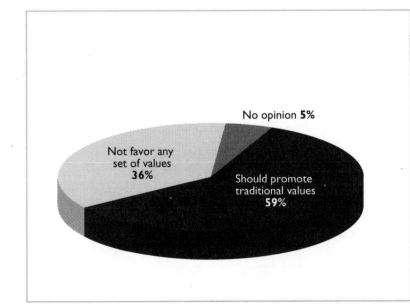

No opinion **5%**

Not favor any set of values **36%**

Should promote traditional values **59%**

American Opinion

Some people think the government should promote traditional values in our society. Others think the government should not favor any particular set of values. Which comes closer to your own view?

Source: The Gallup Poll, January 12–15, 1996

« **Citizens are deeply wary of granting government too much power.** »

cent felt so alienated they could not bring themselves to trust the government in any circumstances.

Polltakers asking the same question at the start of 1994 reported a slightly higher level of trust in government. A breakdown of opinion from the January 1994 poll showed that Democrats (25 percent) were almost twice as likely as Republicans (13 percent) to trust government most of the time, and that those who approved of Clinton were three times as likely to trust government (26 percent) as those who did not (8 percent).

Older people, nonwhites, and poor people were somewhat more likely to trust government than younger people, whites, and the well-to-do. The breakdown found little variation among geographic regions; little difference among those who described themselves as liberal, moderate, or conservative; and only a slight difference between men and women.

People may trust their government in the abstract, but opinion surveys suggest they harbor broad suspicions about the functionaries who run it. In a June 1994 Gallup poll, 58 percent of respondents believed "quite a few" government officials were crooked. Around three of every ten, 29 percent, thought not many were; 6 percent thought hardly any were; and a deeply cynical 5 percent thought all government officials were dishonest.

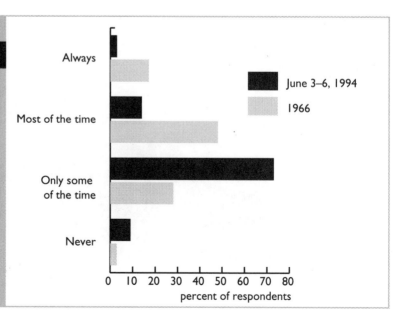

American Opinion

How much of the time do you think you can trust government in Washington to do what is right?

June 3–6, 1994
1966

Always
Most of the time
Only some of the time
Never

0 10 20 30 40 50 60 70 80
percent of respondents

Source: 1994, The Gallup Poll
1966, Michigan National
Election Study

Citizens are also deeply wary of granting the government too much power. Even in the immediate aftermath of the Oklahoma City terrorist bombing in April 1995, Gallup polltakers found that 39 percent of Americans agreed with the statement "The federal government has become so large and powerful that it poses an immediate threat to the rights and freedoms of ordinary citizens." While 58 percent disagreed with the statement, the results suggest there is no consensus for increasing the role of government in American life. When asked in the same poll whether the federal government as a whole had "too much," "about the right amount of," or "not enough" power, 60 percent of respondents said "too much," while only 37 percent said "about right" or "not enough." (To no one's surprise, the specific government agency that scored the highest ranking on the "too much power" scale was the Internal Revenue Service.) Interestingly, only 27 percent of respondents thought their state governments had too much power, while 61 percent felt state government had "not enough" or "about the right" amount of power.

"Reinventing Government"

The Clinton administration established the National Performance Review (NPR) in 1993 to carry out a cam-

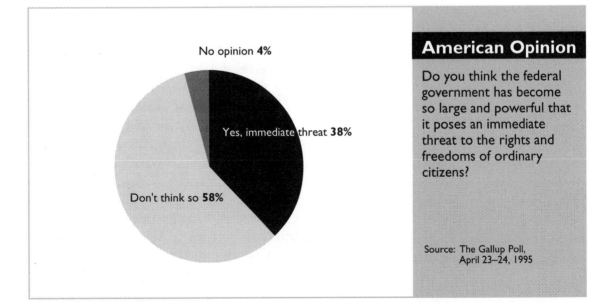

No opinion 4%

Yes, immediate threat 38%

Don't think so 58%

American Opinion

Do you think the federal government has become so large and powerful that it poses an immediate threat to the rights and freedoms of ordinary citizens?

Source: The Gallup Poll, April 23–24, 1995

paign promise to streamline the bureaucracy, increase government efficiency, and cut costs. Under Vice President Al Gore's direction, the NPR pledged to shed government jobs, rescind needless regulations, consolidate programs, and put customers—the citizens—first.

The NPR issued its first report, *From Red Tape to Results: Creating a Government That Works Better and Costs Less*, on Labor Day 1993. With some 800 recommendations, it promised to reduce the 2.1-million–member federal workforce by 250,000 and save more than $100 billion in government expenditures.

Initial responses were broadly favorable, even though some skeptics noted the NPR would be the eleventh major attempt to overhaul the government in this century. "Americans are entitled to a better return on their tax dollars than they are getting from an inefficient, excessively expensive federal bureaucracy," The *Star-Ledger* of Newark, New Jersey, observed.[2] Other opinionmakers warned of the dangers of inertia and politics. "In general everyone is going to like this plan," the *Tulsa World* said. "In detail, every sentence will be fiercely opposed by one or more influential groups."[3]

According to Kettl and other analysts, the NPR has made a start on changing the reform-resistant "culture" of government agencies, it has simplified government rules and processes, and it has encouraged widespread management innovation. The result, claimed Kettl a year after the release of *From Red Tape to Results*, "has been one of the Clinton administration's few clear victories."[4]

The NPR set a series of broad goals: cutting red tape, "empowering" government employees, freeing agency managers to bring the entrepreneurial spirit to the bureaucracy. But in the interests of getting the program off to a fast start, the experts say, Gore's team failed to think some critical questions through. In the short run, the campaign concentrated on "downsizing"—the euphemism, borrowed from corporate America, for abolishing jobs by the thousands. In fact, the federal bureaucracy has been shrinking as a percentage of the labor force for thirty-five years. In 1995, the 2.1 million federal jobs (excluding the military) made up a smaller

« **The National Performance Review has been one of the Clinton administration's few clear victories.** »

share of all jobs than at any other time since the start of World War II. In the view of some civil servants, the NPR had asked bureaucrats to take risks and test innovative ideas at a time when their agencies were already shorthanded—and their own jobs were threatened.[5]

Besides, one critic noted, the near-absence of creative thinking in the bureaucracy is only part of the problem. The NPR report ignored another aspect entirely, according to David Segal of *The Washington Monthly*: the declining quality of the federal workforce. For many years, wrote Segal, the civil service has tended "to attract people who are just looking for steady work with good benefits, rather than folks who are actually filled with an impulse to serve the commonweal."[6]

(continued on page 40)

The Reinvention Machine

Vice President Al Gore began the Clinton administration's campaign to reshape the federal government with a public relations fanfare. He appeared on a network variety show to take a hammer to an overpriced government ashtray. And he turned up on the White House lawn in front of two forklifts loaded with boxes of presumably burdensome and unnecessary government regulations.

The stunts attracted attention to Gore's National Performance Review report, released in September 1993. The report, *From Red Tape to Results: Creating a Government Work Better and Cost Less*, contained some 800 recommendations aimed at taking $108 billion out of the federal budget.

The program achieved substantial results in its first year. Nearly 90,000 positions were trimmed from the civilian government workforce. Programs were consolidated. Bureaucrats were encouraged to try out new ideas. The U.S. Customs Service promised to speed international air travelers through the lines within five minutes.

Some government agencies formed experimental partnerships with private concerns. In the Maine office of the much-abused federal Occupational Safety and Health Administration (OSHA), for example, managers asked the 200 firms with the largest number of injury claims to set up voluntary inspection programs and to correct their own problems. In only two years, the voluntary programs reported close to five times as many hazards as OSHA had found over an eight-year period—and fixed two of every three of them.[1]

To nobody's surprise, Gore's review turned up some classic bureaucratic absurdities. One of the best: a Pentagon-required stress test for a particular type of cake. A confection that broke or cracked after being placed on two 4-inch-diameter cans spaced 6 $\frac{1}{2}$ inches apart failed the government test.[2]

«
How are bureaucratic entrepreneurs to be prevented from running amok?
»

The government, he went on, no longer attempts to recruit top people into the bureaucracy. "It's been thirty years since any president even *tried* to inspire citizens to join the government," Segal wrote. A 1988 report for the Office of Policy Management warned that, far from attracting the best and the brightest, government agencies were drawing "the best of the desperate."[7]

Beyond that, the NPR's vague objectives rely on the independent judgment of too many managers and are open to varying interpretations, analysts suggest.

"Where do procedural due process and proper administrative safeguards become red tape?" Kettl asked. How are bureaucratic entrepreneurs to be prevented from running amok? "What glue will prevent government from disintegrating into a vast network of quasi-independent operators? What process will ensure that the public interest dominates private behavior?"[8]

Some career bureaucrats found aspects of the NPR simplistic, even silly. Wrote Todd S. Purdum in *The New York Times*:

> Managers in some agencies complain that the program has substituted New Age touchy-feeliness for old-fashioned gobbledygook. Some of the vehicles for encouraging employees to take risks and make common sense decisions without waiting for

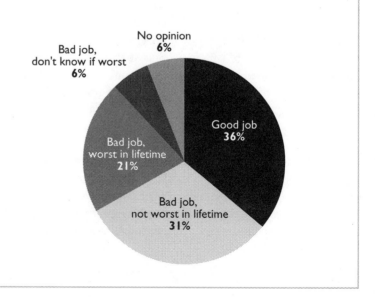

American Opinion

Based on the recent events in Washington, do you think the federal government is doing a good job or a bad job of governing the country? If bad job: Do you think it is the worst job of governing in your lifetime, or do you think there have been other times when it has been when it has been just as bad or worse?

Source: The Gallup Poll, January 5–7, 1996

No opinion
6%

Bad job, don't know if worst
6%

Good job
36%

Bad job, worst in lifetime
21%

Bad job, not worst in lifetime
31%

cumbersome approvals do have a kind of 'hall-monitor tone.' For example, the Interior Department issues 'forgiveness coupons' and the Education Department has 'reinvention permission slips.'[9]

Every survey shows that Americans respond warmly to any offer of more for less. Why shouldn't they? In some specific areas, though, the message of the polls is mixed. People may want the bureaucracy to shrink, but that does not necessarily mean they want their favorite government programs to disappear.

Gallup asked whether respondents would rather have more government services if that meant more taxes; fewer services in order to reduce taxes; or about the same level of services and taxes as now. Taken together, a majority favored more services and taxes (20 percent) or about the same levels of both (35 percent). Around four in every ten (41 percent) said they would accept fewer government services in return for lower taxes.

« **Around 41 percent said they would accept fewer government services in return for lower taxes.** »

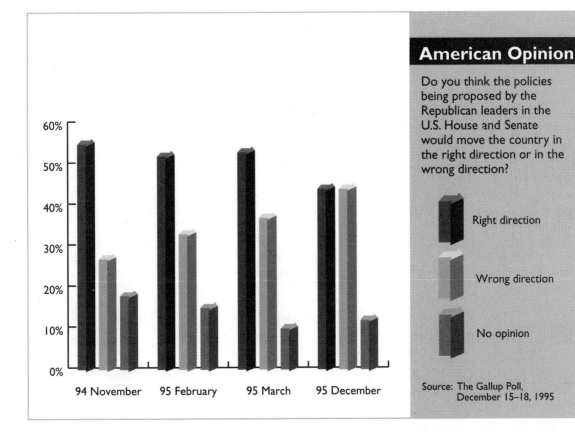

American Opinion

Do you think the policies being proposed by the Republican leaders in the U.S. House and Senate would move the country in the right direction or in the wrong direction?

Right direction

Wrong direction

No opinion

94 November   95 February   95 March   95 December

Source: The Gallup Poll,
December 15–18, 1995

Considerable support remains, too, for the government's protective and regulatory role. A majority judged the amount of government regulation of business and industry as "too little" or "about right." Fewer than four in every ten, 37 percent, thought there was too much government oversight.

The Rise of the States

Growth in government employment, when it has occurred, has come at the state and local levels, which together employ some 17 million civil servants. With the Republican-sponsored shift of federal programs and responsibilities to the states, local government growth seems likely to continue even as resources diminish.

While the Clinton administration and the congressional Republicans agree in a general way on the devolution of power to the states, they are deeply divided over the details. Republicans moved in 1995 to shift such key federal programs as welfare and Medicaid to the states, and to drop the sixty-year-old federal guarantee of basic subsistence for everyone. Democrats countered with charges that the Republicans were pulling the safety net out from under millions of Americans.

Prospects are for increasing conflict as the complex formulas for federal block-grant aid to the states are

> « **Republicans moved in 1995 to shift such key federal programs as welfare and Medicaid to the states.** »

American Opinion

Some people think the government is trying to do too many things that should be left to individuals and businesses. Others think the government should do more to solve our country's problems. Which comes closer to your view?

Source: The Gallup Poll

Mixed/No opinion

Government should do more

Government doing too much

March 1993: 6%, 45%, 49%

January 1996: 7%, 58%, 35%

negotiated—conflict rooted not so much in ideology or political affiliation as in geography. Spending on welfare and health programs varies widely from state to state. The Northeast complains of shifts in federal resources to the Sun Belt. The South argues that New York and Massachusetts have taken more than their share for too long.

"It is preposterous that Texas gets almost half the money that New York gets," said Representative John Bryant, a Texas Democrat. "Why should a grandmother in a New York nursing home receive an average of $4,027 in federal funds while a grandmother in a Texas nursing home receives only $2,356?"[10]

Such disparities usually reflect levels of state contributions to the cost of a program. Under the block-grant system, a state would no longer be rewarded for making a greater commitment than its neighbor. This provision has given rise to Democrats' fears of a "race to the bottom," with poorer states starving once-mandated social programs of funds or shutting them down altogether.

Some public affairs experts challenge the assumption that the states automatically will prove less generous than the national government. "Predictions are more rooted in ideology than in analysis," said Richard P. Nathan, director of the Rockefeller Institute of Government in Albany, New York. "We really don't know how the states will respond."[11]

What seems likely, though, is that state governments will have to expand their roles at a time when many are deeply engaged in their own projects for tax and budget cutting, streamlining, contracting out, and privatizing.

"You must not assume that the Republican success in devolving power to the states ends the debate," said Mickey Edwards, a former Republican congressman who now teaches public policy at Harvard University. "It has just changed from Washington to the states. The danger, of course, is that if the people don't want Washington or [the states] to do the job, is government going to get out of the business altogether? Somebody will have to make decisions."[12]

«

What seems likely is that state governments will have to expand their roles at a time when many are engaged in their own projects for tax and budget cutting.

»

Several states—such as California, Wisconsin, Massachusetts, and New Jersey, all under aggressive Republican governors—have taken the lead in shrinking government and in privatizing government services.

In 1995, for example, New Jersey turned auto registration and driver's license renewal over to a private firm. Massachusetts Governor William Weld proposed issuing lifetime licenses and permanent registrations that would lead to the near-elimination of the state's Registry of Motor Vehicles.[13]

A Look Ahead

Opinion surveys express fairly clearly what people expect from government. Gallup found high levels of support for government involvement in meeting a range of social needs, especially health and medical care. At the same time, though, many question the federal government's effectiveness. In a January 1996 Gallup poll, a majority of respondents, 58 percent, said the government does a "bad job" of governing. Only around a third, 36 percent, credited the federal government with doing a good job.

«
'When things work badly, it is because government tries to do things that are very hard or impossible.'
»

- A majority of respondents, 56 percent, said the government should take a "great deal" of responsibility for health care. Another 31 percent said the government should accept a "fair amount" of responsibility.

- A slight majority, 52 percent, said the government should take a great deal (16 percent) or a fair amount (36 percent) of responsibility for providing a job to all who want one. Fewer than half said the government should take hardly any (34 percent) or no responsibility (13 percent).

- Nearly two-thirds, 64 percent, thought government should take a great deal (17 percent) or a fair amount (47 percent) of responsibility for providing a college education for those who want one. Only about a third, 34 percent, thought government should take hardly any (25 percent) or no responsibility (9 percent).

- A majority, 56 percent, believed government should take a great deal (17 percent) or a fair amount (39 percent) of responsibility for providing day care for working parents. Around four in every ten believed the government should take hardly any (29 percent) or no responsibility (13 percent) for child-care programs.

Will the states do as well as or better than the federal government has done on such issues? How deep does support run for a Republican-engineered shift of power to the states? Americans' views of government's role—and their expectations of what it should deliver—will surely be key issues in the 1996 presidential campaign.

When government fails, it generally fails spectacularly. "Often," says political scientist Donald Kettl, "when things work badly it is because it [government] tries to do things that are very hard or impossible, like preventing drug abuse, training unemployed workers, cleaning up toxic waste, or providing welfare without creating dependence."[14] Americans, he observes, should be realistic about the difficult things.

Republicans will campaign on their plans to reduce or abolish scores of federal programs and turn power, responsibility, and resources from Washington back to the state capitals. The Democrats—or, at any rate, Clinton administration Democrats—claim that they are delivering leaner, more efficient, and less expensive government, without sacrificing federal guarantees dating from the New Deal.

The voters will choose between contrasting prescriptions for governmental reform: one promising to fix the mechanism with some oiling and fine tuning and another that says a top-to-bottom overhaul is required.

Notes: **The Federal Government** The Cause of Our Problems or the Solution?

1. Donald F. Kettl and John J. Dilulio Jr., eds., *Inside the Reinvention Machine: Appraising Governmental Reform* (Washington, DC: The Brookings Institution, 1995), 51.
2. Editorial, *The Star-Ledger*, Newark, N.J., September 8, 1993.
3. Editorial, *Tulsa World*, September 8, 1993.
4. Donald F. Kettl, "Did Gore Reinvent Government? A Progress Report," *The New York Times*, September 6, 1994, A19.
5. Sylvia Nasar, "The Bureaucracy: What's Left to Shrink?" *The New York Times*, The Week in Review, June 11, 1995, 1.
6. David Segal, "What's Wrong with the Gore Report," *The Washington Monthly*, November 1993, 19.
7. Segal, "What's Wrong with the Gore Report," 19–20.
8. Kettl and Dilulio, eds., *Inside the Reinvention Machine*, 13.
9. Todd S. Purdum, "Gore, the Soldier of Streamlining, Returns to Lead Clinton's Charge," *The New York Times*, December 19, 1994, A1.
10. Robert Pear, "Shifting Where the Buck Stops," *The New York Times*, The Week in Review, October 29, 1995, 1.
11. Pear, "Shifting Where the Buck Stops," 1.
12. John Yemma, "State Begins a New Phase in Debate on Government," *The Boston Globe*, November 2, 1995, 1.
13. Yemma, "State Begins a New Phase in Debate on Government," 1.
14. Kettl and Dilulio, eds., *Inside the Reinvention Machine*, 83.

Notes: **The Reinvention Machine**

1. David S. Broder, "15 Ways to Make Government Good" in *The Boston Globe*, November 1, 1995, 17.
2. Todd S. Purdum, "Gore, the Soldier of Streamlining, Returns to Lead Clinton's Charge," *The New York Times*, December 19, 1994, A1.

4 Affirmative Action
Is It Still Needed? Was It Ever?

by
Michael Golay

Most white Americans believe affirmative action has worked so well that preferential programs for minorities and women are no longer needed. Blacks—especially black men—see the matter differently. It is as though the two groups live in separate countries. To blacks, discrimination is endemic. In one opinion survey, more than half the black male respondents claimed they had been passed over for a job, a promotion, or admission to a school because of their race.

Gallup polling in 1995 revealed deep racial and political party fault lines on affirmative action. White men, white women, black men and women, and other minorities disagree fundamentally, even irreconcilably, on specific elements of affirmative action, particularly on government-imposed remedies for discrimination.

Yet, surprisingly, the same polls show considerable support for the *principle* of affirmative action. Is there a contradiction? Well-meaning people may soften the edges of their responses, perhaps more so on racial matters. There seems to be a certain delicacy, or perhaps a lack of candor, in whites' responses to questions about race. In a general way, then, the surveys record a split decision.

"There is no broad consensus for eliminating affirmative-action programs," the Gallup Organization said in a 1995 special report on the issue, "although there is even less support for expanding them."

> **«**
> **There is no broad consensus for eliminating affirmative-action programs.**
> **»**

« **'Affirmative action and even welfare, at the beginning, was a great idea, but it got out of hand.'** »

The views of two Philadelphia men, as told to *The New York Times*, show the breadth of the divide between blacks and whites. Eddie Graham, thirty-seven years old, is a lawyer, and black. "A lot of blacks have gotten to where they are because of affirmative action," said Graham. "For them to say now it's time to end it, that's really a disservice to our younger generation that's coming along."[1]

Rich Romano, thirty-nine years old, is a firefighter, and white.

"Affirmative action and even welfare, at the beginning, was a great idea, but it got out of hand," Romano said. "Now it's gotten to be some kind of entitlement. Everybody thinks they're entitled to everything. No one wants to work hard any more."[2]

Affirmative action ranges from voluntary programs, such as employer outreach and education, to mandatory preferential programs for minorities and women, including hiring and promotion guarantees and set-asides of government contracts.

Such programs are in place at all levels of government and in many private businesses and educational institutions. Major federal agencies—including the Transportation Department, the Defense Department, and the Small Business Administration—set aside contracts and aid programs for minorities and women. Federal agencies enforce preferential hiring and pro-

American Opinion

Overall, do you think affirmative-action programs for the past thirty years have helped racial minorities, have hurt them, or have had no effect one way or the other?

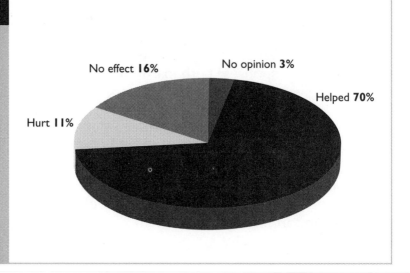

No effect **16%**   No opinion **3%**

Helped **70%**

Hurt **11%**

Source: The Gallup Poll, February 24–26, 1995

motion policies. States reserve federal funds—for highway construction, for example—for minority-owned businesses. State universities and most private colleges and universities practice affirmative action in admissions, hiring, and promotion.

Gallup surveys show that most whites doubt the fairness of practices based on race or gender preferences. Fair or not, though, such practices have unquestionably increased educational and economic opportunity for women and for blacks, Hispanics, and other minority groups. The number of blacks in managerial positions, for instance, has doubled during the era of affirmative action.

"There has been a stunning increase in the number of middle-class blacks and the number of blacks going to college or business or trade schools," says Hugh B. Price, the executive director of the National Urban League. "Our talent bank is exponentially fuller than it was twenty or thirty years ago."[3]

Nannette S. Simon is a case in point. In a letter to *The New York Times*, she identified herself as an African American who dropped out of her California high school in the tenth grade. Later, she passed the high school equivalency exam, scored well on college entrance exams, and through affirmative action won admission to the University of California at Berkeley. She went on to Harvard Law School and is today a securities lawyer in New York City.

"Had I not attended Berkeley," she wrote, "I can only guess that I would be working in a low-paying job and attempting to make ends meet and raise children, like millions of other minority families across the United States."[4]

Still, affirmative action sometimes carries a cost. "I got into law school because I am black," wrote Stephen L. Carter, a constitutional law scholar and a professor at Yale University, in his 1991 book *Reflections of an Affirmative Action Baby*. Carter argues that preference places a tremendous psychological burden on beneficiaries. Could they have gotten where they are without it? Too often, their colleagues doubt them; they often doubt themselves.

« **The number of blacks in managerial positions has doubled during the era of affirmative action.** »

American Opinion		In general, do you think we need to increase, keep the same, or decrease affirmative-action programs in this country?	
	Increase	Keep the same	Decrease
Overall	31%	26%	37%
Whites	26	26	41
Blacks	65	26	6
Racial Gap	−39	0	35
Men	27	24	43
Women	35	28	30
Gender Gap	−8	−4	7
White Men	22	24	48
White Women	29	29	35
Black Men	57	35	4
Black Women	71	19	7

Source: The Gallup Poll, March 17–19, 1995

« **'We should be concentrating on constructive dialogue about how to solve the problems of the real and continuing victims of the nation's legacy of racist oppression.'** »

Carter makes another, more damaging charge. "Among those training for business and professional careers," he wrote, "the benefits of affirmative action fall to those least in need of them." Argues Carter:

We should be concentrating on constructive dialogue about how to solve the problems of the real and continuing victims of the nation's legacy of racist oppression: the millions of struggling black Americans for whom affirmative action and entry into the professions are stunningly irrelevant.[5]

Preference Under Siege

Advocates of affirmative action suffered setbacks on several fronts in 1995.

In March, responding to attacks on affirmative action from the new Republican congressional majority, President Clinton ordered a review of all federal preference programs to determine whether they were working as designed and whether they were fair to white men.

In April, the General Accounting Office raised troubling questions about the effectiveness of a Small Business Administration set-aside program for minorities. A GAO report showed that 25 percent of the contracts in the SBA program went to 1 percent of the 5,000 participants. More than half the companies in the program received no contracts at all.

In May, the U.S. Supreme Court let stand a lower-court ruling that halted a University of Maryland scholarship program reserved for blacks. The court also struck down a Kansas City school desegregation program that required the state of Missouri to fund a program that attracted suburban white students to mainly black city high schools.

In June, the Supreme Court, in a 5–4 decision that shook the foundations of thirty years of affirmative-action policy, ruled in a case involving a Colorado highway contractor that any federal program that classifies people by race is constitutional only if it is narrowly tailored to achieve a compelling government interest. The court said in *Adarand Constructors v. Peña* that evidence of specific discrimination is necessary to justify programs that set aside government contracts for minority-owned businesses.

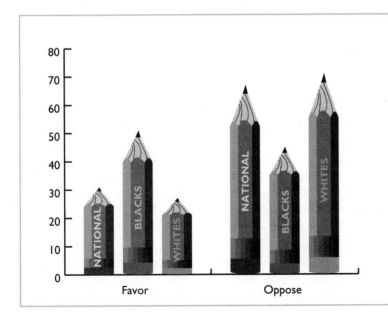

American Opinion

Do you generally favor or oppose making a certain number of scholarships at public colleges and universities available only to minorities?

("No opinion" omitted)

Source: The Gallup Poll, March 17–19, 1995

A white contractor who lost out on a job to a Hispanic-owned company brought the case. The contract, for a guardrail project on a U.S. highway in Colorado, went to the Hispanic-owned company even though it submitted a higher bid for the job.

"Whenever the government treats any person unequally because of his or her race, that person has suffered an injury that falls squarely within the language and spirit of the Constitution's guarantee of equal protection," Justice Sandra Day O'Connor wrote in the court's majority opinion.[6]

In response, the Justice Department advised in a memo to all federal agencies that a general assump-

Gallup's Four Opinion Groups

In breaking down polling results on affirmative action, Gallup analysts identified four broad opinion groups, each of which represents about a quarter of Americans.

- **True believers**, 28 percent, strongly support affirmative action, including remedial programs. Nearly two-thirds say such programs should be increased. Eight in every ten favor quotas. Nearly two-thirds are Democrats; only 29 percent are Republicans. Nearly a third are minorities. Fewer than a quarter are white males. As a group, true believers have less education and income than Americans overall.
- **Antagonists**, 24 percent, strongly oppose affirmative action, even voluntary

outreach programs. Nearly three-quarters say all programs should be scaled back. Only 11 percent believe discrimination is a major problem for women and minorities. Three-quarters say affirmative action is unnecessary and that businesses and schools can be trusted to provide equal opportunity. Seventy-one percent are Republicans; only 21 percent are Democrats. Ninety-eight percent are white; 55 percent are white males.
- **Floaters**, 21 percent, support affirmative action but, paradoxically, discount the prevalence of discrimination. Though they support many remedial programs, only 10 percent of floaters believe job discrimination is

a major problem for minorities and women. Forty-four percent are Republicans and 45 percent are Democrats. Thirteen percent are minorities. As a group, floaters are older, less educated, and poorer than Americans overall.
- **Sympathetic opponents**, 27 percent, are about evenly divided on affirmative action in principle. Forty-six percent favor it; 43 percent oppose. This group supports voluntary outreach but opposes remedial programs, such as set-asides and quotas. A majority, however, believe job discrimination is a major problem for blacks and Hispanics. Half of this group are women, half are men. Forty-nine percent are Republicans, 41 percent are Democrats. Sympathetic opponents are better educated and more comfortably off than the average.

tion of workplace racism or sexism would no longer be sufficient reason for affirmative action. The agencies were told to shut down any programs that enforced quotas, gave preferences for unqualified people, or used reverse discrimination to reach their goals.

In no place has affirmative action come under a more sustained assault than in California, the nation's largest and most racially diverse state. In June 1995, California Governor Pete Wilson, a Republican who only a few weeks before had launched his short-lived candidacy for the party's presidential nomination, issued an executive order abolishing some of the state's affirmative-action programs. In July, at Wilson's urging, the regents of the nine-campus, 150,000-student University of California system voted to eliminate race-conscious affirmative action in admissions, hiring, and contracting. And petitioners were seeking a referendum vote on the so-called California Civil Rights Initiative, which would halt all use of racial preferences in state government.

"It's the end of an era," said Constance Horner of the U.S. Civil Rights Commission. "What tells us that this is the end of an era is that all branches of government—the courts, the Congress, the White House, even the state legislatures—are actively engaged in the same process, and that's a rare event in American politics."[7]

The Clinton Defense

Still, President Clinton mounted an aggressive general defense of affirmative action in 1995. A White House review concluded that affirmative-action programs work well and, on the whole, do not place an undue burden on white males.

"Affirmative action has not always been perfect, and affirmative action should not go on forever," the president said in a major address on the issue in July 1995. "It should be changed now to take care of those things that are wrong, and it should be retired when the job is done.

"I am resolved that that day will come, but the evidence suggests, indeed screams, that that day has not

«
President Clinton mounted an aggressive defense of affirmative action in 1995.

»

come. The job of ending discrimination in this country is not over."

Clinton threw out a catchphrase to summarize his views on affirmative action:

"We should have a simple slogan," he said. "Mend it, but don't end it."[8]

Gallup respondents mostly agreed. In a survey taken shortly after Clinton's speech, only 22 percent said affirmative action should be eliminated. Sixty-one percent said such programs were good in principle but needed reform. Eight percent of those polled thought affirmative action worked fine and ought to be left unchanged.

The political fault lines Gallup analysts identified were evident in the reactions to Clinton's stand.

"He should have said end it; you can't mend it," California's Governor Wilson said. The federal government ought to "get out of the group-preference business," said Senator Bob Dole, a leading candidate for the 1996 Republican presidential nomination.[9]

Perhaps to their surprise, liberal opinionmakers found much to praise in Clinton's defense of the embattled program.

« Clinton's slogan on affirmative action is 'Mend it, but don't end it.' »

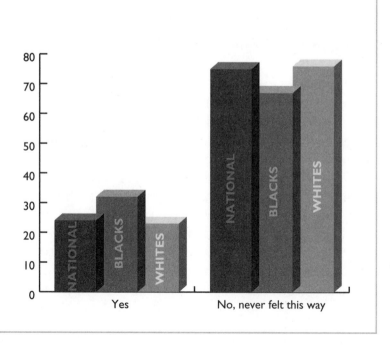

American Opinion

Have you ever felt that a well-qualified person at your workplace was hired or promoted as a direct result of affirmative-action policies—who probably *would not* have been hired *without* affirmative action—or have you never felt this way?

Source: The Gallup Poll,
March 17–19, 1995

"Clinton did the thing that supporters of affirmative action urged the president to do," columnist Derrick Z. Jackson wrote in *The Boston Globe*. "In the guts of his speech, he delivered the facts: unemployment rates of African Americans and Latinos; the wage gap between women and men; the fact that white men with only high school degrees make more than Hispanic women with college degrees.

"Clinton reminded this country how white men make up 43 percent of our work force but hold 95 percent of top corporate jobs," Jackson went on. "He said that out of 90,000 complaints to the federal government of employment discrimination based on race, ethnicity, or gender, fewer than 3 percent were for reverse discrimination."[10]

« 'White men make up 43 percent of our work force but hold 95 percent of top corporate jobs.' »

Affirmative Action: A History

A young black Detroit lawyer named Hobart Taylor, Jr., coined the phrase in 1961, in the early weeks of the Kennedy administration. In an executive order he helped to write, Taylor called for "affirmative action" to assure that job applicants were considered without regard to race or color. The order created a President's Committee on Equal Employment Opportunity, which had the authority to bar federal contractors who discriminated in their hiring practices.

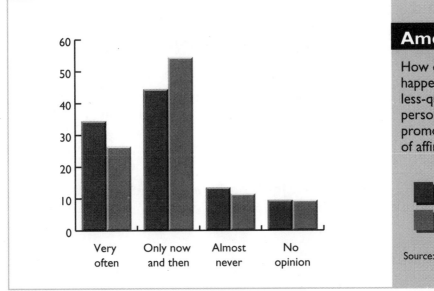

American Opinion

How often does it happen these days that a less-qualified black person gets a job or a promotion only because of affirmative action?

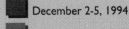 December 2-5, 1994

February 8-9, 1993

Source: The Gallup Poll

At first, however, the term carried no connotation of racial preference, and President Kennedy remained cool to the notion. "I think we ought not to begin the quota system," he said in 1963. "We should look over our employment rolls, look over areas where we are hiring people and at least make sure we are giving everyone a fair chance. But not hard and fast quotas."[11]

In 1964, the landmark Civil Rights Act declared job discrimination illegal and established an Equal Employment Opportunity Commission to hear complaints. Southern Democrats, with their conservative Republican allies, fought a long battle against the measure. Mississippi Senator James Eastland, a leader of the opposition, introduced an argument that would resurface thirty years later.

"The bill would discriminate against white people," Eastland said. "I know what will happen if the bill is passed. I know what will happen if there is a choice between hiring a white man or hiring a Negro, both having equal qualifications. I know who will get the job. It will not be the white man."[12]

To appease the Eastland bloc, the legislation withheld cease-and-desist powers that would have given the commission greater authority to attack discrimination in the workplace. That was part of the problem. Civil rights groups recognized another, greater impediment: Color-blind statutes and programs that relied on persuasion failed to account for persistent and continuing inequities in background, education, and training, let alone the long, sorry history of race and gender discrimination. They did not, in fact, attempt to correct the past.

In a speech in June 1965, President Johnson set a lofty goal for affirmative action: "We seek not just equality as a right and a theory," he said, "but equality as a fact and a result."[13]

On September 24, 1965, after a summer of outbreaks of violent racial uprisings in Los Angeles and other major cities, Johnson issued Executive Order 11246, regarded as the founding document of affirmative action. It gave the federal Department of Labor the au-

> **« A series of court decisions and executive actions constructed a system of race-conscious affirmative action. »**

thority and resources to require employers to aggressively seek out qualified minority candidates.

From this starting point, a series of court decisions and executive actions constructed a system of race-conscious affirmative action. The Supreme Court, in *Griggs v. Duke Power Co.* (1971) and other rulings, held that discrimination should not be considered as the denial of the rights of individuals but as the sum of the unequal effects of racist employment practices. Widespread discrimination in the workplace, the court said, could be assumed.

In 1968, the Johnson administration introduced the Philadelphia Plan, one of the early preferential programs. It called for the hiring of minorities in federal construction contract jobs. Johnson's successor, Richard Nixon, pushed the plan aggressively, at least in part for political reasons. (Nixon reasoned that forcing affirmative action on organized labor would set two core Democratic constituencies, unions and blacks, against

Quotas in Birmingham

America devised affirmative action as a remedy for inequity, but inequities in the remedy are not difficult to find.

In the Birmingham, Alabama, fire department, an inflexible racial-preference program routinely passed over whites for promotions in favor of blacks, even when the whites—on paper, anyway—were clearly more qualified. According to *The New York Times*, Birmingham specifically reserved officer vacancies for blacks during the 1980s. In 1983, out of 95 whites and 18 blacks who took the examination for lieutenant, 89 whites and 9 blacks passed. The two top scorers, both white, were promoted. But the city passed over 76 higher-scoring whites to give the other openings to the three top-rated black candidates. In 1994, a U.S. appeals court ruled the Birmingham program illegal. In April 1995, the U.S. Supreme Court let the lower-court ruling stand.

There is, of course, another side to the story.

Racism was pervasive in Birmingham. During the 1960s, the city's all-white fire department turned high-pressure hoses on black civil rights marchers. Before 1968, there were no blacks in the Birmingham fire department. In 1974, there were only six blacks. Today the 500-member department is 30 percent black.

"The white firefighters are always saying, 'Well, he got that job because he's black,'" Lt. Charles Gordon told Rick Bragg of *The Times*. "But they never question the idea that they got a job because they were white."[1]

each other.) Whatever the motive, the Nixon version of the Philadelphia Plan set strict hiring goals and timetables for the building trades—quotas, in fact.

In its best-known ruling on affirmative action, the reverse-discrimination case of *Bakke v. Regents of the University of California,* in 1978, the Supreme Court ordered the University of California, Davis, to admit a white medical school applicant who argued he had been turned down on the basis of race. In response, the school shut down its minority-preference program. The Court added, however, that universities could make race a positive factor in admissions—an endorsement of race-conscious affirmative action.

The Reagan administration launched the first concerted challenge to the preference system in the 1980s. The Reagan White House argued broadly that discrimination must be proved, not assumed. Conservatives also claimed that racial preferences violate basic principles of fairness in going beyond equality of opportunity and attempting to engineer equality of outcome. America, they said, should guarantee equal opportunity and nothing more.

All the same, the courts continued to uphold race and gender preferences. There matters stood until 1995.

American Opinion

The Need for Affirmative Action

("No opinion" omitted)

Women

Minorities

Source: The Gallup Poll, February 24–26, 1995

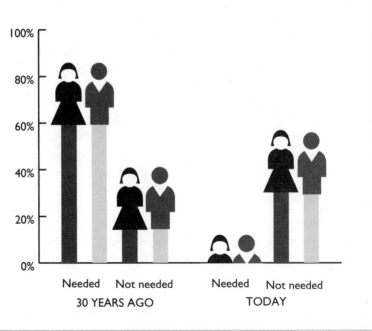

| | Needed | Not needed | Needed | Not needed |
| 30 YEARS AGO | | | TODAY | |

California, Again

Though congressional Republicans initiated the anti–affirmative-action campaign in Washington, California turned out to be the contested ground on which opponents won a series of victories in 1995.

If the voters approve it, the California Civil Rights Initiative would abolish race-conscious affirmative action there. Joe Gelman, a spokesman for the referendum campaign, has invoked Martin Luther King, Jr., and the rhetoric of the 1960s civil rights movement in championing the initiative. "It's consistent with the principles on which the civil rights movement originally stood," Gelman said. It reflects, he went on, paraphrasing King, a vision of "a society judging people on the content of their character rather than the color of their skin."[14]

In pressuring the University of California regents to give up affirmative action, Governor Wilson claimed that students who did not meet minimum academic requirements were being admitted to UC campuses solely on the basis of race. As a result, qualified white students were being turned away, at least from the campus of their first choice. A Wilson ally, Ward Connerly, a Sacramento businessman and one of two blacks on the twenty-six-member board of regents, introduced the resolution to dismantle affirmative action.

"Our system of preferences is becoming entrenched as it builds its own constituency," Connerly said. "Our obsessive preoccupation with race continues to add to the divide."[15]

In fact, no qualified applicant has ever been refused admission to the UC system. Moreover, supporters of affirmative action point out that admissions exceptions are made routinely—for UCLA and UC-Berkeley athletes, for example, and in other areas. They also note that, cumulatively, minorities admitted to UC meet exacting standards of academic achievement, although the dropout rate for blacks is higher than for other groups.

One study showed that black students at Berkeley had a mean grade point average in high school of 3.43

«
The Supreme Court ordered the University of California, Davis, to admit a white medical school applicant who argued he had been turned down on the basis of race.
»

American Opinion	Affirmative Action Approval by Subgroups: For Women			
	Approve		Disapprove	No Opinion
	with quotas	no quotas		
Sex:				
Men	7%	38%	51%	4%
Women	12	43	40	5
Race:				
White	8	38	49	5
Nonwhite	23	55	16	6
Politics:				
Republican	9	30	55	6
Independent	5	50	38	7
Democrat	17	40	42	1

Source: The Gallup Poll, March 10, 1995

out of 4.0. Hispanics had a mean of 3.65. White students compiled a 3.86 mean grade point average. Asians had a near-perfect 3.95.[16]

Asian-Americans generally support abandoning affirmative action in UC admissions, noting that Asian enrollments at Berkeley and UCLA are likely to increase in consequence. Indeed, a Board of Regents study predicted that the number of Asians would rise, the number of whites would hold steady, and the number of blacks and Hispanics would decline.

From 1984 to 1994, white enrollment at all UC campuses fell from 70 percent of the total to 49 percent. Hispanic enrollment nearly doubled, from 7 percent to 13 percent. Asian enrollment climbed from 16 percent to 29 percent. Black enrollment remained steady at 4 percent.

The California regents voted to substitute other criteria for race as a preference—criteria such as growing up in an abusive home or in a bad neighborhood. But supporters of affirmative action say the numbers of blacks and Hispanics at the university's two most popular and prestigious campuses, Berkeley and UCLA, will inevitably decline.

Journalist Nicholas Lemann revisited the Alan Bakke case in mid-1995. Bakke accepted the place the Supreme Court offered him at the Medical School of the University of California at Davis, and he is today a hospital anesthesiologist in prosperous Rochester, Minnesota. According to Lemann, most of the black students admitted under the minority-preference program at Davis are today practicing medicine in underserved areas. One, Dr. Patrick Chavis, an obstetrician/gynecologist in the low-income, mostly black and Hispanic Los Angeles suburb of Compton, freely grants he would not be a doctor without affirmative action. And he offers no apologies for it.

"There's no way in hell—if it wasn't for some kind of affirmative action, there wouldn't be any black doctors," Chavis told Lemann. "Maybe one or two. Things haven't changed that much."[17]

Opinion in Detail

Affirmative action divides Americans neatly along racial and political party lines. Blacks are far more likely than whites to support remedial programs such as quotas and set-asides. Blacks favor expanding affirmative action; whites want no change or a reduction in such programs. Clear majorities of Democrats support most affirmative-action programs; clear majorities of Republicans oppose them.

Overall, more than half (55 percent) of Gallup respondents say they support affirmative action in principle and that such programs should be increased (31 percent) or maintained at present levels (26 percent). About a third (34 percent) are opposed in principle and say affirmative action should be cut back (37 percent).

Overwhelmingly, respondents believe affirmative-action programs were needed when they were introduced thirty years ago. They are, however, ambivalent about their usefulness today. In early 1995, just 41 percent told Gallup such programs were needed; 57 percent disagreed. Shortly after President Clinton

«
Affirmative action divides Americans neatly along racial and political party lines.

»

«
Should a business with few minority employees fill a job opening with a black or a Hispanic instead of an equally qualified white applicant?
»

reaffirmed his support for affirmative action, Gallup polltakers found people about evenly divided on the issue: 49 percent agreed with affirmative action; 47 percent disagreed.

Levels of support vary greatly, depending on the program. Voluntary measures draw nearly unanimous approval from all groups. There is substantially less support for remedial programs, especially among whites.

Nearly three-quarters of respondents agree that companies ought to make special efforts to seek out qualified minorities and women and encourage them to apply for job openings. Eighty-two percent favor job training programs, and 75 percent favor special education classes to prepare minorities for college.

Should a business with few minority employees fill a job opening with a black or a Hispanic instead of an equally qualified white applicant? Respondents divide almost evenly on this question, with 48 percent saying yes, 44 percent saying no.

Respondents were evenly split on the issue of government contract set-asides for minorities and women. Forty-eight percent supported the notion, 48 percent opposed it. But two-thirds of those surveyed opposed setting aside a certain number of college scholarships for minorities.

A clear majority rejects the use of racial quotas in businesses and schools. Nearly two-thirds, 63 percent, oppose job quotas; 57 percent oppose college admissions quotas. More than eight in every ten respondents, 84 percent, oppose advances for minority applicants who are less qualified than whites.

Blacks and whites strongly support voluntary outreach programs, and there is only a minor difference of opinion over the question of job preferences for equally qualified minorities, with blacks more likely than whites to favor the preference. But there is a wide gap between black and white attitudes toward set-asides and quotas. Blacks fervently support both types of affirmative action. Whites oppose them. Blacks are twice as likely as whites (22 percent to 11 percent) to favor job or school preferences for unqualified minorities.

Race, then, is the main cultural fault line, to use Gallup's term. "Blacks and other minorities are most likely to perceive discrimination in society—both in general and in terms of their own personal experiences—than are whites," Gallup says.

Two-thirds of black respondents, 65 percent, believe affirmative-action programs should be increased, compared with only a quarter, 26 percent, of whites. Nearly three-quarters of blacks say black men face major discrimination at work, but fewer than 40 percent of whites agree.

How widespread are race and gender discrimination? Sixty-eight percent of whites agree with the statement that "blacks have as good a chance as white people in your community to get any type of job for which they are qualified." Sixty-two percent of blacks disagree.

As for job discrimination in general, whites are more likely to see job discrimination as a problem for blacks, though not to the extent blacks do. More than seven in every ten blacks (72 percent) say job discrimination is a "major" problem for black men, while about half of all blacks say that about black women (54 percent) and Hispanic men and women (53 percent). Fewer than four of every ten whites (37 percent) say job discrimination is a major problem for black men (39 percent), for black women (39 percent), and for Hispanic men and women (36 percent).

> **«**
> **Race is the main cultural fault line.**
> **»**

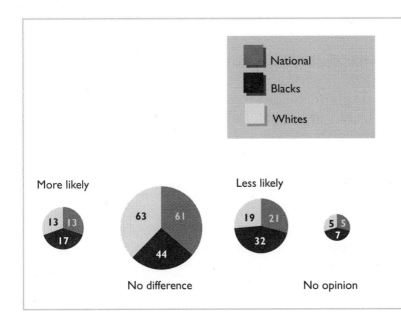

National

Blacks

Whites

More likely

13 13
17

63 61
44

No difference

Less likely

19 21
32

5 5
7

No opinion

American Opinion

If Bill Clinton were to sign a Republican-sponsored bill that reduces existing affirmative-action laws, how would that affect your vote for president in 1996? Would you be more likely to vote for Clinton, would it make no difference to you, or would you be less likely to vote for Clinton?

Source: The Gallup Poll,
March 17–19, 1995

«
**Affirmative action
will be squarely in
the middle of the
presidential
campaign.**
»

Whites and blacks disagree on whether Asian men and women face job discrimination. Thirty-four percent of blacks say yes, compared with 22 percent of whites. Eighteen percent of black respondents and 19 percent of whites say white women encounter job discrimination. More whites (16 percent) than blacks (11 percent) believe white men face job discrimination.

Perceptions of discrimination tend to reflect people's experiences. In a March 1995 Gallup poll, more than half (51 percent) of black men reported at least one instance of racial discrimination. Forty-five percent of black women said they had experienced either sex or race discrimination. Around a quarter of white women (23 percent) said they had experienced at least one instance of sex discrimination.

Substantial numbers of whites and blacks report reverse discrimination. Around a quarter of white men (23 percent) said they had experienced either reverse sex or race discrimination. Fifteen percent of white women said they had experienced reverse racial discrimination. Twenty percent of black men said they had experienced reverse sex discrimination.

The survey results suggest why affirmative action has become such a sensitive political issue. Taken together, significant numbers of people say they have suffered some form of race or sex bias, including reverse bias: 23 percent of white men, 31 percent of white women, 45 percent of black women, and 57 percent of black men.

Political Implications

Gallup calls affirmative action a "cleaving" issue in American politics. Polling results consistently show Democrats are twice as likely as Republicans to support it. People who voted for Clinton in 1992 are substantially more in favor of affirmative action than people who voted for former President Bush or Ross Perot.

What does this suggest for 1996?

"Republicans can satisfy their constituencies by taking a more negative view on affirmative action," Gallup says. "Democrats can satisfy their party base by taking a strongly supportive view. Independents are not strongly in either camp."

As Gallup notes, key Democratic constituencies— blacks and other minorities—believe passionately that government intervention is necessary to bring about equality. They look to the Democratic president to assure the survival of preferential programs. Many see a great danger in any weakening of affirmative action.

"The pessimist in me senses that we are heading to some kind of social conflagration," University of Pennsylvania law professor Lani Guinier told *The New York Times*. (Guinier's nomination for a senior civil rights post in the Justice Department encountered furious opposition from conservatives in 1993.) "The leadership vacuum from both the Supreme Court and the political institutions is creating a void," she went on. "Nature abhors a vacuum, and into that vacuum may move the most extreme voices on each side."[18]

President Clinton has ardently defended affirmative action. The 1995 White House review did not abolish any affirmative-action programs. The president did offer what sounded like a revised definition of affirmative action that might be acceptable to some skeptical whites. "It does not mean, and I don't favor, the unjustified preference of the unqualified over the qualified of any race or gender," he said. "It doesn't mean, and I don't favor, numerical quotas. It doesn't mean, and I don't favor, rejection or selection of any employee or student solely on the basis of race or gender without regard to merit."[19]

Republicans showed some divisions on affirmative action in 1995. Dole, the Senate majority leader (and Republican presidential candidate), introduced a measure that would shut down all federal affirmative-action programs with race and gender preferences. The speaker of the House, Representative Newt Gingrich, urged his Republican colleagues to set the issue aside, at least until they could develop alternative programs to aid minorities. By the end of 1995, Congress had not taken action on any of several proposals to restrict affirmative action.

« **President Clinton has ardently defended affirmative action.** »

"It's premature to predict the death of affirmative action," said Ralph G. Neas of the Leadership Conference on Civil Rights. "Most Americans still favor righting old wrongs. They may have a problem with quotas, but not with justice."[20]

Still, the conditions exist for a spirited political battle over affirmative action. President Clinton has endorsed preference. Republicans will doubtless continue their assault on it. "The issue is out there, and no candidate is going to escape having to take a stand on it," said Clint Bolick of the Institute for Justice, a conservative advocacy group.[21] Affirmative action could develop into a significant issue during the 1996 presidential campaign.

Notes: Affirmative Action Is It Still Needed? Was It Ever?

1. Steven A. Holmes, "As Affirmative Action Ebbs, a Sense of Uncertainty Rises," *The New York Times*, July 6, 1995, 1.
2. Holmes, "As Affirmative Action Ebbs," 1.
3. Holmes, "As Affirmative Action Ebbs," 1.
4. Nannette S. Simon, "A Proud Recipient," Letter to the Editor, *The New York Times*, July 26, 1995.
5. Stephen L. Carter, *Reflections of an Affirmative Action Baby* (New York: Basic Books, 1991), 72; 5.
6. Steven A. Holmes, "Justices Cast New Doubts on Minority Preferences," *The New York Times*, June 13, 1995, 1.
7. Holmes, "As Affirmative Action Ebbs," 1.
8. Todd S. Purdum, "President Shows Fervent Support for Goals of Affirmative Action," *The New York Times*, July 20, 1995, 1.
9. Purdum, "President Shows Fervent Support," 1.
10. Derrick Z. Jackson, "Clinton's Affirmative-Action Speech: The Boldest Move of His Presidency," *The Boston Globe*, July 21, 1995, 23.
11. Herman Belz, *Equality Transformed: A Quarter-Century of Affirmative Action* (New Brunswick, N.J.: Transaction Books, 1991), 22.
12. Nicholas Lemann, "Taking Affirmative Action Apart," *The New York Times Magazine*, June 11, 1995, 40.
13. Lemann, "Taking Affirmative Action Apart," 41.
14. Holmes, "As Affirmative Action Ebbs," 1.
15. B. Drummond Ayres, Jr., "University Regents in California Battle Over Affirmative Action," *The New York Times*, July 21, 1995, 1.
16. William H. Honan, "College Admission Policy Change Heightens Debate on Impact," *The New York Times*, July 22, 1995, 7.
17. Lemann, "Taking Affirmative Action Apart," 66.
18. Holmes, "As Affirmative Action Ebbs," 1.
19. Purdum, "President Shows Fervent Support," 1.
20. B. Drummond Ayres, Jr., "Efforts to End Job Preferences Are Faltering," *The New York Times*, November 20, 1995, 1.
21. Ayres, "Efforts to End Job Preferences Are Faltering," 1.

Notes: Quotas in Birmingham

1. Rick Bragg, "Fighting Bias with Bias and Leaving a Rift," *The New York Times*, August 21, 1995, 1.

5 America's Welfare System
A Hand Up or a Hand Out?

by
Michael Golay

Nearly everyone believes the welfare system has broken down. In one Gallup survey, 90 percent of respondents agreed the system is in crisis, a broad hint that the consensus on welfare formed during the New Deal and confirmed during the Great Society is collapsing. More people than ever before grade reforming welfare as a priority issue. But there is no such unanimity about what's wrong with the system, whether it can be repaired or needs to be rebuilt, or how to rebuild it.

Gallup surveys tracked a rising interest in welfare issues during 1994 and 1995, opinion that both reflected and shaped the Republican political agenda as expressed in the Contract with America. The capture of

Should the current welfare system be replaced?

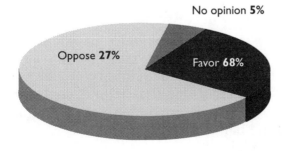

No opinion **5%**

Oppose **27%**

Favor **68%**

American Opinion

Would you favor or oppose replacing the current welfare system with a completely new system to help poor people get off welfare, if that new system would cost the government more money in the next few years than the current system?

Source: The Gallup Poll, May 1994

both houses of Congress in 1994 gave Republicans the opportunity to convert their agenda into law.

In January 1994, only 6 percent of Gallup respondents named welfare as a "Most Important Problem." A year later, in part through the amplifying influence of the Contract with America, 12 percent ranked welfare as the *most pressing problem* facing the nation—the first time the issue had registered in double digits in such rankings. In January 1996, 9 percent put welfare at the top of the list.

Welfare has long been a "hot-button" issue. Still, the 1994 campaign and legislative developments in 1995 focused new attention on what politicians, journalists, and radio talk-show hosts call "the welfare system."

The Republicans' welfare reform measure, which made its way through Congress in 1995, attempted to overturn the sixty-year-old federal-state partnership in providing welfare, canceling the New Deal guarantee of assistance to poor families—the longstanding "entitlement." It reduces benefits in many areas, turns the responsibility for most welfare programs back to the states, and projects savings of $81.5 billion over five years.

The Democratic White House called the bill's cuts in child care, child nutrition, food stamps, and other programs unacceptable. Early in 1996, President Clinton vetoed it.[1]

Gallup surveys found Americans ambivalent about welfare, and particularly about the Republican reform program. Respondents said they favored strict policies to force people off public assistance. But at the same time, they opposed cutbacks and other measures they thought might harm children.

If the public's views seemed inconsistent and even contradictory, so too did the politicians'—especially those of the new majority party in Congress.

Republicans fought among themselves over the formula for dividing federal welfare money among the states. And in a turnabout, conservative Republicans lobbied for regulations that would engineer social change—a "big government" approach usually associated with liberals.

« **Respondents said they favored strict policies to force people off public assistance.** »

Gallup: Where America Stands on Welfare

		Current Recipients?		Future Funding?			
		Need the aid	Cheating system	Increase	Same	Decrease	Terminate
	National	28%	68%	10%	32%	44%	10%
Sex							
	Male	29	67	11	30	44	11
	Female	27	69	9	33	43	10
Age							
	18–19 years	31	67	12	38	43	5
	30–49 years	28	69	8	32	45	13
	50–64 years	28	67	8	27	50	10
	65 & older	24	70	14	29	34	11
Region							
	East	34	63	10	38	41	8
	Midwest	26	60	12	32	44	9
	South	24	72	9	29	45	14
	West	29	68	11	28	44	10
Community							
	Urban	32	65	11	34	40	11
	Suburban	30	66	8	34	47	8
	Rural	21	74	11	27	45	13
Education							
	College postgraduate	43	51	8	31	50	10
	College graduate	41	54	7	35	47	7
	Some college	23	73	6	31	53	7
	No college	24	73	14	30	37	14
Politics							
	Republicans	22	74	7	26	52	12
	Democrats	33	63	17	38	36	8
	Independents	29	67	9	31	44	11
Ideology							
	Liberal	40	58	16	41	31	9
	Moderate	32	64	11	34	43	8
	Conservative	20	75	7	28	50	13
Income							
	$50,000 & over	34	62	7	37	45	10
	$30,000–49,000	26	71	6	28	52	10
	$20,000–29,000	22	74	8	36	11	10
	Under $20,000	30	65	17	30	35	9

Source: The Gallup Poll, April 16–18, 1994

North Carolina Senator Lauch Faircloth asked his Republican colleagues to try to change people's sexual behavior by banning cash welfare for unwed mothers younger than eighteen. "The problem that is destroying the country is illegitimacy," Faircloth said. "We've got to put a control on it and stop subsidizing it."[2] Faircloth's views struck even some Republicans as punitive.

Were the main Republican reform goals—imposing work requirements, reducing teen pregnancy, transferring power to the states, and saving money—incompatible? Some analysts thought so. Lawrence M. Mead, who has advised Republicans on welfare policy, told *The Boston Globe:* "If you make states responsible for welfare, you have given up federal power to attack illegitimacy and impose work requirements. If you cut the budget alone, you haven't reformed welfare."[3]

Democrats, divided over whether to fight to preserve the welfare entitlement, failed to rally behind an alternative proposal of their own, though they did develop an effective strategy for attacking the Republicans. Congressional welfare reform, Democrats argued, will cause widespread hardship among children. "The bill is cruelty to children," said Senator Daniel Patrick Moynihan, a New York Democrat and an expert on welfare policy. "There are provisions there that make you think 'what kind of society are we?' "[4]

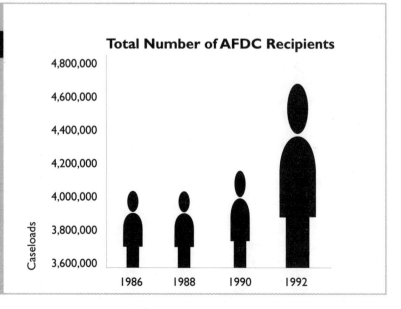

As a Matter of Fact

Between 1986 and 1992 the number of AFDC recipients rose from 3.7 million to 4.8 million, an average annual increase of 27.2 percent.

Source: Office of Family Assistance

Total Number of AFDC Recipients

Caseloads

4,800,000
4,600,000
4,400,000
4,200,000
4,000,000
3,800,000
3,600,000

1986   1988   1990   1992

"The System" as It Is

What are the key elements of American welfare policy and administration? Who benefits? Does welfare create a dependent class of poor people? Shouldn't more people get off "the system" and go to work? How much does welfare cost?

The program of direct cash aid to the poor, the main element of the welfare system, came into existence on August 14, 1935, when President Franklin D. Roosevelt signed the Social Security Act.

A response to the mass economic and social deprivation of the Great Depression, Social Security guaranteed old people a basic income against all eventualities. It also provided federal cash payments for "widows and orphans." This quaintly phrased entitlement evolved into today's Aid to Families with Dependent Children (AFDC) welfare program, which pays benefits to 14.3 million poor people—10 million of them children.

Recent studies of welfare reveal its complex dynamics. Some families may go on and off several times over the course of a few years, with the entries and exits determined by the availability of jobs, the costs of day care and access to medical insurance, the addition of a child, the breakdown or repair of a marriage. Around 30 percent spend less than three years on AFDC after

> «
> **The majority of recipients at any point in time are long-termers.**
> »

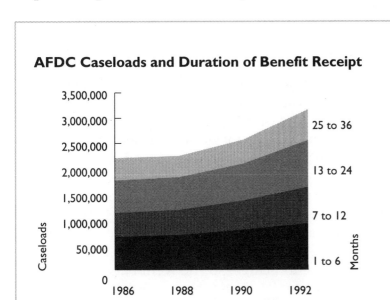

AFDC Caseloads and Duration of Benefit Receipt

As a Matter of Fact

At any given moment, about 65 percent of AFDC recipients have been on the rolls eight years or longer.

Source: Office of Family Assistance

first enrolling; 30 percent of first enrollees end up on AFDC for eight years or more.

The majority of people starting welfare at any given point in time and the majority of people who ever go on welfare stay on for only a comparatively brief period—three or four years. Yet the majority of recipients at any point in time are long-termers, and most of the money is spent on them.

Government studies show that 65 percent of AFDC recipients have been on the rolls eight years or longer. Does the system perpetuate this dependent class? Does it encourage the formation and expansion of single-parent families, which are nearly always headed by women? Is it transmitted as a way of life from one generation to the next?

There are no conclusive answers, in part because so much depends on unprovable assumptions about psychology and human nature. Economic behavior, however, can lend itself to more objective analysis. If a single mother can choose between working full-time and collecting welfare, she'll probably stay home if working—with day-care and medical-insurance costs deducted from a low-wage paycheck—leaves her little or no better off than staying home. Given these choices, it's a rational economic decision, at least in the short term.

Why do people—young women, primarily—go onto welfare? According to government reports, the immediate cause for 45 percent of recipients is a divorce or separation. For 30 percent, it is having a child out of wedlock. For 12 percent, an unexpected fall in earnings has made supporting a family impossible.[5]

Gerri Tyson of Chicago turned to welfare when her marriage fell apart. She thought the spell would be temporary, she told Isabel Wilkerson of *The New York Times*. "I was going to be on for six or seven months and someone was going to wave a magic wand and everything would automatically fall into place," Tyson said.

As it turned out, she collected welfare for six years. Her ex-husband could not be relied on for child support. Tyson held down jobs from time to time, but something always came up—a rent increase, problems arranging child care—so she went back on the dole.

«

If a single mother can choose between working full-time and collecting welfare, she'll probably stay home if working leaves her little or no better off than staying home.

»

Now, with the children older, she believes she may finally have broken the cycle. Her job in a federal youth program pays $420 every two weeks.[6]

In financial as well as psychological terms, Tyson appears better off. Illinois benefits average less than $400 a month. AFDC benefits vary widely from state to state and, in some states, from county to county. In no state, however, do they enable a family to rise above the federal government definition of the poverty line. New York grants $577 a month to a poor family of three; Mississippi grants $120. The average for all the states is around $370 per month.

A number of noncash welfare programs are available to AFDC families. Some 27.4 million Americans receive food stamps, including nearly every family on AFDC. School lunch programs provide at least one nutritious meal a day for millions of poor children. About a quarter of all those on welfare receive some form of housing assistance.

The combined programs provide family incomes that range from 46 percent of the poverty line in Mississippi to 95 percent in Connecticut and Vermont.[7]

Living on Welfare

Statistics convey only a shadow of the reality. In their 1994 study *Welfare Realities*, Mary Jo Bane and

« **In no state, however, do [AFDC benefits] enable a family to rise above the federal government definition of the poverty line.** »

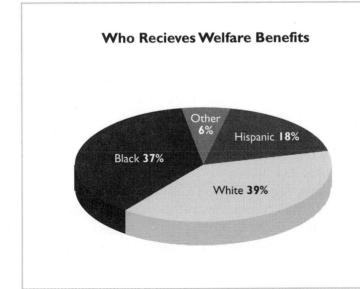

Who Recieves Welfare Benefits

Other 6%
Hispanic 18%
Black 37%
White 39%

As a Matter of Fact

Statistics compiled from government reports for 1993.

Source: 1994, House Ways and Means Committee *Green Book*

Facts About AFDC

- AFDC delivers cash benefits to 5 million American families— more than 14 million people.
- Two-thirds of the beneficiaries are children.
- Most AFDC families are headed by young single women. More than half the women on AFDC became mothers at age nineteen or younger.
- Roughly 39 percent of the recipients are white, 37 percent are black, and 18 percent are Hispanic.
- The average size of a family on AFDC is 2.9 people.
- Nearly half of all AFDC recipients live in six states: California, New York, Illinois, Ohio, Michigan, and Pennsylvania.
- AFDC cost $25.2 billion a year in 1993. The federal government contributed $13.8 billion of the total, or $156 per year for each federal taxpayer. With the state share added in, AFDC cost the average taxpayer around $300 per year.

David T. Ellwood describe the typical welfare recipient as a never-married mother in her twenties or thirties with one or two children. (A generation earlier, the typical recipient had been divorced or separated from the father of her children.) She may not have a high school diploma. She probably has no specific job training or skills, and has had little or no experience in the job market.

Bane and Ellwood, Harvard professors on leave to work in the Clinton administration's Department of Health and Human Services, which manages America's welfare system, say AFDC works harder to enforce eligibility rules than to help welfare families achieve self-sufficiency.

"Welfare as we know it is structured so that those who work are no better off than if they had remained on welfare," Bane and Ellwood say.[8]

That appears to be true more often than not. So far, though, things have worked out all right for Linda Baldwin, a Chicago mother of four who went on welfare at age seventeen and stayed for ten years. She now works with Gerri Tyson in the Chicago youth program and is self-supporting. But like most of the working poor, she is never far from disaster.

"I told my children, 'I suggest nobody in my family breaks or hurts anything 'cause I can't pay for it,'" she said.[9]

A young mother's first approach to the system begins at the state agency that administers AFDC. She stands in line to put her name down on a waiting list for a screening interview. Eventually, and there is always a wait, she is called for an interview that will determine whether she is eligible for benefits.

Has she ever been on welfare before?

Is the father available?

Any disabilities?

Is she pregnant?

How many children does she have? What are their ages? Do they live with her? Can she prove this? Can she produce Social Security numbers, wage stubs, rent receipts, utility receipts, birth certificates, school attendance records, a marriage certificate, divorce records?

Chances are, she will have to go out in search of at least some of the verifications. The stops might include the school administration offices, the state health department, city hall, the motor vehicles registry, the labor department, a parish church. If she fails to deliver the required proofs, she will be denied. The authorities are quite strict about this. Bane and Ellwood found one family that had been dropped from AFDC because the mother neglected to turn in a school attendance certificate for one of her children. It was August and the school was closed, but the family was struck off the rolls anyway.

Once she has been accepted, the young woman is assigned to an "eligibility technician," who monitors her case from then on. Every three months, her eligibility must be verified. If the young woman has found a part-time job in the interval, so much the worse for her. Here is where the system appears to penalize even modest efforts toward self-reliance.

The woman has increased her income and at the same time jeopardized her eligibility, becoming what is known in welfare agency jargon as "error-prone." Frequent verifications mean more trouble and expense for the beneficiary and more work for the eligibility technician. It is simpler for everyone if she just stays home.

In any case, she could keep only part of her part-time paycheck. Work can be costly, for welfare benefits

- The federal share of AFDC spending accounts for 1 percent of the federal budget.

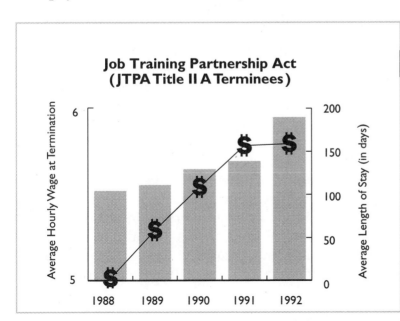

Job Training Partnership Act (JTPA Title II A Terminees)

Average Hourly Wage at Termination

Average Length of Stay (in days)

1988 1989 1990 1991 1992

As a Matter of Fact

Job-training programs strive to increase participants' future earning and reduce their dependence on welfare. States and localities administer the programs according to federal guidelines.

Source: 1994, House Ways and Means Committee Green Book

«
**The challenge is
to find a way to
make work pay.**
»

generally are reduced dollar-for-earned-dollar. Bane and Ellwood, using Illinois benefit structures, calculate that a woman working half-time at the $4.25-an-hour minimum wage and following AFDC rules would end up with about $100 a month more than if she didn't work at all. Of course, many poor people work part-time or for money under the table and fail to report the extra income. In this way, they might actually rise to or above the poverty line.

The challenge, then, is to find a way to make work pay, to bring more people like Gerri Tyson and Linda Baldwin into decent jobs. A single mother would need to earn nearly twice the minimum wage, with medical benefits and affordable day care, to be materially better off working than on welfare. In other words, she would need the skills to make $7 to $8 an hour, and a job would have to be available at that pay scale.[10]

Welfare itself provides only the barest subsistence, and the constant-dollar value of benefits has eroded significantly over time. In 1972, AFDC and food stamp benefits together totaled $9,359 (in 1986 dollars) for a family of four. By 1986, the value had fallen 20 percent, to $7,519.[11]

Updated to 1993 dollars and figured by the month, the average benefit declined from $676 in 1970 to $373 in the mid-1990s.

A Short History of Reform

The modern history of welfare reform begins in the early 1960s. The first wave broke in 1962, with the passage of the Social Security Amendments, which emphasized social work—making an effort to get at the root causes of poverty—over the mere distribution of benefits. The idea was to fight poverty with counseling.

As eligibility requirements were eased, the welfare caseloads increased sharply, rising 36 percent between 1962 and 1967. Many caseworkers found themselves overwhelmed by their clients' seemingly intractable problems. Burnout became endemic. Sometimes the clients themselves did a slow burn, angered by social workers' intrusive and meddlesome ways. The welfare-rights movement called social workers' practices and values into question and lobbied for strict quantitative standards that would apply to everyone.

So a second reform wave broke in the late 1960s. The main features were uniformity, accountability, and impersonality. Welfare agencies were places where one set of clerks determined someone's eligibility and another set wrote out the checks.

"We've been trying to get the people who think like social workers out and the people who think like bank tellers in," one Massachusetts welfare official said.[12]

The late-sixties reforms built in job training as a component of AFDC. The Work Incentive (WIN) program of 1967 required welfare recipients to enroll in work and training programs. By 1986, 1.6 million AFDC clients registered with WIN. Somehow, though, it had become a paper program. Computers registered people automatically when they applied for benefits. Only 220,000 people were actually receiving any job-training assistance in 1986, and only about 130,000 WIN participants had been able to work their way off welfare.

And right along, welfare caseloads and spending continued to rise. Caseloads more than doubled between 1967 and 1972. The system became increasingly bureaucratized. The numbers told all. Those who met the eligibility requirements and complied with the rules were in, and those who didn't were out. The system actively discouraged independence, or so it seemed.

The third wave broke in 1988, with the passage of the Family Support Act, touted as the most comprehensive reform measure since the New Deal. It sought to replace AFDC with a new program that emphasized work, child support, education, and training. Going to school and finding work were not to be just another eligibility requirement but a potential way out of welfare.

The act required the states to establish training, placement, and day-care programs and gave the states more flexibility in trying out new ideas.

Real training and placement are costly. In the short term, they are often a lot more expensive than welfare.

«
'We've been trying to get the people who think like social workers out and the people who think like bank tellers in.'

»

And the federal government contracted to meet only 60 percent of the costs of these new programs. During the recessionary late 1980s, few states could afford to increase their welfare budgets. So even the most effective state programs reached only about 15 percent of the grown-up welfare population.

Critics find many existing training programs wasteful and irrelevant. Writing in *The New York Times,* community activists Johnny Ray Youngblood and Michael Gecan said of the Job Training Partnership Act of 1983: "Contractors gave training in fields such as cosmetology, where jobs are scarce. Others didn't offer job training at all but something called 'job readiness preparation'—instruction on writing résumés, dressing for interviews and building self-esteem."[13]

Still, there have been a number of modest successes. Several states took advantage of their newly given freedom to experiment. Under Governor Tommy Thompson, a Republican, Wisconsin became a laboratory for innovative welfare policy. Thompson actually got the jump on the Family Support Act. Elected on a promise of welfare reform in 1986, he attacked the problem at once. And the record shows that Wisconsin's welfare caseload has fallen 25 percent since 1987. But it has been a struggle. Studies show that short-term welfare spending in Wisconsin actually increased in some areas. The cost of training programs rose from $1 million in 1986 to $57 million in 1995. Wisconsin requires AFDC recipients to enroll in training programs set up under the Family Support Act. Along with attending class, participants must actively look for work—and accept any job they're offered. The state claims a 54 percent participation rate, compared with a national average of 11 percent. Nearly one in every five Wisconsin participants is working, compared with one in a hundred nationally. The state now claims welfare savings of $16 million a month.[14]

Some states have put into motion plans to limit welfare payments. In Massachusetts, for example, Republican Governor William Weld sought a two-year limit on aid to employable parents and their children.

> «
> **Nearly one in every five Wisconsin participants is working, compared with one in a hundred nationally.**
> »

Connecticut has long offered one of the most generous welfare packages. Governor John G. Rowland, also a Republican, has called for a 21-month limit on welfare, which would be the country's strictest.

Clinton and GOP Welfare Reform

President Clinton campaigned in 1992 on a promise to "end welfare as we know it." He spoke of day care and real jobs and of ending cycles of poverty and dependency, but Democrats made scant effort to address the issue in 1993 and 1994.

In mid-1995, in response to the House Republicans' Personal Responsibility Act, the Democratic congressional leadership introduced a bill requiring welfare recipients to work and limiting benefits to five years. The bill preserved the entitlement and pledged to increase welfare spending whenever the number of needy people increased.

Clinton did not endorse the Democratic proposal, though he did say he preferred to save the entitlement. The House measure formally withdrew it. It also reduced benefits in a number of areas, froze spending at the 1994 level of $16.8 billion, and called for the distribution of lump sums (or block grants) to the states. So long as they met federal goals for putting welfare recipients into jobs, training, or schools, the bill stipulated, the states could spend the money much as they chose.

The House–Senate compromise hammered out in the autumn of 1995 canceled the entitlement, in effect repealing part of the Social Security Act of 1935. It required welfare recipients to find work after two years. In a concession to the less stringent Senate bill, the conference committee bill obliged the states to maintain 75 percent of their own welfare spending. The House version contained no state spending requirement.[15]

A predictable divide of opinion formed on the issue.

Liberal editorialists favored maintaining the federal guarantee of subsistence to everyone who qualifies. "The welfare reform bill . . . is more about saving money than it is about saving poor families," *The Boston Globe* suggested. The Republican measure, said the *Pittsburgh*

« **The Democratic congressional leadership introduced a bill requiring welfare recipients to work and limiting benefits to five years.** »

Post-Gazette, "reforms welfare in the same sense that a wrecking ball refurbishes buildings."[16]

Liberals and conservatives joined to attack the block grant provision, though for different reasons.

"The block grant is the secret device for cutting welfare benefits," said Professor Paul E. Peterson, director of the Center for American Political Studies, at Harvard. "It is a way of avoiding blame for loading deficit reduction on the backs of the poor."[17]

Sun Belt Republicans challenged the formula for dividing up the grants, seeking larger shares for their states, which have populations that are growing. Northern states with stable or declining populations should get less, they argued. "There is no reason why the federal government should be subsidizing poor children in one state more than another," said Senator Kay Bailey Hutchison, a Texas Republican.[18] But she failed to note that the federal contribution is keyed to the level of state spending. And Northern states spend a lot more on welfare than Southern ones do. For example, Massachusetts grants $579 a month for a family of three. The monthly benefit in Texas is $184.

Conservatives say the existing system is irreparable and the new one will save money as well as generate innovative ideas that could finally break cycles of dependency and give poor people a genuine opportunity to make something of their lives.

> « Liberals and conservatives joined to attack the block grant provision, though for different reasons. »

As a Matter of Fact

In the last twenty years, federal welfare expenditures have increased by approximately 1000 percent. Totals include Aid for Families with Dependent Children (AFDC), Supplemental Security Income (SSI), and Food Stamps.

Source: 1994, House Ways and Means Committee Green Book

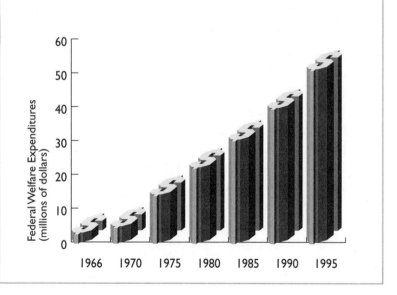

Federal Welfare Expenditures (millions of dollars)

1966   1970   1975   1980   1985   1990   1995

"In welfare, you get what you pay for," said Robert Rector, a policy analyst at the conservative Heritage Foundation. "We paid for nonwork and nonmarriage and we've gotten dramatic increases in both."[19]

Liberal analysts suspect the states, freed of federal oversight, will neglect the poor and their problems. Only the federal government can be trusted to guarantee a minimum standard, they say.

State officials insist they know best. "The current system screams, 'We don't trust the states, and we don't trust the people at the local level,'" said Massachusetts Governor Weld.[20] Weld, one of the more aggressive governors on the welfare issue, introduced a series of proposals in 1995 to tighten the system, among them a halt in cash payments to teen mothers and the fingerprinting of welfare recipients to discourage fraud.

As the year neared its close, liberals stepped up the pressure on Clinton to veto the Republican welfare measure. "What a tragic irony it would be for this regressive attack on children and the poor to occur on your watch," Marian Wright Edelman, director of the Children's Defense Fund, wrote in an open letter to the president.[21]

In the event, Clinton vetoed the welfare measure twice—as part of the Republicans' overall budget package in December 1995 and as a free-standing bill on January 9, 1996.

Opinion in Detail

In exercising the veto, the president acted in evident defiance of public opinion. In a January 1996 Gallup poll, nearly two-thirds of respondents, 64 percent, favored large cuts in welfare funding and a shift in responsibility for programs to the states—the outline of the Republican plan. Only 30 percent supported small cuts and continued federal responsibility for welfare.

Other recent Gallup polling suggests support for time limits and other restrictive measures is on the increase, though most respondents do not favor reductions in aid to children. In vetoing the Republican bill,

«

'We paid for nonwork and nonmarriage and we've gotten dramatic increases in both.'

»

Clinton highlighted aspects he asserted would be too hard on children.

In December 1994, 58 percent of Gallup respondents said people who had not found a job or become self-sufficient after two years should be denied welfare benefits. But 78 percent said the children of such people should continue to receive help from the government.

In 1994 polling, less than half of the respondents—48 percent—said welfare spending should remain steady or go up. Forty-six percent thought it should go down or be withdrawn entirely. Gallup broke down responses by age, sex, region, and so on. Fifty-five percent of men and 53 percent of women favored reducing or ending welfare. Forty-eight percent of eighteen-to-twenty-nine-year-olds and 45 percent of those sixty-five and older favored reducing or ending payments.

Southerners expressed less support for welfare spending than Easterners, Midwesterners, or Westerners. Whites expressed less support than blacks. Highly educated people expressed less support than those with no college. People who described themselves as conservatives expressed considerably less support than those who described themselves as liberals.

It is clear that support for welfare has slipped among all categories of voters. In December 1972, shortly after Richard Nixon's reelection to the presidency, Gallup found that nearly three-quarters of those surveyed—71 percent—favored maintaining or increasing existing levels of welfare spending. Only 24 percent thought spending should be reduced or ended altogether.

Polling in 1994 and 1995 also found a high level of suspicion of welfare recipients. When Gallup asked whether most people on welfare were genuinely in need of help or were taking advantage of the system, 68 percent of respondents said most were cheating. Only 28 percent agreed the recipients truly needed assistance.

Breaking down the response, Gallup found a surprising uniformity of opinion. Sixty-seven percent of respondents eighteen to twenty-nine years old thought most welfare people were cheaters; 70 percent of those sixty-five and older thought so. Sixty-nine percent of

«
What is clear is that support for welfare has slipped among all categories.
»

whites thought recipients were cheating; 62 percent of blacks thought so. Sixty-seven percent of male respondents thought most recipients were taking advantage of the system; 67 percent of women thought so.

People in the upper and lower income categories were more generous in their views of those on welfare than people in the middle-income ranges. People with higher educational levels also were more apt to give recipients the benefit of the doubt. Only 51 percent of respondents with some postgraduate work thought most people on welfare were taking money they did not deserve, but 73 percent of those with no college at all thought most recipients were cheaters.

A sharp divergence of views came between those who called themselves "liberal" and those who called themselves "conservative." Fifty-eight percent of liberals believed widespread welfare cheating had been going on; 75 percent of conservatives were certain this was so.

In fact, there is little evidence to support the charge of widespread welfare fraud. In recent years, stricter accounting systems have reduced fraud and cheating as well as honest mistakes.

A New York City campaign to uncover fraud by fingerprinting welfare recipients turned up only a few cases of cheating. In two months of operation in 1995,

> **«**
> **Sixty-eight percent said most welfare recipients were cheating.**
> **»**

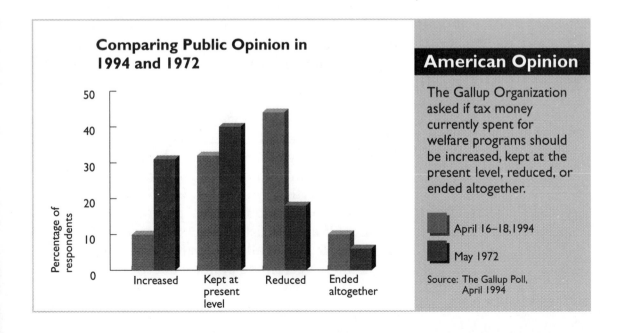

Comparing Public Opinion in 1994 and 1972

Percentage of respondents

Increased | Kept at present level | Reduced | Ended altogether

American Opinion

The Gallup Organization asked if tax money currently spent for welfare programs should be increased, kept at the present level, reduced, or ended altogether.

April 16–18, 1994

May 1972

Source: The Gallup Poll, April 1994

fewer than a third of one percent of all applicants—43 of 148,052—were found to have filed duplicate claims.

Gallup surveys found overwhelming support for government programs to provide child care so mothers could look for work and for job training that would teach them new skills. But only about half those surveyed—54 percent—thought the government itself should supply jobs when there weren't enough private sector jobs to go around.

A slightly higher percentage (58 percent) said all benefits should be cut off for people who had not found a job or become self-sufficient after two years. Sixty-two percent favored limiting all adults to a total of five years on welfare. Fifty-six percent said benefits should be denied to legal immigrants until they have lived in the United States for five years.

Fewer than half the respondents—46 percent—supported barring increases in payments to women who give birth while on welfare.

« **Welfare reform may develop into an important issue in the 1996 presidential campaign.** »

A Look Ahead

How close did the Republican Congress' reform package match Americans' ideas of what is needed to fix the welfare system?

The answer should emerge during the 1996 presidential campaign. Clinton's veto of the welfare bill no doubt satisfied the liberal wing of his own party, and particularly the African-American component, traditionally a key Democratic constituency. Even a small drop in turnout among black voters could deprive him of victory in critical states such as California, Illinois and New York.

Still, had Clinton signed the bill he could have taken credit for redeeming his 1992 pledge on welfare. Republicans will surely remind voters of his failure to deliver on a major campaign promise. In turn, they can claim they did everything in their power to reform a costly, ineffective and unpopular social program. All the same, the Republicans run risks, too. Democratic efforts to portray Republicans as callous toward children and the elderly could have a telling political effect.

Notes: America's Welfare System A Hand Up or a Hand Out?

1. Alison Mitchell, "On Welfare, Clinton Faces a Litmus Test," *The New York Times*, November 20, 1995, B9.
2. Judith Havemann and Helen Dewar, "Heated Debate on Welfare Reform Threatens to Melt GOP Solidarity," *The Washington Post*, June 19, 1995, 4.
3. Peter G. Gosselin, Mass. Funds for Welfare Threatened," *The Boston Globe*, July 2, 1995, 1.
4. "In Congress So Far," *Nation's Business*, June 1995, 22.
5. Data drawn from House Ways and Means Committee, *1994 Green Book*.
6. Isabel Wilkerson "An Intimate Look at Welfare: Women Who've Been There," *The New York Times*, February 17, 1995, 1.
7. Mary Jo Bane and David T. Ellwood, *Welfare Realities: From Rhetoric to Reform* (Cambridge, Mass.: Harvard University Press, 1994), 136.
8. Bane and Ellwood, *Welfare Realities*, xiii.
9. Wilkerson, "An Intimate Look at Welfare."
10. Bane and Ellwood, *Welfare Realities*, 154.
11. Bane and Ellwood, *Welfare Realities*, 111.
12. Bane and Ellwood, *Welfare Realities*, 16.
13. Johnny Ray Youngblood and Michael Gecan, "Jobs for Nobody," Op-Ed, *The New York Times*, June 30, 1995.
14. "Two Good Programs," *Nation's Business*, June 30, 1995, 24.
15. Robin Toner, "Senate Approves Welfare Plan That Would End Aid Guarantee," *The New York Times*, September 20, 1995, 1.
16. Editorials, *The Boston Globe*, March 30, 1995; *The Pittsburgh Post-Gazette*, March 28, 1995.
17. Celia Dugger, "Why Lump Sums Mean Some Lumps," *The New York Times*, The Week in Review, May 28, 1995.
18. Havemann and Dewar, "Heated Debate on Welfare Reform."
19. Dugger, "Why Lump Sums Mean Some Lumps."
20. Bob Hohler, "Weld Assails Clinton for Welfare Comments," *The Boston Globe*, June 8, 1995, 8.
21. Mitchell, "On Welfare, Clinton Faces a Litmus Test."
22. Kimberly J. McLarin, "Fingerprinting Finds Most People Are Telling the Truth," *The New York Times*, September 29, 1995, B1.

6 Crime and Justice
Broad Support for Stern, Sure Punishment

by
Michael Golay

The Democratic White House and the Republicans in Congress pressed rival crime-fighting programs in 1994 and 1995. The Gallup Organization's opinion surveys suggest that the political debate focused the public's attention on crime and criminals as never before. Whether the condition persists as new issues come to the fore remains to be seen.

Crime rates have been skyrocketing since 1960. Street crime, particularly drug-related crime, is practically endemic in America's major cities. The number of reported incidents of family violence is rising sharply. U.S. homicide rates are among the highest in the world: seven times as great as Finland's, twenty times as great as Germany's, forty times as great as Japan's.[1]

Yet, until recently, few Americans put crime at the head of the Gallup Organization's running list of most important problems—nearly always fewer than 10 percent of those polled. That changed dramatically in 1994, when the Clinton administration revved up the engines of the presidential publicity machine to build support for its package of crime-fighting bills.

In August 1994, as Congress debated the Clinton crime measure, more than half the respondents to a Gallup survey—52 percent—listed crime as the most important problem facing America.

By January 1995, after President Clinton had signed the crime bill into law and before the new Republican majority had launched its effort to repeal many of its provisions, the figure had fallen to 27 percent. Even with that precipitous drop, though, Americans' level

« **U.S. homicide rates are among the highest in the world.** »

of concern about crime remained four or fives times higher than the historical norm. In a January 1996 poll, 18 percent ranked crime as the most important.

In Gallup polling between 1976 to 1993, crime rarely ranked as the most important problem for more than 5 or 6 percent of the respondents. In a July 1990 survey, only 1 percent put it at the top of their list. In June 1994, more than eight of every ten respondents told Gallup they agreed with the statement that crime was "a very serious threat to Americans' rights and freedoms." By that year's end, more than 80 percent of those polled were saying they supported tougher anticrime legislation.

Polltakers believe the debate on Capitol Hill created the surge, perhaps a temporary spike, in the survey results. Even so, the findings appear to reflect accurately an underlying anxiety among Americans, one that has been building for a long time.

"People have always been concerned about crime," writes Stanford law professor Lawrence M. Friedman in his book *Crime and Punishment in American History*. "But there is reason to believe people are more upset about crime today than ever before—more worried, more fearful. They are most afraid of sudden violence or theft by strangers; they feel the cities are jungles; they are afraid to walk the streets at night."[2]

Perceptions and Trends

While no one would deny America has a crime problem, there are indications the situation is improving—at least temporarily—just as public concerns are rising.

Two of America's murder capitals, New York City and Houston, reported a decline in homicide rates in 1995. Nationally, the murder rate for adults age twenty-five and older fell 10 percent between 1990 and 1993. In one famously drug-ridden New York City district, a long-term police crackdown yielded a 35 percent increase in drug arrests from 1993 to 1994. With tougher sentencing requirements and new laws such as the "three-strikes" provision for repeat felons, more con-

«

'People are more upset about crime today than ever before—more worried, more fearful.'

»

victs are off the streets for longer stretches of time. Still, there are grounds for concern.

African Americans—especially young African-American males—are arrested, accused, tried, convicted, and punished at a greater rate, in proportion to the overall population, than young white males. In mid-1995, nearly 7 percent of all adult African-American males were in jail or prison, compared with 1 percent of adult white males.[3] An October 1995 study reported that on any given day, one of every three African-American men in their twenties is either in prison, on probation, or on parole—a sharp rise from one in every four only five years earlier.[4]

Poverty, lack of opportunity, and America's legacy of racial intolerance help explain the disparity, although there is no consensus on the issue. Before the civil rights revolution of the 1960s, the police and courts massively and overtly discriminated against African Americans. Many people believe the system is still biased, even if inadvertently. Some criminologists say the police and courts have always been harder on poor people, whatever their race. African Americans are also more likely than other groups to be poor.

The boom in drug trafficking over the past two decades is another part of the answer. A significant portion of the increase in the rate of incarceration is attributable to harsher punishments for drug traffick-

«

Some criminologists say the police and courts have always been harder on poor people, whatever their race.

»

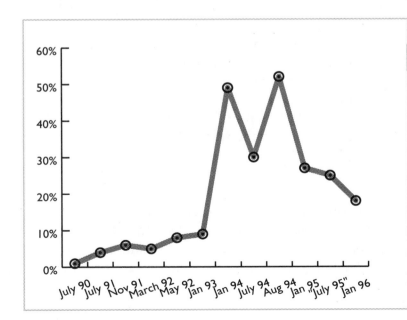

American Opinion

Percentage of respondents who rate crime as the most pressing problem facing the United States.

Source: The Gallup Poll, January 16–18, 1995

ing and use, according to a study prepared by a non-profit advocacy group called the Sentencing Project and based primarily on U.S. Justice Department figures. Such harsh punishments, which are often mandatory, fall more heavily on African Americans, the study found. While African Americans account for 13 percent of drug users, the report went on, they account for 35 percent of arrests for drug possession, 55 percent of convictions, and 74 percent of prison sentences.[5] Commentators attributed the disparity in large measure to two factors: enforcement of antidrug laws is concentrated in urban centers (where more African Americans live), and poor people are more likely than middle-income people to resort to crime to support their drug habits.

Even though some categories of violent crime are down, juvenile crime is rising at alarming rates. In September 1995, the U.S. Justice Department reported that arrest rates for children aged ten to seventeen increased 100 percent between 1983 and 1992. Reports of neglect and abuse of children nearly tripled, to 2.9 million, between 1980 and 1992, according to the Justice Department survey. Juvenile homicides involving handguns increased fivefold between 1984 and 1993. Guns began to appear in schools as well as on the streets.

Over the next decade, the teenage population is expected to rise 20 percent. So the projection is for a plague of juvenile crime: arrests of young people for violent crimes could double by 2010, according to the Justice Department.

"This report," said Attorney General Janet Reno, "is a road map to the next generation of crime."[6]

Most Americans, Gallup reported, exaggerate the amount of juvenile crime. Statistics show that juveniles commit roughly 13 percent of all violent crimes. In a September 1994 poll, respondents thought people younger than eighteen committed more than 40 percent of all violent crimes in the United States.

Those surveyed support harsher penalties for juvenile offenders. Sixty percent favored the death sentence for juveniles who commit murder. (In 1959, only 11 percent of respondents said juvenile killers should be executed.) Half the respondents said first-time ju-

« **Those surveyed support harsher penalties for juvenile offenders.** »

venile offenders should face the same penalties as grown-up first-timers. And more than eight of every ten said repeat underage lawbreakers should be treated as harshly as repeat adult felons. Only 31 percent said there should be less emphasis on punishing young criminals and more emphasis on rehabilitating them.

Dealing with Crime

There are no comprehensive solutions to crime, only more or less effective strategies for containing it. During the 1990s, the most insistent voices have called for deterrence: for tougher laws, more police, more prisons. As fear of crime waxes, support wanes for programs that attack poverty and other social ills some say are the root causes of crime. Support rises for harsh sentences, including the ultimate penalty, and falls for programs of rehabilitation and redemption.

In a January 1995 Gallup poll, more than eight of every ten respondents—84 percent—said Congress should make tougher anticrime legislation a top priority or a high priority. Other Gallup surveys show steadily increasing support for the death penalty. People appear more willing to restore lapsed forms of punishment, such as whipping and hard labor. In the spring of 1994, when authorities in Singapore sentenced a young American convicted of vandalism to be beaten

« **People appear more willing to restore lapsed forms of punishment, such as whipping and hard labor.** »

How successful would you say rehabilitation programs have been at controlling juvenile crime?

No opinion 3%

Very successful 1%

Moderately successful 24%

Not successful at all 23%

Not very successful 49%

Source: The Gallup Poll, September 6–7, 1994

American Opinion

In most places, there are criminal justice programs that treat juveniles differently from adults who commit the same crimes. These programs emphasize protecting and rehabilitating juveniles rather than punishing them.

> «
> **Criminologists debate the effectiveness of more police and stricter enforcement in curbing crime.**
> »

with a cane, Gallup asked whether such a form of corporal punishment would deter crime if used in America. Nearly two-thirds of respondents, 62 percent, thought it would.

Criminologists debate the effectiveness of more police and stricter enforcement in curbing crime. The results of a New York City campaign against the drug trade in the Washington Heights district of northern Manhattan suggest such measures can work, at least in a limited way.

In the early 1990s, New York City sent more police onto the streets of Washington Heights and cracked down aggressively on dealers. At the same time, private wars among the many small dealers operating in the neighborhood left dozens dead and many others in jail or working elsewhere. The combination—aggressive policing and the drug traders' own civil wars—made Washington Heights a safer and quieter place. To avoid police harassment, surviving dealers moved their business indoors. The number of murders dropped from 119 in 1991 to 56 in 1994.

Nobody believes the drug trade in Washington Heights has been seriously damaged. Still, life for the law-respecting majority appears to be better there. "It's more secretive and better hidden now," police officer Richard Wells told *The New York Times*. "It was so blatant before."[7]

American Opinion

Should a teenager who commits murder and is found guilty by a jury get the death penalty, or should he be spared?

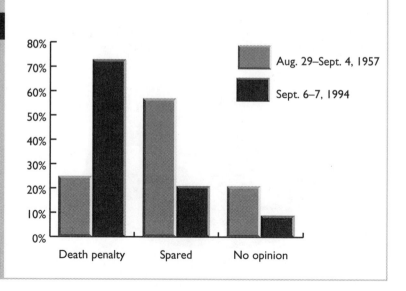

- Aug. 29–Sept. 4, 1957
- Sept. 6–7, 1994

Death penalty   Spared   No opinion

Source: The Gallup Poll, April 20, 1995

Crime and Politics

Many criminologists argue that crime is a local problem, and that therefore federal efforts to curb it are generally ineffective.[8] The American legal system assigns states and localities the primary responsibility for dealing with most forms of violent crime. Nevertheless, both national political parties strove in 1994 and 1995 to persuade Americans they had solutions to offer.

Delivering on a 1992 campaign pledge, President Clinton pushed through a major package of crime legislation in late 1994, before the Republicans won their congressional majority. The measure banned nineteen types of assault weapons, mandated life prison terms for repeat offenders convicted of federal crimes (the "three-strikes" provision), and reserved federal funds to enable localities to put 100,000 additional police officers on the streets. (As of late 1995, the measure had funded 25,000 police jobs.) It also called for preventive social programs that might help fight crime.

Gallup surveying in 1994 found strong support for specific elements of the Clinton package. Seventy-nine percent of respondents favored federal spending for more local police; only 18 percent were opposed. Seventy-four percent supported the three-strikes provision; 21 percent were opposed. Seventy-one percent supported the assault-weapons ban; 26 percent were opposed.

> «
> **Both parties strove in 1994 and 1995 to persuade Americans they had solutions to offer.**
> »

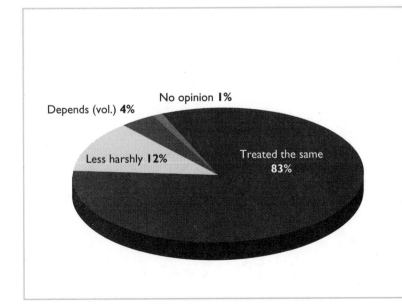

No opinion **1%**

Depends (vol.) **4%**

Less harshly **12%**

Treated the same
83%

American Opinion

Do you think that juveniles convicted of their second or third crimes should be given the same punishment as adults convicted of their second or third crimes—or should juveniles be treated less harshly?

("vol." refers to a volunteered response)

Source: The Gallup Poll, September 6–7, 1994

Federal funds for social programs such as midnight basketball and other activities for poor children drew somewhat less support. Although 65 percent of respondents favored programs of this type, nearly a third— 31 percent—opposed them.

Overall, though, only a bare majority of respondents supported the Clinton crime measures. In a Gallup poll in September 1994, after congressional approval of the crime bill, 50 percent of respondents said they favored the legislation, 33 percent said they opposed it, and 17 percent had no opinion.

Republicans have traditionally considered law and order to be their issue. The GOP attempted in 1995 to overturn the Democrats' crime package and substitute one of its own.

The Republicans promised to replace the Clinton administration's five-year, $13.8 billion crime-fighting package with $10 billion in block grants to be dealt out to the states to spend as they chose, whether for new police or jails or other measures. Supporters of the Republican plan said local leaders knew their communities' needs better than officials in Washington. Some city officials wondered how they would pay for the new officers once federal funds run out.

The Republican crime package called for more prisons, longer sentences, fewer legal loopholes through which accused criminals could escape, and less money

> «
> **Overall, though, only a bare majority of respondents supported the Clinton crime measures.**
> »

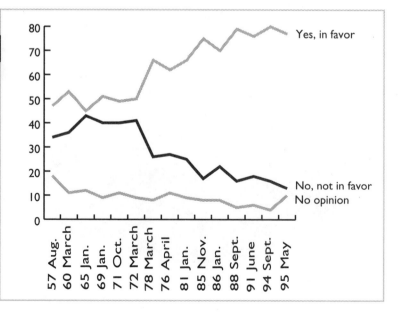

American Opinion

Are you in favor of the death penalty for a person convicted of murder?

Yes, in favor

No, not in favor
No opinion

Source: The Gallup Poll,
May 11–14, 1995

for youth and social programs. It called, too, for measures to give the police authority to search without a warrant and to speed the long, slow journey from death row to the execution room.

Congress approved the Republican crime measure, but Clinton killed it in December 1995 when he vetoed the overall spending bill for the federal Justice Department.

The Death Penalty

In *Furman v. Georgia* in 1972, the U.S. Supreme Court voided every death-penalty law in the country. The ruling capped a long campaign against capital punishment in America. But in many states, new laws were drawn up almost overnight to meet the high court's test of fairness.

At the time of the ruling, there had been no executions in the United States since 1967; there were none until 1977, when a killer named Gary Gilmore stood before a firing squad in Utah. In the interval, states set up elaborate judicial machinery to restore the death penalty. In many states, the chief feature of the new laws provided for what amounted to a second trial, after conviction, to determine punishment. The rewritten Georgia law bound a judge to consider aggravating circumstances (a particularly brutal killing, for

> «
> **In *Furman v.
> Georgia* in 1972,
> the U.S. Supreme
> Court voided
> every death-
> penalty law in the
> country.**
> »

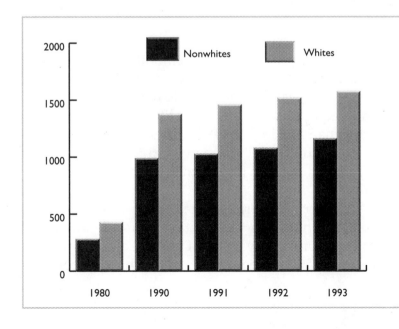

As a Matter of Fact

Total prisoners in America under death sentence

Source: U.S. Bureau of Justice Statistics

example) as well as mitigating circumstances (a de-based childhood, perhaps) in each case before handing down a capital sentence.

The Supreme Court's acceptance of the Georgia statute inaugurated an era of seemingly endless appeals from increasingly crowded death rows. Thirty-seven states have restored the death penalty. The undisputed leader is Texas, which in October 1995 carried out its 100th execution since 1982. Thirteen states had executed no one as of mid-1995. Roughly 2,500 men and women await execution on America's death rows.

In parallel with the evolution of new laws, the trend of public opinion has swung toward support of the death penalty for murderers. In 1936, Gallup found that 62 percent of respondents favored it. For the next two decades, support held steady at around two-thirds, with a slight rise in recent years. In May 1995, support for the death penalty for murderers had reached 77 percent, while only 13 percent opposed it and 10 percent had no opinion on the issue.

At the same time, Americans want to streamline the process. In 1933, Giuseppe Zangara shot at President-elect Franklin D. Roosevelt as he rode down a Miami street in an open car; a bullet found Roosevelt's motoring companion, Chicago mayor Anton Cermak, and wounded him mortally. Twenty-two days after the shooting, Zangara confessed. Eleven days after that, Florida's executioners put him to death in the electric chair.

Today, the average wait between condemnation and execution is seven years and ten months. Retrials, writs of habeas corpus, appeals, stays, and other legal maneuvers can delay a convict's date with the executioner for a dozen years and more. California reinstated the death penalty in 1977. In 1992, the state carried out its first execution under the new statute. In early 1995, nearly 400 men and a few women were on California's death row.

Whatever the merits of the death penalty as a deterrent, it is not likely to save taxpayers any money. A 1993 Duke University study of North Carolina murder cases found it cost about twice as much to try, convict,

<< **In October 1995, Texas carried out its 100th execution since 1982.** >>

sentence to death, and execute a killer as it did to secure a first-degree murder conviction with a sentence of twenty years to life in prison. Critics of the death penalty say the money for capital cases could be better spent elsewhere. Those who favor limiting appeals to speed the process say the same thing.

Philip J. Cook and Donna B. Slawson's analysis of North Carolina murder trials determined it cost the state $329,000 more for each case to secure the death penalty. Even after subtracting projected prison costs, they found, the net additional charge exceeded $160,000. The actual cost for each North Carolina execution came to $2.1 million.

"Common sense says that it's cheaper to supply a few jolts of electricity than to shell out the equivalent of tuition at Harvard for incarceration for the next twenty years," Cook and Slawson wrote. "But when all the costs are weighed, just the opposite is true. The death penalty is more expensive because of the constitutional protections embodied in the judicial determination that death as a punishment is different."[9]

Franklin E. Zimring, director of the Earl Warren Legal Institute at the University of California, Berkeley, put the matter succinctly. "Lawyers," he said, "are more expensive than prison guards."[10]

Ardent supporters of capital punishment say money is not the main issue. "I don't look at it as a money saver or a money waster or whatever," New York Assemblyman Anthony S. Seminerio, a Democrat, said. "I don't care if it costs more. I don't care, as long as the guy pays with his life."[11]

For most opponents, the death penalty is, in the last analysis, a moral issue. Whether death or life imprisonment is more or less expensive is beside the point. Whether or not capital punishment deters is irrelevant. It is simply wrong, they say, for the state to put people to death.

Three Strikes

The public's demand for tougher, longer felony sentences is filling up America's prisons and jails, which

«

'Lawyers are more expensive than prison guards.'

»

held 1,103,534 inmates as of June 30, 1995.[12] In 1992, there were 14 million arrests for all causes, and many of those convicted doubtless received sterner punishments than they would have a few years earlier.

State and federal three-strikes laws are designed not so much to deter as to punish, to put career criminals on ice, where the only damage they can do thereafter is to their own perverse kind. As of late 1995, fourteen states had enacted three-strikes provisions that will keep criminals with three felony convictions in prison for the rest of their lives.

Supporters say such laws are necessary to destroy criminal careers. Critics of the federal law, which went into effect in October 1994, say it is cosmetic, costly, and discriminatory. It will have small impact, they say, because so few crimes fall under U.S. jurisdiction. The law seems to target middle-aged criminals who, so the argument runs, are nearing the end of their violent years. One study estimated the law would cost the government $700,000 more over the lifetime of each prisoner older than fifty. And, the skeptics add, it falls most heavily on poor people, for they are unable to afford a high-quality legal defense.[13]

In August 1995, an Iowa drifter named Tommy Lee Farmer became the first habitual criminal to be sentenced to prison for life under the federal three-strikes law. Accused of holding up a supermarket in Waterloo, Iowa, Farmer ended up in federal court when the prosecutor argued that because the supermarket is part of a multistate chain, the robbery interfered with interstate commerce.

Farmer, forty-three years old, had served hard time for murder and armed robbery convictions dating back to 1978—around fifteen years in prison for crimes for which he had received an aggregate sentence of thirty-five years. Freed on parole, he landed back in court on a domestic-abuse charge and, later, for the supermarket robbery.

"Tommy Farmer is the perfect poster child, or man, for the three-strikes law," U.S. Attorney Stephen J. Rapp, the prosecutor, said. "He has been through the criminal justice system and didn't learn his lesson."[14]

As it happened, Farmer had not heard of the three-strikes law when his jailers led him into federal court in October 1994. Farmer wondered what sort of deterrent it would be to felons who, like himself, failed to keep current about developments in criminal justice.

"It's going to make a few guys think," he said, "but some other guys don't even watch TV or care; they don't know nothing about the law."[15]

California's three-strikes provision, mandating a sentence of twenty-five years to life in prison, went into effect in March 1994. Supporters cited a drop of nearly 7 percent in the California Crime Index during the first months of the new law.

Still, there were a number of unintended consequences. The law caused major backlogs in court dockets, as many more defendants than usual declined to plea-bargain. In San Francisco, juries refused to return guilty verdicts when they learned it would be a defendant's third strike. Jails filled to overflowing. Court costs rose dramatically. A Los Angeles judge estimated the new law would increase the courts' cost of operation by $79 million in 1995.[16]

The California statute makes no distinction among the 500 or so felonies, violent or otherwise, on the books. In an initial study, the state found that 70 percent of all second- and third-strike cases were for nonviolent crimes. (In California, a second conviction brings double the standard sentence.) The most numerous crimes, according to the survey, were drug possession and burglary.[17]

The Simpson Case

Through television and the press, Americans in 1994 and 1995 followed the arrest, trial, and acquittal of O.J. Simpson for the murder of his wife, Nicole Brown Simpson, and her friend Ronald Goldman. The proceedings—from pretrial hearings to jury selection to arcane testimony about DNA to the competence and racial attitudes of the Los Angeles police—crept along at a crablike pace, as much sideways as ahead, with every nuance and development reported in stupefy-

«

In San Francisco, juries refused to return guilty verdicts when they learned it would be a defendant's third strike.

»

Simpson Poll Results Reveal Stark Racial Divide

From the outset, Gallup polling found sharp differences between African Americans and whites over the innocence or guilt of O.J. Simpson. Poll results also showed how wide and deep distrust of the police and the criminal justice system runs in the African-American community.

A majority of African Americans believed charges that Simpson murdered his wife, Nicole Brown Simpson, and her friend Ronald Goldman were false. A majority of whites believed they were true. A majority of African Americans expressed sympathy for Simpson. Most whites were unsympathetic.

A Los Angeles jury acquitted Simpson of the murder charges on October 3, 1995. Again, respondents divided along racial lines. Many whites disagreed with the verdict. Many African Americans celebrated it.

In the aftermath, one African-American juror in the case, Brenda Moran, said she accepted a defense argument that the Los Angeles police had planted evidence against Simpson, with racism as the motive. Some jurors, she said, believed the police were both racist and incompetent.

One observer, the lawyer and novelist Scott Turow, suggested that the history of racial animus in Los Angeles was reflected in the verdict in the Simpson case.

"The jurors were impaneled knowing from the start that this was business as usual in Los Angeles," Turow wrote. "Nothing the prosecutors could do could convince them that this case was not corrupted by the police

ing detail. Jurors heard 126 witnesses and saw 1,105 pieces of evidence during the nine-month trial. The transcript ran to 45,000 pages. What were people taking away from the Simpson judicial marathon?

"The trial showcases much of what is right, and much of what is wrong, with the U.S. justice system," the *Los Angeles Times* editorialized at the outset of the proceeding.[18]

Gallup surveys appear to confirm the second part of the *Times*'s claim, if not the first. "Do you think the criminal justice system in the O.J. Simpson trial is working basically as it should, or do you think it has broken down?" Gallup asked in June 1995, one year after the killings.

Fifteen percent of the respondents thought the system was working properly. More than eight of every ten—82 percent—said it had broken down.

department's world-renowned racial hostility."[1]

In a March 1995 Gallup survey, two-thirds of African-American respondents agreed with the statement that the system of American justice is biased against African Americans. A clear majority of whites—59 percent—disagreed.

In the same survey, only 24 percent of African Americans said they believed Simpson to be definitely or probably guilty. But two-thirds of white respondents thought so.

Fully one-third of African Americans characterized Simpson as the victim of a racist criminal justice system. Only 12 percent of whites saw him that way. And only 20 percent of African American respondents thought the police would have worked as hard on the case if the victims had been African American. Sixty percent of whites said race made no difference in the detectives' zeal to solve the case.

Much of the racial component in the long Simpson trial turned on the racist views of Los Angeles police detective Mark Fuhrman. Simpson's lawyers charged that racism led Fuhrman to plant evidence—specifically, a bloody glove—linking Simpson to the murders, and that the police department fell in with the conspiracy.

Robert Shapiro, one of Simpson's lawyers, said after the verdict that he had objected to the defense team's strategy of "playing the race card" but that the lead lawyer, Johnnie B. Cochran, Jr., overruled him. Cochran is African American.

"He believes everything in America is related to race," Shapiro said of Cochran. "I do not."[2]

A former Black Panther sat on the Simpson jury. As he left the courtroom after the verdict had been read, the juror raised a clenched fist, the African-American power salute, in Simpson's direction.

The polltakers reported that respondents had more trust in prosecutors than in defense attorneys. They were skeptical about the competence of the police. Many believed that jurors were likely to let their racial attitudes color their judgment. Most thought intense media attention made a fair outcome less likely. Most—two-thirds, roughly—believed Simpson to be guilty of the murders. Whites were far more likely than African Americans to say the charges were true. (See "Simpson Poll Results Reveal Stark Racial Divide," above.)

The jury needed only three hours to clear Simpson of the double murder charges. A Gallup poll the evening of the verdict, October 3, 1995, found that a majority of respondents—56 percent—disagreed with the jury's finding of not guilty. Only a third of those polled thought the jurors, ten women and two men, had reached the right conclusion. Fifty-seven percent of respondents told Gallup the jurors had acted too quickly. Thirty-seven percent said they had not rushed to judgment. More than a third of respondents told Gallup they believed racial issues had such influence over the mostly African-American panel (nine of the twelve were African-American) that they determined the verdict.

In June 1995, Gallup asked respondents whether, as a result of the Simpson trial, respondents had more, less, or the same level of confidence in various aspects of the criminal justice system. Below are some of the findings:

- On the ability of judges to treat both sides fairly, 18 percent had more confidence, 49 percent had the same, 31 percent had less confidence.

- On the ability of defense attorneys to represent their clients without using unethical or irresponsible tactics, 7 percent had more confidence, 29 percent had the same, 61 percent had less confidence.

- On the ability of prosecutors to try their cases without using unethical or irresponsible tactics, 11 percent had more confidence, 36 percent had the same, 49 percent had less confidence.

« **Most respondents thought intense media attention made a fair outcome less likely.** »

American Opinion

As a result of the O.J. Simpson trial, do you have more confidence, less confidence, or do you feel about the same level of confidence in the following aspects of the criminal justice system?

Source: The Gallup Poll, June 5–6, 1995

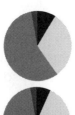
That jurors can reach a verdict in a trial without letting their racial attitudes affect their judgment

That the proper verdict is reached whether a defendant is rich or poor

That the criminal justice system can come to a fair decision even when the media pay a great deal of attention to the trial

More confident

Same confidence

Less confidence

No opinion

- On whether police generally do a good job investigating crimes, 19 percent had more confidence, 47 percent had the same, 33 percent had less.

- On whether jurors could reach a verdict without letting their racial attitudes affect their judgment, 9 percent had more, 31 percent had the same, 57 percent had less confidence.

- On whether the criminal justice system could come to a fair decision even when the media pay a great deal of attention to the trial, 7 percent had more confidence, 24 percent the same, 67 percent had less confidence.

- On whether a proper verdict could be reached regardless of whether the victim is rich or poor, 7 percent had more confidence, 23 percent had the same, 67 percent had less confidence.

After the verdict, 73 percent of those polled said the jury would have convicted Simpson had he been unable to afford the expense of his high-powered team of defense attorneys. His legal bills ran into the millions, possibly as much as $10 million.

"What this verdict tells you is how fame and money can buy the best defense, can take a case of overwhelming incriminating physical evidence and transform it into a case riddled with reasonable doubt," said Peter

« **The jury needed only three hours to clear Simpson of the double murder charges.** »

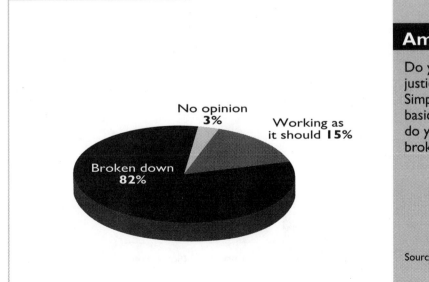

American Opinion

Do you think the criminal justice system in the O.J. Simpson trial is working basically as it should, or do you think it has broken down?

No opinion 3%

Working as it should 15%

Broken down 82%

Source: The Gallup Poll, June 5–6, 1995

Arenella, a law professor at the University of California at Los Angeles.

The trial and acquittal of O.J. Simpson appears to have shaken many Americans' faith in the police and courts, especially white Americans'. Still, there is abundant evidence that confidence in American justice has been eroding for some time. "Hardly anyone has a good word to say about it," the sociologist Lawrence Friedman wrote in 1993. [19]

Views on Domestic Violence

The Simpson case appears to have influenced people's attitudes about family violence, which had been evolving in any case. Historically, the police and courts viewed wife beating as a lesser infraction than an assault on a stranger and were reluctant to intervene in domestic disputes. That has changed as domestic violence has escalated—half the women murdered in the United States are victims of their husbands or boyfriends. There have been many successful claims of self-defense in cases of battered women accused of killing their tormentors.

Recent Gallup surveys found most people said they would take action if they knew a man who beat his wife. Nearly two-thirds said they would have a private word with the batterer; 72 percent said they would report him to the police.

> « The Simpson case appears to have influenced people's attitudes about family violence. »

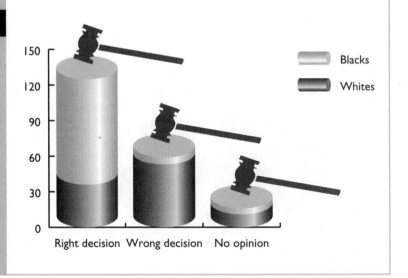

American Opinion

Based on the facts presented in the O.J. Simpson case, do you think the jurors made the right decision or the wrong decision?

Blacks
Whites

Right decision   Wrong decision   No opinion

Source: The Gallup Poll, October 19–22, 1995

Around half the respondents said they knew personally of a situation in which a husband or boyfriend had roughed up a woman. More women (55 percent) than men (43 percent) knew of such cases. More than two-thirds said the police fail to do enough to protect women. More women (73 percent) than men (62 percent) thought this way. Finally, nearly two-thirds of the respondents said the authorities should have taken stronger steps against Simpson in 1989, when he battered his wife. Once again, women (69 percent) felt more strongly on the question than men (57 percent).

A Look Ahead

Many experts on crime and punishment say more police, longer sentences, and more prisons are merely palliative. After all, America already locks up a greater percentage of its citizens than any other nation.[20] In any event, Americans appear willing to go only so far in fighting crime. Speedy executions are unlikely to become commonplace. Nobody in America will have a hand lopped off as a punishment for thievery. Effective gun control is by most accounts a political impossibility. And there are limits to how much taxpayers are willing to spend on police, courts, and prisons.

President Clinton launched his 1996 television advertising campaign by touting the legislation that is to

> «
> **Polling suggests that people become alarmed when politicians focus on the crime issue.**
> »

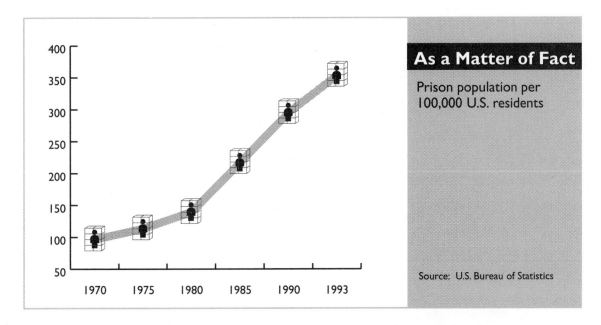

As a Matter of Fact

Prison population per 100,000 U.S. residents

Source: U.S. Bureau of Statistics

put 100,000 more police officers on the streets. The Republicans continue to call for more prisons, longer sentences, and fewer restrictions on the police and courts.

Whether crime becomes a major issue in the 1996 campaign seems to depend on the politicians. When they focus on the issue, polling in 1994 and 1995 suggests, people become alarmed—and the alarm registers in the survey results. When the debate moves on to another subject, public concerns appear to abate.

Notes: **Crime and Justice** Broad Support for Stern, Sure Punishment

1.   Lawrence M. Friedman, *Crime and Punishment in American History* (New York: Basic Books, 1993), 451.
2.   Friedman, *Crime and Punishment*, x.
3.   Michael J. Sniffen, "US Inmate Population Soars in '95," Associated Press report in *The Boston Globe*, December 4, 1995, 3.
4.   Charles Sennott, "Big Rise Recorded in Black Men in Criminal System," *The Boston Globe*, October 5, 1995, 3.
5.   Sennott, "Big Rise Recorded."
6.   Fox Butterfield, "Grim Forecast Is Offered on Rising Juvenile Crime," *The New York Times*, September 8, 1995, 16.
7.   Matthew Purdy, "Drug Turf Is Safer as Dealers Avoid Streets," *The New York Times*, January 2, 1995, 1.
8.   Friedman, *Crime and Punishment*, 460–63; Katharine Q. Seelye, "Anti-Crime Bill as Political Dispute: President and GOP Define the Issue," *The New York Times*, February 21, 1995, 16.
9.   Sam Howe Verhovek, "Across the U.S., Executions Are Neither Swift Nor Cheap," *The New York Times*, February 22, 1995, 1.
10. Verhovek, "Across the U.S."
11. Verhovek, "Across the U.S."
12. Sniffen, "US inmate population soars."
13. Fox Butterfield, "A Criminal Résumé Tailor-Made to Fit the New Three-Strikes Law," *The New York Times*, September 11, 1995.
14. Butterfield, "A Criminal Résumé."
15. Butterfield, "A Criminal Résumé."
16. Fox Butterfield, "3 Strikes Law in California Is Clogging Courts and Jails," *The New York Times*, March 23, 1995, 1.
17. Butterfield, "3 Strikes Law."
18. Editorial, *Los Angeles Times*, January 20, 1995.
19. Friedman, *Crime and Punishment,* 457.
20. Sniffen, "U.S. Inmate Population Soars."

Notes: **Simpson Poll Results in Stark Racial Divide**

1.   Scott Turow, "Simpson Prosecutors Pay for Their Blunders," *The New York Times*, Op-Ed, October 4, 1995.
2.   David Margolick, "Jury Clears Simpson in Double Murder; Spellbound Nation Divides on Verict," *The New York Times*, October 4, 1995, 1.

7 Gun Control
Most Say "Yes" Softly, but Loudest Say "Never"

by

Michael Golay

For two decades, Gallup surveys have found a substantial majority of Americans—a consistent two-thirds, most of the time—to be in favor of gun control. A hard-core minority, a just-as-consistent 20 to 30 percent, opposes stricter firearms laws. A powerful and determined anti–gun-control lobby, led by the National Rifle Association (NRA), amplifies the minority's voice, giving it an influence far out of proportion to its actual strength.

The passage of the Brady bill and the ban on assault weapons, the NRA's counterattack on the new restrictions, fears about the government's potential for the abuse of power, the Oklahoma City terror bombing, and the focus of attention on the armed extremist groups known as citizen militias shaped public opinion on guns in 1995. (See also "Oklahoma City Bomb Shock," page 127)

Gallup polling in the spring of 1995 revealed that 62 percent of respondents thought firearms laws should be toughened. Another 24 percent said existing laws should be left unchanged. Taken together, the two figures suggest an overwhelming approval rating for the Brady measure and the assault-weapons ban. Only 12 percent said they believed gun laws should be made less strict.

These results are consistent with longer-term Gallup findings. While there is scant sentiment for banning all guns, Gallup reports, most Americans favor regulations that make acquiring guns more difficult.

> **«**
>
> **Most Americans favor regulations that make acquiring guns more difficult.**
>
> **»**

The Brady Law and the Assault-Weapons Ban

The Brady Law is the namesake of James S. Brady, the White House aide who was grievously wounded in the 1981 assassination attempt on President Ronald Reagan. Brady made a partial recovery and with his wife Sarah went on to found Handgun Control Inc., one of the most visible of the lobby groups favoring more restrictions on firearms.

The Brady Law, which became effective on February 28, 1994, mandates a five-day waiting period for gun buyers; requires background checks that aim to deny guns to felons, fugitives, illegal aliens, juveniles, and the mentally ill; and raises the fee for the most common federal gun dealer's license, a three-year permit, from $30 to $200.

In March 1995, independent studies found that the Brady Law had denied gun permits to as many as 45,000 convicted felons. Nobody challenges the figure. In fact, it is probably higher. But the opposing gun lobby vigorously disputes what it means.[1]

"I believe the Brady bill has reduced the number of crimes those felons would have committed," said district attorney J. Tom Morgan, of De Kalb County, Georgia. "It shows criminals do go to stores to buy guns, and they obviously don't buy handguns to go duck hunting."[2]

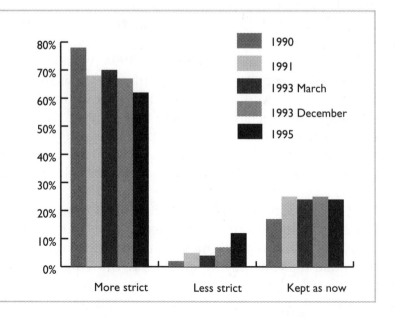

American Opinion

In general, do you feel that the laws covering the sale of firearms should be made more strict, made less strict, or kept as they are now?

1990
1991
1993 March
1993 December
1995

Source: The Gallup Poll

All the same, there is as yet no direct evidence of the law's impact on violent crime. "The test," said James Q. Wilson of the University of California at Los Angeles, "is whether felons have been stopped from buying guns and then killing people with them. And that we don't know."[3]

The Brady Law makes no provision for punishing felons for attempting to buy firearms. "They weren't arrested," Bill Bridgewater, the executive director of the National Alliance of Stocking Gun Dealers, said of the 45,000 former convicts caught in the Brady net. "So all they had to do was go out on the street corner at midnight and pay more to get a gun."[4]

The assault-weapons ban, which took effect on November 28, 1994, prohibits the sale of nineteen types of semi-automatic firearms, including the best-known type, the AK-47. (A semi-automatic weapon discharges a large number of rounds with multiple squeezes on the trigger. An automatic weapon fires a large number of rounds with a single squeeze.) The immediate effect of the ban was to drive up the street price of AK-47s, from about $80 to between $400 and $500.

Public support for this legislation is also high, although does not appear to be as high as that for the Brady Law. In April 1995, Gallup found 68 percent of Americans in favor of the ban on "assault-style" semi-automatic guns, with close to one-third (29 percent)

> **«**
> **There is no direct evidence of the law's impact on violent crime.**
> **»**

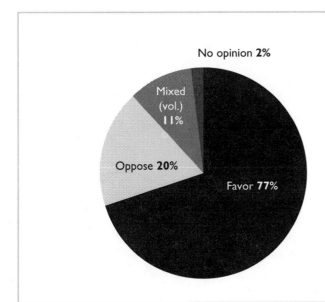

No opinion 2%
Mixed (vol.) 11%
Oppose 20%
Favor 77%

American Opinion

Would you generally favor or oppose a ban on the manufacture, sale, and possession of certain semi-automatic guns known as assault rifles to reduce crime?

("vol." refers to a volunteered response)

Source: The Gallup Poll, August 15–16, 1994

> « The 3.5-million-member National Rifle Association launched an all-out campaign in 1995 to overturn the Clinton gun-control initiatives. »

opposed. Public support for the Brady Law has held steady, at close to 90 percent, since Gallup first asked questions about it in 1988. In December 1993, in the most recent Gallup measure, 87 percent of Americans indicated they supported the Brady bill, while only 11 percent opposed it. Even most gun owners broadly approve of the Clinton administration's gun-control measures. Seventy-nine percent of gun-owning respondents supported the Brady bill; 66 percent supported the assault-weapons ban.

Virtually all law-enforcement agencies are in favor of gun control. Newspaper editorialists strongly backed the Brady bill and the assault-gun measure. As the *St. Petersburg Times* noted, millions of ordinary gun owners have no objection to most restrictions. "Such people," the newspaper said, "do not favor cop-killing bullets. They do not oppose the Brady law. They do not think a ban on assault weapons is a crazy notion."[5]

Yet, in the face of this consensus, the 3.5-million-member National Rifle Association launched an all-out campaign in 1995 to overturn the Clinton gun-control initiatives. The new Republican Congress pledged in early 1995 to repeal the Brady Law and the assault-weapons ban. And the Republicans appeared to have the votes; the National Rifle Association gave "A" ratings on weapons issues to 225 members of the House of Representatives. Given the long odds, congressional

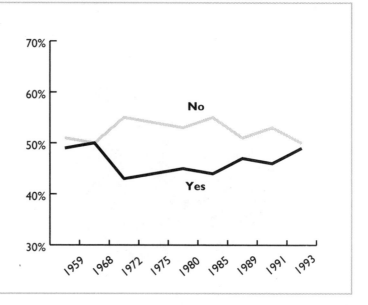

American Opinion

Do you have a gun in your home?

Source: The Gallup Poll,
December 17–21, 1993

Democrats abandoned efforts for new gun-control measures to close ranks for a last-ditch defense of the threatened law. President Clinton promised to use the veto to preserve the assault-weapons ban.

Gun-lobby rhetoric escalated to new levels of intensity, culminating in an NRA fundraising letter that stigmatized the U.S. Bureau of Alcohol, Tobacco and Firearms (BATF) agents as "jackbooted government thugs." The letter's overwrought language prompted the well-publicized resignation of former President George Bush, a longtime member of the NRA.

The letter, over the signature of NRA executive vice president Wayne R. LaPierre, Jr., charged that the assault-weapons ban "gives jackbooted government thugs more power to take away our constitutional rights, break in our doors, seize our guns, destroy our property and even injure and kill us." [6]

From the other side, too, came repeated sharp bursts of rhetorical firepower. "The NRA is all about spreading death," columnist Bob Herbert wrote in *The New York Times* in a commentary on the gun lobby's attack on the Brady bill. "Its music is the sound of endless guns firing and the agonized screams of the men, the women, the children, and the babies whose bodies absorb the bullets."[7]

As in the past, both sides used personal anecdotes, often tragic, sometimes with triumph-of-justice endings, to publicize their viewpoints.

«
President Clinton promised to use the veto to preserve the assault-weapons ban.
»

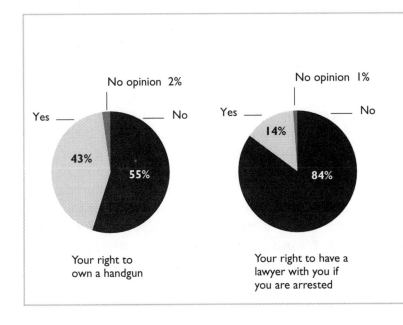

No opinion 2%

Yes —   — No

43%   55%

Your right to
own a handgun

No opinion 1%

Yes —   — No

14%

84%

Your right to have a
lawyer with you if
you are arrested

American Opinion

Would you be willing to give up any of the following rights in the effort to reduce crime in the United States?

Source: The Gallup Poll,
June 1994

«

The two dominant political parties remain deeply divided over gun control, with little apparent room for compromise.

»

At a March 1995 congressional hearing on repeal of the assault-weapons ban, Sharon-Jo Ramboz told how, when she was in her teens, an intruder broke into her parents' house, beat her, and left her for dead. Years later, after she had married, another stranger penetrated her home.

"I calmly walked to our closet where the firearm was stored," Mrs. Ramboz, now thirty-six years old, said. "I took my Colt AR-15 semi-automatic rifle [and] inserted the magazine while I was in the closet. I walked to the top of the stairs. Then I pulled back the bolt and, letting it go, chambered a round."[8]

The loud click in the quiet house startled the prowler. Perhaps associating it, rightly, with the loading of a firearm, he turned and fled.

Byrl Phillips-Taylor had an altogether different story. An eighteen-year-old high school boy armed with a rapid-fire AK-47 assault rifle shot and killed her son Scott, seventeen. Outside the congressional hearing room, she described her reaction to Mrs. Ramboz's pro-gun testimony, especially the use of her children's pictures to illustrate her points.

"It's made me physically sick," Mrs. Phillips-Taylor said. "What was I supposed to do, arm my poor child?"[9]

Although firearms were not a factor in the bombing of the Alfred P. Murrah Federal Building in Oklahoma City on April 19, 1995, the specter of antigovernment terrorists made it politically difficult for the GOP-controlled Congress to stay on schedule with a vote to undo gun-control legislation passed the year before. Shortly after the bombing, Republican Senate Majority Leader Bob Dole moved to postpone the repeal vote. "It's still on track, but it's not on a fast track," the NRA's LaPierre said in accepting the delay.[10] Bob Walker, at Handgun Control, Inc., had a different take: "Part of the public reaction to the bombing is, 'Do we want to give in to a small band of militants on this issue?'"[11]

The two dominant political parties remain deeply divided over gun control, with little apparent room for compromise. Democrats generally favor tougher gun laws; Republicans generally oppose more restrictions. The repeal issue is likely to resurface, whatever the opinion polls say. In any case, the gun lobby views the results through its own special lens. "We represent a majority of the American people who have lost faith in their government and fear government abuses," NRA chief lobbyist Tanya Metaksa said.[12]

A comprehensive Gallup survey in 1993 on gun issues broke down public opinion on gun control this way: About 20 percent favored an all-out ban, while a much smaller minority (6 percent) favored no restrictions whatsoever on gun ownership. The vast majority fell in between, favoring some restrictions, although they were divided on how extensive these should be. Overall, about four in every ten Americans (41 percent) came down on the "con" side of the debate, favoring either minor restrictions or no restrictions at all; while a majority (58 percent) came down on the pro–gun-control side, supporting major restrictions or a full gun ban.

Gallup survey results reflect Americans' attachment to handguns for protective and hunting purposes. They also hint at a lack of faith in the government's ability to enforce weapons restrictions. As the gun-lobby slogan has it, "If guns were outlawed, only outlaws would have guns."

In an August 1994 poll, Gallup asked respondents whether, if handguns were outlawed for everyone except the police, they would feel more safe, they would

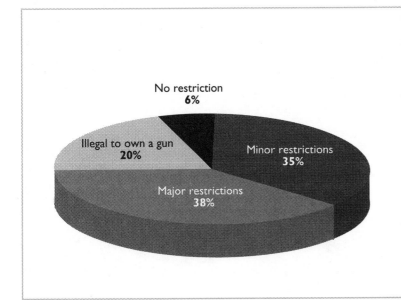

No restriction
6%

Illegal to own a gun
20%

Minor restrictions
35%

Major restrictions
38%

American Opinion

Would you favor **minor** restrictions—such as a five-day waiting period to buy a gun, and gun registrations—or would you favor **major** restrictions that would also ban ownership of some guns altogether?

Source: The Gallup Poll,
December 17–21, 1993

> «
> **Gallup survey results reflect Americans' attachment to handguns for protective and hunting purposes.**
> »

feel less safe, or it would make no difference. A substantial majority, 74 percent, said they would feel less safe or that such a ban would make no difference. Only 25 percent said they would feel safer if the police, and nobody else, could carry handguns legally. This response held fairly steady even when Gallup altered the question significantly: "Would you feel safer," the polltakers asked, "if you could be *certain* only the police would have handguns?" Only 32 percent of Americans said they would feel safer.

In fact, Gallup surveys show that about 50 percent of Americans have a firearm in their household; close to one-third of adult Americans personally own a handgun.

The Second Amendment

Opponents of restrictive gun laws say the Second Amendment to the United States Constitution gives citizens an unconditional right to bear arms. They anchor their argument in what most legal scholars say is a misreading of the amendment. "There is a kind of legendary impression of the Second Amendment that has no basis in its history or its text," said Harvard Law professor Laurence Tribe. The impression, Tribe and others say, confuses private ownership and community security.[13] The amendment, ratified in 1791, reads

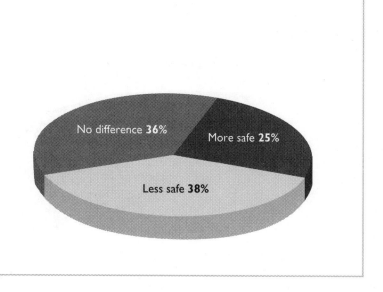

American Opinion

If handguns were outlawed for everyone except the police, would you feel more safe, would you feel less safe, or wouldn't it make a difference?

No difference **36%**

More safe **25%**

Less safe **38%**

Source: The Gallup Poll, August 15–16, 1994

this way: "A well regulated Militia, being necessary to the security of a free State, the right of the people to keep and bear Arms, shall not be infringed."

Most Americans may have but a hazy notion of the Second Amendment, but a 1995 Gallup survey found that a great majority is clear about one thing: there is no constitutional right to buy and store large quantities of weapons. When asked the question, 71 percent of the respondents said the Constitution does not convey such a right. Only 24 percent said Americans have a constitutional right to maintain large weapons caches.

A History of Gun Control

After a half century of debate over the Second Amendment, the United States has more gun laws than any other country on earth. The ironic counterpoint is that there also are more firearms, and more deaths and wounds from them, in the United States than anywhere else. In their book *The Citizen's Guide to Gun Control*, Franklin S. Zimring and Gordon Hawkins note that the inhabitants of Belfast, Northern Ireland, during the worst of "the troubles" there, were statistically four times safer—that is to say, four times less likely to die from a gunshot—than the inhabitants of Detroit, one of the most crime-ridden of America's cities.[15]

«
There is a kind of legendary impression of the Second Amendment that has no basis in its history or its text.
»

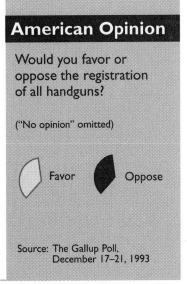

Handgun Registration, by Gun Owners

All gun owners

Long gun owners only

National adults

All handgun owners

American Opinion

Would you favor or oppose the registration of all handguns?

("No opinion" omitted)

Favor   Oppose

Source: The Gallup Poll, December 17–21, 1993

Between 1973 and 1993, U.S. weapons manufacturers produced 40 million handguns. By accident or by design, firearms claim the lives of more than 35,000 Americans each year. According to U.S. Justice Department figures, firearms were used in two-thirds of all homicides in 1993. In that year, 1.3 million Americans faced an assailant armed with a gun—in eight of every ten such incidents, a handgun.[16]

Gun owners fall into two broad categories, or rather two distinct gun cultures: people who own sporting arms for hunting or target shooting, and people who own guns—most often, handguns—for protection or defense.

Whether handguns are effective in the defense of a home is open to question. In fact, a gun-owning homeowner is statistically more likely to shoot himself accidentally than to be shot by a burglar. That said, guns doubtless arm their owners with a sense of security, even if false. As Zimring and Hawkins observe, "If their guns do not give them any real measure of protection, they have no other way of dealing with their fears."[17]

Firearms have been a feature of American life from the start, and a prominent theme in the national mythology. A report prepared for the National Commission on the Causes and Prevention of Violence in 1968 put it this way:

> For many years the armed citizen-soldier was the country's first line of defense; the "Kentucky" long rifle opened the frontier; the Winchester repeater "won the West"; and the Colt revolver "made men equal." Firearms no longer play a significant role in keeping food on American tables, yet Americans own and use firearms to a degree that puzzles many observers. If our frontier has disappeared, our frontier tradition remains.[18]

Where there were guns, so too were there regulations to control them. The colony of Massachusetts banned the carrying of weapons in public places before the Revolution. In 1813, Kentucky prohibited the carrying of concealed weapons. In New York, strict gun-

«

The United States has more gun laws than any other country.

»

control laws have been on the books since 1911. Today, a miscellany of 20,000 federal, state, and local gun laws regulates the sale and use of firearms in America.

Congress passed the first federal gun-control law, a ban on the mail-order shipment of concealable weapons, in 1927. The National Firearms Act of 1934 drew a bead on so-called "gangster" weapons—sawed-off shotguns, machine guns, silencers. The 1938 Federal Firearms Act added a broad range of mild new regulations.

Thirty years later, the assassinations of Martin Luther King, Jr., and Robert F. Kennedy impelled Congress to pass the first comprehensive federal gun-control legislation. The Gun Control Act of 1968 restricted interstate traffic in guns; prohibited certain high-risk groups, such as felons and the mentally ill, from owning guns; banned the private ownership of bazookas and submachine guns; curtailed the import of the cheap, short-barreled pistols known as Saturday-night specials; and required most gun dealers to obtain a federal license.

In 1986, during the Reagan era of deregulation, the National Rifle Association campaigned successfully to weaken restrictions on interstate sales and to ease regulations on gun dealers. Though the 1986 measure left the rest of the 1968 law intact, most observers viewed the outcome as a symbolic victory for the NRA, which

«
A gun-owning homeowner is statistically more likely to shoot himself accidentally than to be shot by a burglar.

»

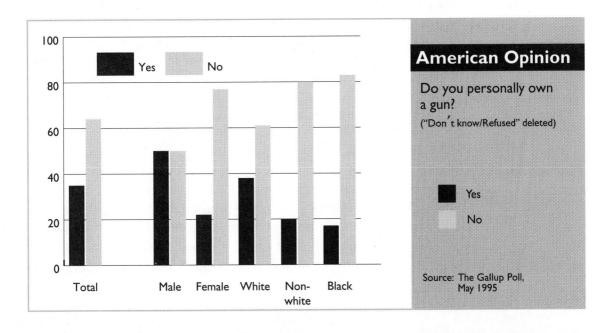

American Opinion

Do you personally own a gun?
("Don't know/Refused" deleted)

■ Yes
▢ No

Source: The Gallup Poll, May 1995

did not again find it necessary to mount an intensive lobbying effort until after Bill Clinton's election in 1992.

Most of America's gun laws are "place and manner" restrictions: bans on carrying arms within a city's limits or in a car, for example, or on carrying concealed weapons or discharging firearms in crowded areas. There are many more regulations for handguns than for rifles and other long-barreled sporting arms. Many states and localities prohibit felons, fugitives, and other high-risk groups from owning guns.

In 1981, the Chicago suburb of Morton Grove, Illinois, became the first U.S. locality to adopt an outright ban on the sale and ownership of handguns. The law even forbade the keeping of handguns at home. In a series of rulings, the courts validated the Morton Grove ordinance; ultimately, the U.S. Supreme Court let stand an appeals-court ruling that upheld the ban.

The Gun Lobby

The National Rifle Association's vocal opposition to gun control in recent years has made it a lightning rod for controversy, but for most of its history it was anything but controversial. The NRA was founded by a group of former Union army officers in 1871 with a view to improving the legendarily poor marksmanship of the soldiers they had commanded during the Civil War. For many years, the organization consisted largely of hunters and sportsmen whose interests ran to target practice and the monitoring of game laws. During the 1960s, the NRA's focus shifted. A new, politically minded leadership converted the organization into a powerful single-issue lobby intent on protecting Americans' presumed constitutional right to bear arms.

The NRA opposed the Brady bill and the ban on assault weapons every step of the way. "The final war has begun," the NRA's LaPierre declared in June 1994 in *American Rifleman*, the organization's magazine.[19] But just as the opinion surveys showed broad support for gun control, they also reflected skepticism about the NRA and its message. In August 1994, during congres-

« **In 1986, the NRA campaigned successfully to weaken restrictions on interstate sales and to ease regulations on gun dealers.** »

sional debate on the Clinton-crime control bill, which included the assault-weapons ban, a Gallup poll found that 56 percent of those surveyed believed the NRA had a negative impact on the debate. Only 32 percent judged the NRA contribution to be positive.

In May 1995, in the aftermath of the Oklahoma City bombing and of the "jackbooted thugs" remark so repugnant to former President Bush, 52 percent of those surveyed said they disapproved of the NRA's public statements and advertisements. Only 22 percent said they approved. (More than a quarter—26 percent—registered no opinion on the matter.)

Some observers traced a decline in membership reported in mid-1995 to the stridency of the NRA's statements. One former board member expects more cancellations. "I think these ads are embarrassing to the traditional market of the NRA—Joe Gun Owner," said Dave Edmondson, who served on the NRA board from 1986 to 1992. "So when the time comes for annual renewal, these people are not going to write a check, and we're going to lose people in droves."

Beyond the Capitol, NRA lobbyists have supported efforts in many states to ease or remove local restrictions on guns. In August 1995, Texas repealed a 125-year-old law that made it illegal for ordinary citizens to carry concealed weapons. Eight other states have overturned similar bans within the past two years.

«
The National Rifle Association's vocal opposition to gun control in recent years has made it a lightning rod for controversy.
»

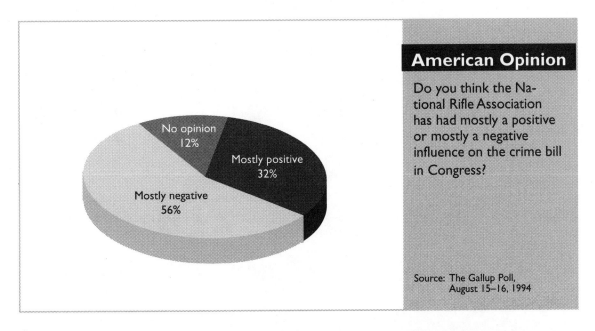

American Opinion

Do you think the National Rifle Association has had mostly a positive or mostly a negative influence on the crime bill in Congress?

No opinion
12%

Mostly positive
32%

Mostly negative
56%

Source: The Gallup Poll,
August 15–16, 1994

> «
> **Proponents say that expanding the right to bear arms will make America a safer place to live.**
> »

Proponents say that expanding the right to bear arms would make America a safer place to live. There is a deterrent effect, so the argument goes, anytime a criminal cannot be reasonably certain that a potential victim is unarmed.

One firearms advocate even argued that more guns in the hands (or, rather, the holsters and handbags) of citizens would make the country a more mannerly place. "An armed society is a polite society," Jim Wilson wrote in the magazine *Shooting Times*. Gun owners "treat others with respect, tolerance and consideration. And they expect to be treated the same way in return. The handguns that they pack are for those who just don't get the message until they look down the bore and get a glimpse of those pearly gates."[20]

A Look Ahead

The Oklahoma City bombing muffled the gun lobby's clamor, at least temporarily, though the NRA remains committed to pushing its 225 "A"-rated members of Congress into overturning the 1994 gun-control legislation.

Preserving the assault-weapons ban is near the top of President Clinton's list of priorities, which makes him anathema to the NRA. One of his chief Republican challengers, Bob Dole, the Senate majority leader,

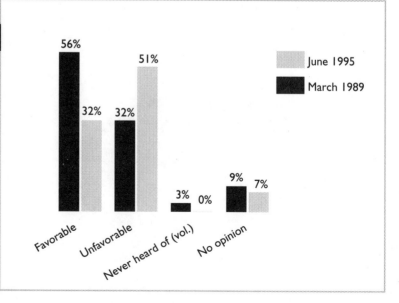

American Opinion

Since 1989, the public's opinion about the NRA has shifted to primarily unfavorable.

("vol." refers to a volunteered response)

Source: The Gallup Poll

June 1995
March 1989

Favorable 56% / 32%
Unfavorable 32% / 51%
Never heard of (vol.) 3% / 0%
No opinion 9% / 7%

has shifted his position under pressure from the NRA and has called for repeal of the ban. After the Oklahoma City bombing, Dole decided to table a vote on repeal.

The NRA accepted the delay without protest. At the same time, it renewed its attack on Clinton, using the provocative language that has become commonplace in the debate. Gallup surveys, however, offer little evidence that the NRA has enough credibility with the voters to threaten Clinton's reelection chances. In fact, strident NRA attacks on Clinton could just as easily backfire against the organization, given its relatively low approval ratings in Gallup's May 1995 poll.

Notes: Gun Control Most Say "Yes" Softly, but Loudest Say "Never"

1. Fox Butterfield, "Handgun Law Deters Felons, Studies Show," *The New York Times,* March 12, 1995, 23.
2. Butterfield, "Handgun Law Deters Felons."
3. Butterfield, "Handgun Law Deters Felons."
4. Butterfield, "Handgun Law Deters Felons."
5. Editorial, *The St. Petersburg Times,* May 15, 1995
6. Fox Butterfield, "Rifle Association Has Long Practice in Railing Against Federal Agents," *The New York Times,* May 8, 1995.
7. Bob Herbert, "In America, Guns for Everyone," *The New York Times,* Op-Ed, April 1, 1995.
8. Katharine Q. Seelye, "A Life Saved, A Life Lost: Gun Issue Gets Personal," *The New York Times,* April 1, 1995, 26.
9. Seelye, "A Life Saved, A Life Lost."
10. Steven A. Holmes, "Bombing Alters the Landscape for Gun Lobby," *The New York Times,* April 28, 1995, 1.
11. Holmes, "Bombing Alters the Landscape."
12. Butterfield, "Rifle Association Has Long Practice."
13. Michael Rezendes, "Reading their Rights: Gun Lobby Challenging Second Amendment's Interpretation," *The Boston Globe,* September 10, 1995, 1.
14. Franklin E. Zimring and Gordon Hawkins, *The Citizen's Guide to Gun Control* (New York: Macmillan, 1992), 146.
15. Zimring and Hawkins, *The Citizen's Guide to Gun Control,* 7.
16. Zimring and Hawkins, *The Citizen's Guide to Gun Control,* 32.
17. Zimring and Hawkins, *The Citizen's Guide to Gun Control,* 69.
18. Butterfield, "Rifle Association Has Long Practice."
19. Butterfield, "Rifle Association Has Long Practice."
20. Sam Howe Verhovek, "Why Not Unconcealed Guns?," *The New York Times,* The Week in Review, September 3, 1995, 1.

8 Oklahoma City Bomb Shock
The Government's Ability to Prevent Attacks Is Questioned

by
Michael Golay

The April 19, 1995, bombing of the Alfred P. Murrah Federal Building in Oklahoma City unnerved many Americans. A terror assault in such a place—in stolid, honest, uncomplicated Middle America—seemed to leave everyone feeling vulnerable. "If any statement was made, it's that any place can be targeted," said Drew University political scientist Douglas Simon. "After all, this wasn't New York or Los Angeles. It was the heartland of America."[1]

At first, suspicion fastened on terrorists from abroad, most probably the Middle East. Then the arrest of Timothy McVeigh, a young drifter and army veteran from upstate New York with ties to an extremist paramilitary group, forced a mortifying reassessment. As Serge Schmemann of *The New York Times* pointed out, the general view had to be radically revised.

"The heartland abruptly lost its innocence," Schmemann wrote. "Newspapers and television shows plunged into the murky world of the extreme right, of paramilitary groups with names like The Order, Aryan Nation Group, White Aryan Resistance, Posse Comitatus, Bruder Sweigen or Duck Club, whose members rail against Jews, African Americans, communists, Muslims, and bankers, train with weapons, and above all, despise the federal government."[2]

Public reaction to the bombing came in waves, with the initial focus on the wreckage quickly followed by a sober reflection on the motives behind the attack and the implications it could have on civil liberties for av-

> **« What implications could the attack have on American civil liberties? »**

> **« Clinton's proposed legislation would give the government broad new powers to fight terrorism. »**

erage citizens in this country. How likely are such attacks to happen again, people wondered, and what personal restrictions and invasions will Americans endure in order to prevent them? Later in 1995, Washington gave at least a partial answer to the second part of the question.

In the aftermath of the bombing, the Clinton administration proposed legislation giving the government broad new powers to fight terrorism. It contained provisions that would increase the government's authority to plant wiretaps, make it easier to deport illegal aliens suspected of terrorism, expand the armed services' role in some terror cases, and limit the appeals of convicted terrorists sentenced to death.

The measure moved quickly in June 1995 through the Senate and the House Judiciary Committee. Then even some supporters began to have doubts. Skepticism increased after congressional hearings in August and September on federal agents' raids on armed compounds in Waco, Texas, and Ruby Ridge, Idaho. An unlikely alliance of gun lobbyists, conservative Republicans, and liberal Democrats with civil liberties concerns campaigned against the bill.

"Since the Oklahoma City bombing, we've had hearings on Waco and Ruby Ridge which demonstrate the ability of the federal government to overreach," said Laura Murphy of the American Civil Liberties Union.

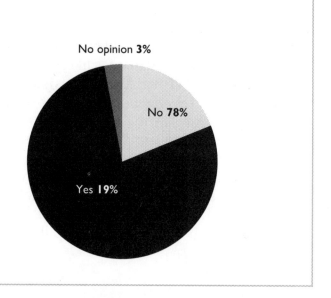

American Opinion

Do you think ordinary citizens should be allowed to arm and organize themselves in order to resist the power of the federal government?

No opinion 3%

No **78%**

Yes 19%

Source: The Gallup Poll,
April 23–24, 1995

"The thinking, which has crossed party lines, is that if law enforcement can do these things without a counterterrorist bill, imagine what would happen with one."[3]

Opponents managed to stall the measure, and passage seemed unlikely, at least in its original form.

The timing of the Oklahoma City attack, which fell on the second anniversary of the 1993 raid by the federal Bureau of Alcohol Tobacco and Firearms (BATF) on the Branch Davidian compound near Waco, raised the question of whether McVeigh, the primary suspect, had committed the unthinkable act as a "payback" for that deadly federal raid. The apparent antigovernment motive and paramilitary activities of the suspects focused public attention the BATF and raised specific questions about paramilitary "citizens militias" and gun ownership. While not used in the attack, guns played a central role in the terrorists' culture, and the BATF's aggressive firearms enforcement tactics may have spurred the Oklahoma City bombing. As a result, controversy over federal efforts to police illegal weapons also became a prominent aspect of the Oklahoma City media coverage and of Americans politics in 1995. (See "Gun Control," page 111, for this aspect of the debate.)

Gallup polls taken a few days after the bombing captured public reaction at each stage, first to the crime and then to the larger question of domestic terrorism. One such poll found Americans to be far less wary of the government than of armed citizen militias. Seventy-two percent of respondents said the federal government should investigate paramilitary groups, even though that might infringe on their constitutional rights. Only 23 percent said the government should leave such groups alone.

Citizen Militias

Militias are active in around twenty states. Estimates of their numbers range upward to 25,000. They practice assaults and defensive tactics and distribute amateurish videos and handbooks on weapons and terrorism. The enemy, in large terms, is something

«

One poll found Americans to be far less wary of the government than of armed citizen militias.

»

« **One militia group accused Hillary Clinton of belonging to a coven of witches.** »

called the New World Order. Specific targets are the United Nations, the Clintons, and the BATF.

A rumor that the U.N. had taken over Yellowstone National Park agitated members of the Montana Militia. California paramilitary units prepared to mobilize when word spread that the barbed wire of the perimeter fence at an abandoned air base had been turned inward, so the base could be converted into a concentration camp for government adversaries. Another militia group accused Hillary Clinton of belonging to a coven of witches.

Few Americans knew or cared much about the BATF before the bungled raid on the Branch Davidian compound on February 28, 1993, and the fire fifty-one days later that consumed eighty cultists. Waco made the BATF—which licenses gun dealers, polices gun sales, and tracks down illegal gun shipments—the demon of the armed right. A paranoiac fear of the federal government is a feature of the far-right worldview. Its expression ranges from a quiet determination to resist the supposed enemy to the shrill tones of an all-consuming suspicion and dread.

"We don't want our children to lose their freedom," Susan Timko told a newspaper reporter covering a far-right fair called Gunstock '95 near her suburban Detroit home. "When they're our age, I don't want to see them living under suppression."[4]

A radio talk-show host named Mark Scott told the Gunstock crowd the Central Intelligence Agency had been involved in the Oklahoma City bombing. "It was committed by CIA contractors" bent on "disarming the American patriot movement," he said.[5]

An Idaho congresswoman seemed to validate right-wing fears of the government when she pledged to sponsor a bill requiring federal agents to obtain written permission from local officials to carry firearms. Representative Helen Chenoweth, a Republican, said armed federal agents intimidate ordinary citizens. "They shouldn't be armed unless they're deputized by the local sheriff," she said.[6]

Federal efforts to police illegal weapons resulted in a catastrophic raid in Idaho in 1992, engendering fear and loathing among the paramilitary groups of the radical right as well as concern among civil libertarians, editorial writers, and politicians. U.S. agents were seeking to arrest white supremacist Randall Weaver on a weapons charge in August 1992 when events spiraled out of control outside the Weaver stronghold at Ruby Ridge. The FBI laid siege to the Weaver place after Weaver's fourteen-year-old son Sammy and a federal marshal were killed in an August 21 gunfight. A few days later, an FBI sharpshooter killed Weaver's wife, Vicki, as she stood holding the couple's infant daughter in her arms. An Idaho jury in 1993 acquitted Randall Weaver of murder charges in connection with the federal marshal's death. Weaver served a total of four months on the original weapons count—that he had sold two sawed-off shotguns to an undercover BATF agent.

Congressional hearings in August and September 1995 called the BATF and FBI competence into question in both the Ruby Ridge and the Waco incidents. There were charges that the FBI had massively overreacted at Ruby Ridge, particularly in issuing a "shoot on sight" directive before offering the Weavers an opportunity to surrender. And there were allegations of an FBI coverup to protect the high-level officials who had approved the rules of engagement for Ruby Ridge.

In August 1995, the U.S. Justice Department paid the surviving Weavers $3.1 million in damages in an

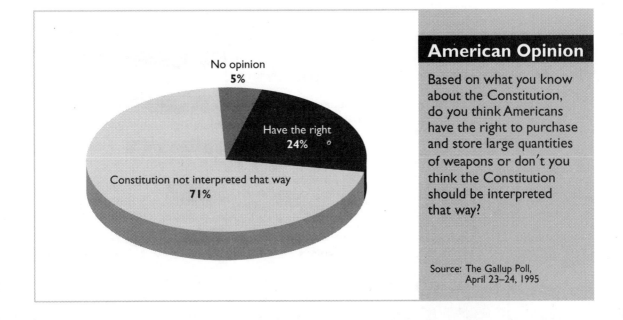

No opinion
5%

Have the right
24%

Constitution not interpreted that way
71%

American Opinion

Based on what you know about the Constitution, do you think Americans have the right to purchase and store large quantities of weapons or don't you think the Constitution should be interpreted that way?

Source: The Gallup Poll,
April 23–24, 1995

out-of-court settlement of the family's $200 million wrongful-death suit. The government did not, however, admit wrongdoing in the matter.

Reaction to Oklahoma City

« **There is widespread initial support for several antiterrorism measures, even some that limit the freedom and privacy of individuals.** »

In the wake of the Oklahoma City bombing, the Gallup poll found Americans mostly resigned to the fact that acts of terrorist violence will occur in the United States, but also sharply split on whether the government can prevent such attacks. Nearly nine in every ten Americans (89 percent) believed terrorist acts are likely to happen again in the near future, though only 28 percent believed one would happen in their community. Only 45 percent believed the government could do anything to stop them. Forty-six percent said little or nothing could be done.

Nevertheless, there was widespread initial support for several antiterrorism measures, even some that limit the freedom and privacy of individuals. The public supported setting up security checkpoints in office buildings (87 percent) and favored restricting entry into the United States from countries with known ties to terrorists (75 percent). Slightly smaller majorities also supported restricting access to U.S. federal buildings (62 percent) and increasing surveillance of foreigners in the United States (63 percent).

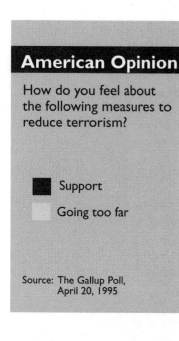

American Opinion

How do you feel about the following measures to reduce terrorism?

■ Support

▫ Going too far

Source: The Gallup Poll,
April 20, 1995

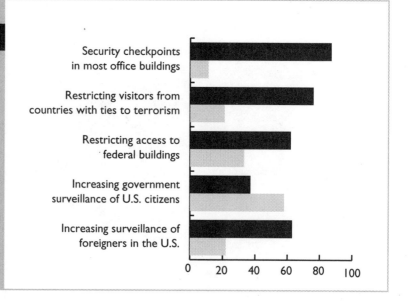

Security checkpoints in most office buildings

Restricting visitors from countries with ties to terrorism

Restricting access to federal buildings

Increasing government surveillance of U.S. citizens

Increasing surveillance of foreigners in the U.S.

0   20   40   60   80   100

The only antiterrorism measure that a majority of respondents opposed called for increasing government surveillance of U.S. citizens. Fifty-eight percent said this would go too far, and only 37 percent were in favor.

Even so, it is clear from Gallup data that terrorism remains a public concern only in the abstract. Although the level of fear about terrorism happening in one's own life is slightly higher in 1995 than it was in 1993 after the bombing of the World Trade Center in New York, this fear had not yet become pervasive, with only 16 percent reporting that they felt personally at risk (up from 12 percent in 1993). Eighty-four percent of Americans said they are not afraid of becoming a terrorist victim, and 83 percent said they don't expect to change any of their habits or activities to reduce their chances of becoming a victim.

Spreading the Blame

In the immediate aftermath of the bombing, suspicion fell first on foreign terrorists. Then, on April 20, 1995, came the arrest of McVeigh and the revelation of his ties to paramilitary groups in Michigan and Arizona. Before McVeigh's arrest, a Gallup survey showed that nearly two-thirds of respondents would be more disturbed to know that those responsible for the attack were U.S. citizens than if they were foreigners. Like

« **Democrats and members of the news media blamed Republicans and talk-show hosts for their criticisms of the federal government.** »

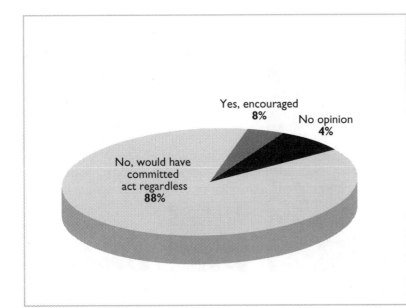

Yes, encouraged
8%

No opinion
4%

No, would have committed act regardless
88%

American Opinion

Republican leaders in Congress publicly criticized the size and power of the federal government. Do you think this encouraged the people responsible for the bombing in Oklahoma City or that they would have committed that act regardless of what the Republican leaders said?

Source: The Gallup Poll,
April 21–23, 1995

the anguished self-doubt created in Israel by the November 1995 murder of Prime Minister Yitzhak Rabin, Americans' realization that the Oklahoma City bombing was homegrown induced a period of profound national introspection.

In the case of Rabin's assassination in Israel, his widow and others argued that Likud party leaders and other Rabin opponents were partially responsible for the murderous actions of the young, impressionable ideologue who was arrested for the crime. After Oklahoma City, some Democrats and members of the news media made a similar argument, blaming Republicans and talk-show hosts for their criticisms of the federal government. In an April 1995 survey, respondents soundly rejected the connection. Only 8 percent believed the anti–big–government rhetoric of Republican leaders in Congress might have encouraged the people responsible for the Oklahoma City bombing; 88 percent said the terrorists would have committed the act regardless.

News reports about the paramilitary activities and anti-Waco views of McVeigh and other suspects in the case provoked a national discussion about a significant segment of Americans deeply dissatisfied with the current size and power of the federal government, and in particular with federal law-enforcement authorities.

As a consequence of this coverage, the Gallup poll asked several questions meant to measure the preva-

« Seventy-two percent said the federal government should investigate paramilitary groups. »

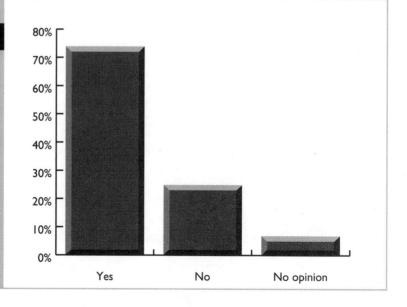

American Opinion

Do you think the federal government should actively investigate and infiltrate groups that arm and organize themselves against the federal government even if doing so may infringe their constitutional rights?

Source: The Gallup Poll, April 23–24, 1995

Yes   No   No opinion

lence and intensity of antigovernment sentiment which that attack seemed to represent.

The post–Oklahoma City bombing survey in late April 1995 found an overwhelming 78 percent of respondents who said they do not believe individual citizens have the right to arm and organize themselves to resist the federal government. Fewer than one in every five (19 percent) thought they did. Seventy-two percent of respondents said the federal government should investigate paramilitary groups, even if that infringes on their constitutional rights. Only 23 percent said the government should leave such groups alone.

At the same time, nearly four in every ten Americans responded in the affirmative to a question intended to define the proportion of Americans harboring exceptionally high levels of fear of the federal government. A startling 39 percent of Americans agreed with the statement that "the federal government has become so large and powerful that it poses an immediate threat to the rights and freedoms of ordinary citizens"; 58 percent disagreed.

The BATF

Americans' recent introduction to the Bureau of Alcohol, Tobacco and Firearms has been double-edged:

> **«**
> **A startling 39 percent of Americans agreed that 'the federal government has become so large and powerful that it poses an immediate threat to the rights and freedoms of ordinary citizens.'**
> **»**

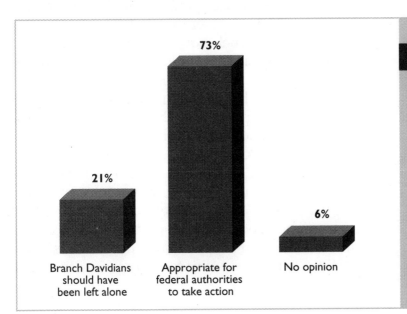

73%

21%

6%

Branch Davidians should have been left alone

Appropriate for federal authorities to take action

No opinion

American Opinion

Which one of the following comes closer to your own view—the people at the Branch Davidian compound should have been left alone to live as they pleased, or it was appropriate for the federal authorities to take action against the Branch Davidians based on what the authorities believed was happening?

Source: The Gallup Poll, April 23–24, 1995

« The public had significantly more concern about the power of major corporations and banks than it had about the BATF. »

they generally supported its 1993 raid on the Branch Davidians in Waco, Texas, but have since heard fiery debate over its use of excessive force there and in other places. In 1995, the BATF came under the scrutiny of the congressional investigatory hearings for its fatal raids on the Weaver family compound at Ruby Ridge and against the Branch Davidians in Waco.

Despite the heated debate over the BATF's tactics, Gallup polls indicate only one in five Americans might be sympathetic to the view expressed in 1995 by the National Rifle Association's often-repeated charge that BATF agents are "jackbooted government thugs." Most Americans (73 percent) believe BATF authorities acted correctly in moving against the Texas cult; only 21 percent say the government should have left the Branch Davidians alone to live as they pleased.

Gallup polling later in 1995, however, found the BATF viewed somewhat less positively. Thirty-nine percent said the BATF had too much power, while only 23 percent said it did not have enough power. But more than a third (34 percent) held the view that the BATF has about the right amount of power, and more than half of Americans (57 percent) were generally supportive of the much-maligned agency.

In context with a variety of public and private institutions tested in August 1995, a Gallup poll suggests that the BATF is only moderately controversial. Among twenty separate groups tested in the Gallup survey, the BATF ranked tenth in terms of perceptions of its having "too much power," with Americans far more inclined to view the agents of mass media as overly powerful. A majority considered advertising, television news, the entertainment industry, and newspapers as too powerful. The public also had significantly more concern about the power of major corporations and banks than it had about the BATF.

At a time when a majority of Americans view the federal government generally as having too much power, the country's top law-enforcement agency for guns does not appear to be a primary target of the public's wrath—that's a position apparently reserved for the IRS. Of the five specific federal agencies included

American Opinion	What Americans Think of the Power Held by Twenty Institutions			
	Too Much Power	About Right	Not Enough	Don't Know / Refused
Majority Say "Too Much"				
The IRS	63	32	3	2
The Advertising Industry	62	33	4	1
The Federal Government	60	29	8	3
Major Corporations	58	31	7	4
TV News	56	36	7	1
The Entertainment Industry	55	35	8	2
"Too Much" Outweighs "Not Enough"				
The CIA	42	37	9	12
Newspapers	41	48	10	1
Banks	41	49	7	3
The BATF	39	34	23	4
Courts	37	34	27	2
Labor Unions	36	35	24	5
The FBI	32	48	16	4
State Government	27	58	13	2
"Not Enough" Outweighs "Too Much"				
Churches	23	46	28	3
The United Nations	21	35	39	5
Local Government	17	62	18	3
The Military	17	57	23	3
Local Police	13	55	31	1
State Police	12	61	24	3

Source: The Gallup Poll, August 11–14, 1995

on Gallup's list of institutions, the IRS and CIA receive significantly higher levels of criticism than does the BATF. At the same time, the BATF's power is viewed more negatively than that of either the FBI or the military. Only the military was viewed on balance as having *too little* rather than too much power.

Notes: Oklahoma City Bomb Shock The Government's Ability to Prevent Attacks Is Questioned

1. Serge Schmemann, "New Images of Terror: Extremists in the Heartland," *The New York Times*, April 24, 1995, 8.
2. Schmemann, "New Images of Terror."
3. Stephen Labaton, "Bill on Terrorism, Once a Certainty, Derailed in House," *The New York Times*, October 3, 1995, 1.
4. James Bennet, "At Michigan Rally, Unyielding Anger at the Brady Bill," *The New York Times*, May 15, 1995, 10.
5. Bennet, "At Michigan Rally."
6. Steven A. Holmes, "Bombing Alters the Landscape for Gun Lobby," *The New York Times*, April 28, 1995, 1.

9 Foreign Affairs
Americans Shun Policeman's Lot

by
Michael Golay

In a post–Cold War world where U.S. interests are not always manifest and where villains and victims can be difficult to distinguish, many Americans are reluctant to hazard the use of the nation's military power to influence events in troubled places.

Gallup polling in 1994 and 1995 found most Americans opposed to sending in U.S. armed forces to restore the legitimate government of Haiti. Substantial majorities opposed a U.S. military role in Bosnia, a skepticism that extended to the offer of troops to join America's allies in monitoring a peace agreement there.

When North Korea defied international law in refusing to allow inspections of its nuclear facilities, fewer than half of those polled believed America should use force to compel cooperation, even in concert with other powers. And opinion divided about evenly on whether U.S. forces should come to the aid of longtime ally South Korea in the event of an attack from the North.

Surveys suggest Americans are uncertain about the nation's role in a changing world. No directing principle has replaced the old Cold War rivalry, stable and therefore comfortable in its way, with the former Soviet Union. Few see vital American interests at stake in

« Americans are uncertain about the nation's role in a changing world. »

> «
>
> **Some patterns of Cold War thinking remain largely unaltered.**
>
> »

distant conflicts in obscure places, and fewer still would risk American lives for such problematic objectives as enforcing peace in the Balkans, Haiti, or Somalia.

In an exception that tends to prove the rule, public opinion continues to support the use of U.S. military power against Iraq. There, Americans find the issues sharply etched. There is oil, and there is an aggressor, the Iraqi dictator Saddam Hussein. There is, too, a recent memory of a standoff air war, waged with stealth aircraft and "smart" bombs, a land battle of maneuver fought in a desert, and astonishingly light American casualties.

Saddam survived the U.S.-led Persian Gulf War of 1991 and rapidly rebuilt his military machine. In October 1994, in response to Iraqi troop movements in Kuwait's direction, President Clinton dispatched U.S. forces to the gulf and signaled his readiness to use them. According to Gallup, nearly three-quarters—74 percent—of those polled approved of the U.S. reaction. Almost as many, 72 percent, said they would support U.S. military action to drive Saddam from power.

As it happens, some patterns of Cold War thinking remain largely unaltered. In September 1994, Gallup asked whether or not the United States should spy on various countries. Sixty-three percent thought America should continue spying on Russia and 60 percent on China, the traditional Cold War adversaries. Only 17

American Opinion

The Clinton administration has stated that if the U.S. were to send United States troops to Bosnia, they would be withdrawn within one year. How confident are you that U.S. troops would be withdrawn within one year as planned?

Source: The Gallup Poll, October 19–22, 1995

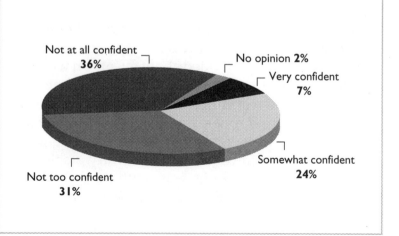

Not at all confident
36%

No opinion **2%**

Very confident
7%

Somewhat confident
24%

Not too confident
31%

percent thought the U.S ought to spy on Britain, its longtime partner in the Atlantic "special relationship."

New Isolationism?

Around half the respondents in a January 1994 Gallup poll said they followed U.S. relations with other countries "somewhat closely." That vague construction suggests Americans know there is a conflict in the Balkans and that Israel and the Palestine Liberation Organization continue to negotiate peace. It does not necessarily suggest a deep engagement with such issues. The other half in the poll divided evenly: 23 percent follow events abroad "very closely," 23 percent "not too closely."

Historically, Americans have been wary of foreign involvements, especially those requiring military commitments. More recently, this isolationist impulse has been a legacy of the Vietnam War, as well as a consequence of the collapse of the Soviet order, the revival of nationalism, particularly in Eastern Europe, the rise of international terrorism, and situations such as Somalia's, where famine, anarchy, and civil war combine to create a crisis that seems to defy solution.

When the use of force is in prospect, senior American military leaders often are as cautious as the public they serve. Some U.S. commanders, including the then-

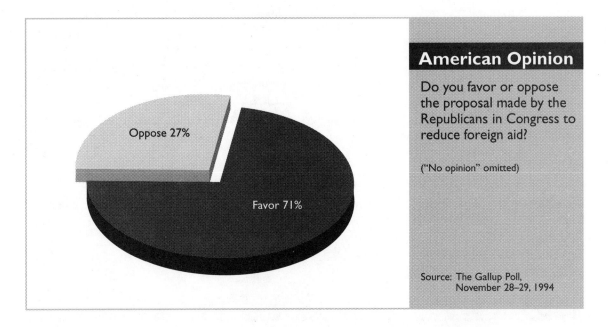

Oppose 27%

Favor 71%

American Opinion

Do you favor or oppose the proposal made by the Republicans in Congress to reduce foreign aid?

("No opinion" omitted)

Source: The Gallup Poll,
        November 28–29, 1994

chairman of the Joint Chiefs of Staff, General Colin Powell, supported sanctions over force during the Persian Gulf crisis of 1990–91. Powell also argued against using American and NATO airpower as a check to Serbian aggression in the former Yugoslavia in 1991 and 1992.

Military officials are wary, too, of close association with United Nations operations. In Somalia, the initial American role of humanitarian relief flared into a search-and-destroy campaign against one of the Somali warlord factions. In military jargon, that was "mission creep"—in this instance, an escalation under U.N. auspices beyond direct U.S. political control and lacking broad support at home.

The corollary to this post–Cold War phenomenon is a great apprehension among American political leaders of the electoral cost of even a modest number of U.S. casualties in pursuit of a poorly articulated for-

Vietnam

The Gallup Poll found strong support for the Clinton administration's decision in 1995 to pursue normal relations with Vietnam.

The United States fought a communist uprising in what was then South Vietnam from the late 1950s until 1973, and 58,000 Americans died there. As a young man, President Clinton evaded the draft and opposed the war, and he proceeded cautiously before announcing the establishment of ties with Vietnam in July 1995.

According to Gallup, 61 percent of respondents favored the establishment of normal diplomatic relations, while 29 percent opposed it. In 1993, only 48 percent had supported ties with Vietnam, while 42 percent were opposed.

Some Republican leaders, including Senate majority leader Robert Dole, opposed normalization, charging the Vietnamese had been uncooperative on the issue of accounting for missing American servicemen. Gallup found, though, that support for the change in policy cut across party lines, with majorities of Democrats and Republicans alike favoring it.

Nearly three-quarters of those polled, 71 percent, said America had been mistaken in sending troops to fight in Vietnam. Only 23 percent thought the United States had been right to fight there. When Gallup had asked the same question in mid-1965, only 24 percent had thought the United States had made a mistake in going into Vietnam. By 1971, 60 percent of respondents thought so.

Finally, more than half of those polled, 52 percent, said the U.S. role in Vietnam was "fundamentally wrong and immoral." Forty-three percent thought America's actions were well intentioned though mistaken.

eign policy objective. Many people ask bluntly whether restoring order in Haiti and shoring up a fragile peace in Bosnia are worth even a single American life.

At a Capitol Hill hearing on Bosnia, Senator James Inhofe, an Oklahoma Republican, asked Defense Secretary William Perry and Secretary of State Warren Christopher whether peace in the Balkans justified "hundreds of young Americans dying over there." Perry and Christopher both answered yes.[1]

According to the surveys, Americans answer no. In an October 1995 Gallup poll, two-thirds of respondents said they would favor a U.S. mission in Bosnia supposing that no Americans would be killed. Supposing twenty-five Americans would be killed? Only 31 percent favored sending U.S. forces to Bosnia. Supposing four hundred Americans would be killed? Twenty-one percent favored a Bosnia deployment; 72 percent were opposed.

"Americans have become accustomed to short battles with defined outcomes," noted an Iowa editorialist writing about Bosnia for the *Cedar Rapids Gazette*. "They would be unwilling to supply their sons and daughters despite Clinton's pleas for humanitarian assistance."[2]

As the Iowan suggests, morally lofty or politically abstract goals have lost much of their power to animate Americans. A threat to oil supplies is more likely to mobilize opinion than a call to defend democracy or

« **'Americans have become accustomed to short battles with defined outcomes.'** »

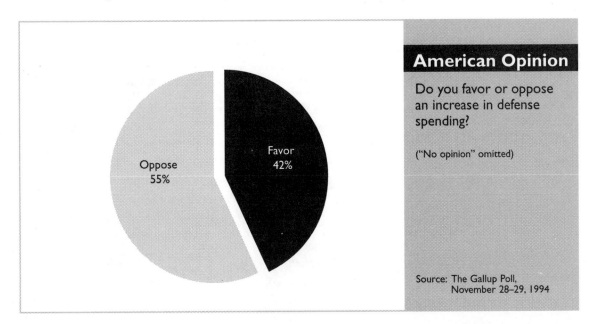

American Opinion

Do you favor or oppose an increase in defense spending?

("No opinion" omitted)

Oppose 55%

Favor 42%

Source: The Gallup Poll, November 28–29, 1994

to keep dominoes from falling. The surveys suggest the public expects a clear statement of the country's direct interest in an overseas issue. Beyond that, Americans want to know how much a prospective military operation would cost, and when—an actual date, preferably—it would end and the forces return home.

President Clinton acknowledged these realities even as he attempted, late in 1995, to arrange a U.S.-sponsored end to the war in Bosnia. In October, in what was regarded as a diplomatic coup, Clinton's envoys persuaded the warring factions to agree to a cease-fire. On November 21, 1995, Serbia, Croatia, and Bosnia initialed a peace accord; they met to sign a formal treaty in Paris in December. Soon after, 20,000 U.S troops began taking up positions in Bosnia as part of a NATO force that would guarantee the settlement.

The president also offered a hedge: "The United States will not be sending our forces into combat in Bosnia," Clinton said. "We will not send them into a peace that cannot be maintained. But we must use our power to assure that peace."[3]

Bosnia

Civil war in Bosnia has left 250,000 people dead and some 3 million homeless since 1991. To many Ameri-

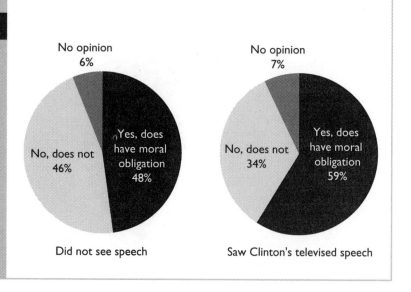

American Opinion

Do you think the United States has a moral obligation to help keep the peace in Bosnia, or not?

No opinion 6%

No, does not 46%

Yes, does have moral obligation 48%

Did not see speech

No opinion 7%

No, does not 34%

Yes, does have moral obligation 59%

Saw Clinton's televised speech

Source: The Gallup Poll, November 27, 1995

cans, the issues there seem baffling—they believe that a lot of murky Balkan history has created a problem too complex to comprehend. In fact, the British journalist Ed Vulliamy observes, the dynamics of tribal war in Bosnia are devastatingly simple. Writes Vulliamy in his book *Seasons in Hell*:

> [The fighting] is the result of the resurrection in our time of the dreams and aggrieved historical quests of two great Balkan powers of medieval origin, Serbia and Croatia, and the attempt to re-establish their ancient frontiers with modern weaponry in the chaos of post-communist eastern Europe. Where the frontiers of these two dreams overlap or do not fit together, there is either war or compromise. Either way, there exists a third people who do not fit, who do not belong to either Serbia or Croatia, and whose homeland is a third, ethnically mixed, country which emerged between the two great Balkan powers, called Bosnia. Bosnia is shared between Serbs, Croats, and the third people, Slavic Muslims.[4]

According to Gallup surveys, the public doubts whether America has any stake in all this. There are doubts, too, about whether intervention will be effective in any case. And few seem to respond to the argument, sometimes offered, that U.S. credibility as NATO's leader is at issue.

« **The dynamics of tribal war in Bosnia are devastatingly simple.** »

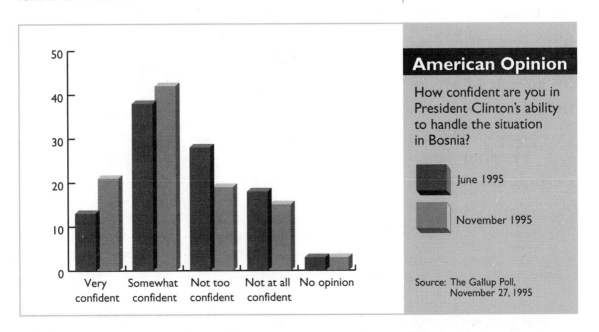

American Opinion

How confident are you in President Clinton's ability to handle the situation in Bosnia?

June 1995

November 1995

Very confident Somewhat confident Not too confident Not at all confident No opinion

Source: The Gallup Poll, November 27, 1995

Television pictures have shown the world the dead and maimed strewn around the Sarajevo market after a Bosnian Serb artillery attack. Newspaper photographs have caught sniper victims in their final moments: an old woman dying in the street at a Sarajevo bus stop, a child crumpled and bleeding on a playground.

Evidence that Bosnian Serb and rival Croatian forces engaged in orgies of murder, torture, and rape is indisputable. Both sides carried out mass killings, rape, and torture in pursuit of what they describe with the chilling euphemism "ethnic cleansing." Tens of thousands of people were driven from their homes. In many cases, the victims, caught and ground between Croat and Serb expansionists, were the Bosnian Muslims.

The evidence has not, however, built significant support for the use of American forces in Bosnia even for humanitarian purposes, still less to impose a settlement on the warring factions. Even so, President Clinton tried in 1995 to sway public opinion in favor of American intervention in Bosnia. "In Bosnia, as elsewhere, if the United States doesn't lead, the job will not be done," he said.[5]

Gallup polling in June 1995 found Americans opposed to an expanded U.S. involvement in Bosnia. They saw no compelling moral or political reason to aid the Bosnian Muslims. They overwhelmingly opposed the Republicans' proposal to lift the arms embargo and permit the Bosnian government to buy weapons with which to defend its territory.

Whether they were molding opinion or trailing along in its wake, newspaper editorialists agreed that Americans should not be imperiled in Bosnia, and that at any rate it was too late to help.

"It is devastating to admit that the world has failed Bosnia—that a historic opportunity to punish aggression and prevent a bloodbath has utterly passed," wrote an editorialist for *The Miami Herald*. "But that is the grim fact. To risk American lives—or, indeed, any foreign lives—in a hopeless crusade to unwrite history would now be irresponsible at best, and maybe catastrophic."[6]

«
Both sides carried out mass killings, rape, and torture in pursuit of what they describe with the chilling euphemism 'ethnic cleansing.'
»

In the June 1995 poll, two-thirds of Gallup respondents believed Clinton had not pursued a well-thought-out policy on Bosnia. More than one-third thought the United States already had become too involved there. While 60 percent said the United States had a moral obligation to protect the U.N. peacekeeping force (then under intense military pressure from the Bosnian Serbs), only 29 percent thought America had any duty, moral or otherwise, to screen Bosnian citizens from Serb attacks.

Nearly two-thirds—63 percent—said the United States had no interest in the outcome in Bosnia. Polltakers found a striking age discrepancy on the question. Of respondents old enough to have fought in World War II, only 18 percent thought the national interest required a U.S. presence in Bosnia. About a third (36 percent) of respondents ages eighteen to twenty-nine believed important U.S. concerns were at risk there.

Bosnia looked like a quagmire to most Americans in the summer of 1995. By the autumn, though, the prospects for a settlement had changed greatly for the better. With the Croatian army's entry into the war on the Bosnian government side and a sustained NATO

« **Bosnia looked like a quagmire to most Americans in the summer of 1995.** »

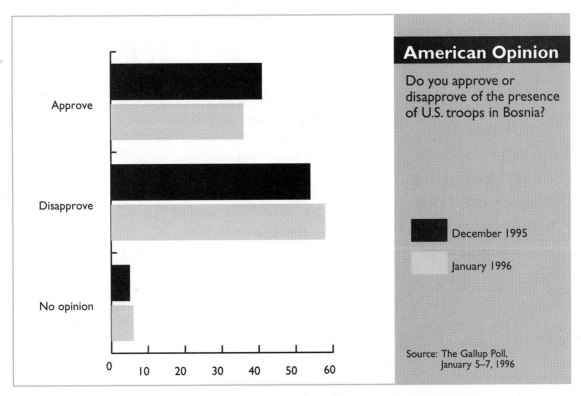

American Opinion

Do you approve or disapprove of the presence of U.S. troops in Bosnia?

December 1995

January 1996

Source: The Gallup Poll, January 5–7, 1996

Approve

Disapprove

No opinion

0 10 20 30 40 50 60

air offensive against the Serbs, the balance tilted sharply toward the Bosnian Muslims.

In late summer, Croat and Bosnian Muslim forces reclaimed territory lost earlier to the Serbs, reducing the Serbian share of Bosnia's land area from 70 percent to 49 percent. Having gained their territorial objectives, the Croats were willing to negotiate. At the same time, the Bosnian Serbs became more tractable, too, figuring that if they fought on, they were likely to lose still more.

In September, the Bosnian government accepted in principle the creation of an autonomous Serbian substate within Bosnia. In October, the warring parties pledged to stop fighting and start negotiating; President Clinton repeated his offer of U.S. forces to monitor an agreement. And in besieged Sarajevo, the lights went on again.

In the end, the Bosnian Muslims, fearing an eventual permanent partition of the country, were the most difficult group to conciliate. Promised military assistance and economic aid for reconstruction, the Muslims reluctantly agreed to go along. The November accord preserved Bosnia as a single state, confirming Sarajevo as the undivided capital of the whole, but with two distinct self-governing halves: a Muslim-Croat federation and a Serb republic.

> «
> **The agreement 'offers tangible hope that there will be no more days of dodging bullets, no more winters of freshly dug graves.'**
> »

The negotiators may have fashioned an imperfect peace. But at least the agreement held out the possibility of a permanent end to the fighting. Said Secretary of State Christopher: "It offers tangible hope that there will be no more days of dodging bullets, no more winters of freshly dug graves, no more years of isolation from the outside world."[7]

All the same, Americans remained skeptical. In a January 1996 Gallup poll, only 36 percent of respondents approved of the presence of U.S. forces in Bosnia; 54 percent disapproved.

In a December 1995 survey, only 40 percent said they were confident the United States would achieve its goals in Bosnia with few or no casualties. (On February 3, 1996, the American command reported its first fatality in the field, an Ohio soldier who had stepped on a landmine.) A majority of respondents, 57 percent, doubted the U.S mission would succeed, or that the cost in lives would be small.

Haiti

Americans were split too over the issue of Haiti, a desperately poor and backward Caribbean island nation lacking a democratic tradition and with a history of phenomenally abusive and corrupt misgovernment.

"If all other diplomatic efforts, including economic sanctions, fail to restore a democratic government in Haiti," Gallup asked in September 1994, "do you think the United States should send military troops to Haiti along with troops from other countries, or should the U.S. *not* send military troops to Haiti at all?"

Fifty-two percent of respondents said the United States should stay out of Haiti entirely. Only 44 percent said they supported U.S. intervention as part of a multinational force.

Some 20,000 troops, mostly American, landed in Haiti in September and October 1994 to return President Jean-Bertrand Aristide to office. A military coup had forced Aristide into exile in 1991. President Clinton

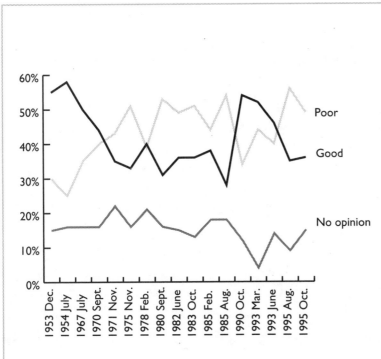

American Opinion

In general, do you think the United Nations is doing a good job or a poor job in trying to solve the problems it has had to face?

Source: The Gallup Poll,
October 19–22, 1995

employed main force after negotiations, economic sanctions, and other forms of persuasion had failed to resolve the matter.

Public support for U.S. intervention remained soft, even after the most critical and dangerous early phase of the operation had passed without military incident or casualties. Just after the landing, 54 percent of Gallup respondents said they supported the operation. A few weeks later, only 48 percent approved.

In March 1995, after Aristide had been returned to office and when Haiti appeared to be on course for elections scheduled for later in the year, only 34 percent of those polled said they approved of the U.S. mission. Fifty-nine percent said they disapproved.

The Public Split on Gays in the Military

President Clinton's compromise on the question of homosexuals in the military drew a mixed reaction in the Gallup Organization's polling on the issue.

The policy—known as "Don't ask, don't tell, don't pursue"—allows homosexuals to serve in the military so long as they do not make their orientation public or engage in homosexual activity. Approved late in 1993, the compromise went into effect on February 28, 1994.

Gallup found opinion split roughly evenly on the issue. In a January 1994 poll, 50 percent said they supported the "Don't ask, don't tell" policy, 47 percent were opposed, and 3 percent had no opinion.

At the same time, Gallup reported low approval ratings for President Clinton on issues involving gays and lesbians. Fewer than a third of those surveyed, 32 percent, endorsed Clinton's handling of such issues. Fifty-seven percent disapproved, and 11 percent offered no opinion.

A federal judge struck down the compromise policy in March 1995, rejecting the government's argument that military morale and performance would suffer if openly homosexual men and women were permitted to serve.

"Congress may not enact discriminatory legislation because it desires to insulate heterosexual service members from statements that might excite their prejudices," Judge Eugene H. Nickerson wrote.[1] The ruling, handed down in Federal District Court in Brooklyn, New York, applied only to the six military personnel who brought the lawsuit. This and similar challenges were expected to make their way eventually to the U.S. Supreme Court, which would settle the issue.

In April, United Nations peacekeepers took over for the U.S. force in Haiti. Parliamentary elections in June were confused and in some cases inconclusive, but they were largely peaceful. In December 1995, a presidential election took place that was generally reported as fairly, if somewhat ineptly, conducted—there were only minor incidents.

Public opinion may never have warmed to the intervention in Haiti, but the newspaper editorialists gave Clinton credit for a foreign policy success. "President Clinton can take pride in the Haiti operation," the *Los Angeles Times* wrote. "Against the wishes of an America made leery by Somalia, the Administration accomplished what it set out to do: U.S. intervention ended a corrupt and illegal military rule, restored the democratically elected president, and stanched the flow of illegal immigrants to this country."[8]

Russia

Though interest in Russia has waned, Gallup surveys suggest Americans continue to regard the one-time Cold War rival as the nation's chief foreign policy priority.

In a 1994 poll, four of every ten respondents (41 percent) ranked Russia as America's leading overseas priority. Twenty-seven percent rated Western Europe

> **« Americans continue to regard Russia as the nation's chief foreign policy priority. »**

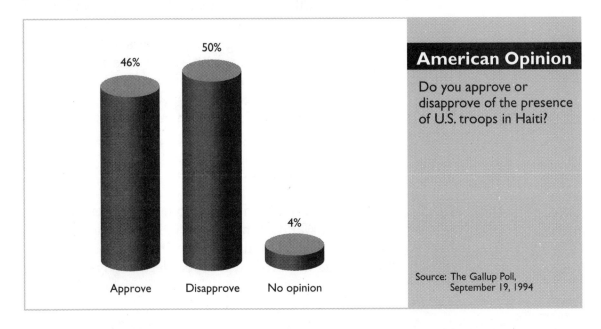

46% 50% 4%

Approve   Disapprove   No opinion

American Opinion

Do you approve or disapprove of the presence of U.S. troops in Haiti?

Source: The Gallup Poll, September 19, 1994

most important; 22 percent thought U.S. diplomats should pay closest attention to Asia.

In an April 1995 poll, more than six of every ten respondents (64 percent) believed NATO, Europe's Cold War bulwark against the Soviets, should be maintained. A sizable minority, 22 percent, thought the Atlantic alliance had outlived its usefulness.

More than half—54 percent—said Russia no longer posed a significant military threat. Yet in April 1995, nearly half of those polled—48 percent—judged U.S. force levels in Western Europe, then at 100,000, "about right" for the circumstances. Thirty-nine percent thought the United States had too many troops in Europe; only 7 percent thought there were too few.

Gallup found that most poll respondents had slight concern for the security of the former Iron Curtain countries of Eastern Europe. Four of every ten believed the United States should stay neutral in the event Russia tried to reestablish control of the region. Twenty-eight percent said they would support sending military and economic aid should Eastern Europe be threatened, but only 27 percent favored the use of U.S. military forces to challenge a hypothetical Russian aggression.

Overall, Russia graded low as a military threat to America. In a June 1994 Gallup survey, only 21 percent of respondents viewed Russia as the first or second most serious threat to U.S. security. Forty-two percent saw Iraq as the major threat. Only 30 percent rated China first or second among potential U.S. enemies.

Russia's embattled president, Boris Yeltsin, fell increasingly out of favor with Americans in 1994 and 1995, according to Gallup. In January 1994, two-thirds of those polled considered Yeltsin an ally of the United States. By April 1995, fewer than half—48 percent—thought of him that way.

Foreign Trade, Free Trade

To the Clinton administration, the proper study for post–Cold War diplomats is global economics. Foreign trade is as critical a national security issue today as ever the balance of terror was three decades ago. Import-

> «
> **Import-export figures are to the mid-1990s what nuclear throw weights were to the mid-1960s.**
> »

export figures are to the mid-1990s what nuclear throw weights were to the mid-1960s. U.S. exports more than doubled from 1985 to 1994, and export goods now account for fully 10 percent of the gross domestic product.

President Clinton has made free trade, with its promise of more and better jobs for Americans, a centerpiece of his foreign policy. The issue has become entwined with American domestic politics as well. Free-traders clash with labor groups and with those who lead the foreign policy agenda with human rights issues: prison labor in China; government repression of labor organizers in Indonesia; wages, working conditions, and environmental neglect in Mexico.

Clinton has tried to avoid linking politics and trade. The administration did not permit concerns about human rights, labor, and environmental issues to block approval of preferential trading status for China or stall the campaign for the North American Free Trade Agreement (Nafta) and the General Agreement on Tariffs and Trade (GATT). Laura Tyson, chairwoman of the President's Council of Economic Advisors, put the administration's bottom-line argument this way: "Ralph Nader [the consumer advocate] is willing to

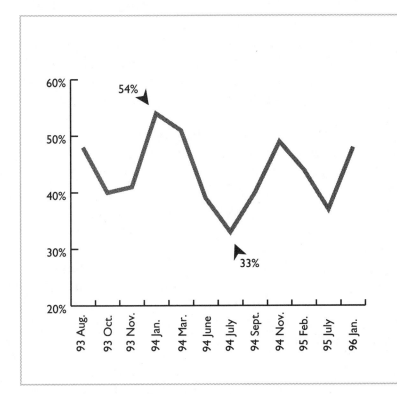

American Opinion

Percentage of respondents who approve of the way Clinton is handling foreign affairs.

Source: The Gallup Poll

have the United States pay a higher price for goods because we eliminate imports from countries that don't adhere to environmental standards we consider to be acceptable," she said. "But he doesn't tell us the price tag consumers should be willing to pay."[9]

The polls suggest Americans are unsure of their ground on such issues and are willing to give equal time to both sides of the argument.

In November 1994, just before Congress approved GATT, Gallup asked a representative sampling of Americans whether they viewed free trade more as an opportunity for American economic growth or as a threat to the economy from foreign imports. Fifty-three percent regarded free trade as an opportunity, up from 44 percent in September 1992. Thirty-eight percent considered it a threat, down from 48 percent in the earlier poll.

Gallup respondents divided almost evenly on Nafta. In a survey taken in November 1993, around the time Congress approved Nafta, 43 percent approved the treaty, 41 percent were opposed, and 16 percent had no opinion about it.

Clinton administration economists forecast the creation of 170,000 jobs in the first year of Nafta, which removed most trade barriers among the United States, Canada, and Mexico. As it happens, the short-term result has been a loss of jobs—at least 40,000 of them, by a U.S. Department of Labor reckoning. They were mostly factory jobs that migrated to Mexico, where wages can be as little as one-seventh of those north of the border.

Sometimes, though, the figures tell only part of the story. *The New York Times* gave the example of the Key Tronic Corp., a Spokane, Washington, computer keyboard manufacturer that took advantage of Nafta to lay off 277 assembly workers and shift their jobs to Ciudad Juarez, Mexico. Lower production costs—wages in Ciudad Juarez are one-fourth of those in Spokane—enabled the company to cut the price of its keyboards, generating more sales. But because Key Tronic's parts continue to be manufactured in the Spokane area, increased demand for keyboards created new jobs there.[10]

« **After a sharp dip following the near-collapse of Mexico's financial system, trade appears to be again on the increase.** »

Overall, U.S. exports to Mexico, now even with Japan as America's second-largest trading partner (Canada is the largest), rose 21.7 percent in the first nine months of Nafta, with imports from Mexico up 22.8 percent. After a sharp dip following the near-collapse of Mexico's financial system during the peso crisis of late 1994, trade appears to be again on the increase.

Some analysts believe the real issue for American jobs is the trade deficit, not free-trade agreements. Administration economists estimate that each $1 billion in exports creates 20,000 jobs. Labor union economists counter that each $1 billion in imports abolishes 20,000 jobs. The U.S. trade deficit in 1994 approached $160 billion.

With its 22,000 pages of rules and regulations covering 124 nations, GATT provides for the gradual elimination of tariffs, quotas, local content requirements, and other barriers to trade. Not surprisingly with an issue of such density, most survey respondents admitted to ignorance about GATT. Only 41 percent told Gallup they had followed the issue closely. Nearly six in every ten, 59 percent, said they had not paid much attention to the GATT debate. Fewer than one in every four, 23 percent, supported the agreement. Fourteen percent opposed it. Nearly two-thirds—63 percent—admitted they did not know enough about the treaty to form an opinion.

« **A majority expressed strong 'buy American' views.** »

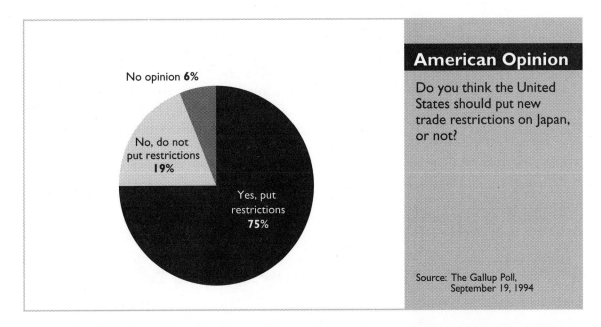

No opinion **6%**

No, do not put restrictions **19%**

Yes, put restrictions **75%**

American Opinion

Do you think the United States should put new trade restrictions on Japan, or not?

Source: The Gallup Poll, September 19, 1994

«

**Many question
whether Clinton
has a clear vision
of America's role
in the world.**

»

Survey respondents showed no such reticence when asked about trade with Japan. In March 1994, 60 percent of those polled faulted President Clinton for not being strict enough with Japan on trade. Fewer than a third (31 percent) graded his approach "about right." And more than three-quarters—78 percent—thought the United States should place new trade restrictions on the Japanese.

A majority in the same poll expressed strong "buy American" views. Given a choice, 59 percent of respondents would purchase an American product over a similar Japanese-made one at the same price even if the Japanese version was of higher quality. Thirty-nine percent said they would buy the Japanese article.

American trade negotiators probably had the survey results in mind in June 1995, when they nearly touched off an economic war with Japan over automobiles. The United States sought an agreement to expand American access to the Japanese car and car-parts market. When the Japanese balked, President Clinton threatened $5.9 billion in tariffs on Japanese luxury cars.

A last-minute compromise averted a trade war. The accord makes it easier for U.S. manufacturers to sell car parts to Japanese repair shops and increases the number of Japanese dealers offering American cars. Japan's five major automakers also pledged to increase their production in American plants.

A Look Ahead

Few analysts consider the conduct of foreign affairs to be President Clinton's long suit. Critics have found him to be vacillating, hesitant, changeable. In opinion surveys, his approval ratings have been low, usually below 50 percent. Many respondents question whether Clinton has a clear vision of America's role in the world.

Still, Clinton makes a case for his record in foreign affairs. He says he is an experimenter, not a vacillator, and that he seeks new approaches for a changing world and a new century. He claims as successes the intervention in Haiti, peace talks in Northern Ireland, timely approval of $20 billion in loans to Mexico during the peso crisis, and the latest Israeli–PLO accord.

Barring unforeseen events, foreign policy probably will not become a major preoccupation in the 1996 presidential campaign. The great variable is Bosnia. Two Republican presidential aspirants, Robert Dole and Phil Gramm, were persistent critics of the administration's Bosnia policy. "American power cannot solve every awful problem in the world," said Senator Gramm.[11] (Gramm aborted his candidacy in February 1996.) On the other hand, Dole in the end helped Clinton win a crucial Senate vote providing limited support for the deployment of U.S. troops to enforce the Bosnia peace accord.

Clinton runs considerable risks with American sponsorship of the peace process there. Previous cease-fires quickly broke down. In Bosnia, even allies detest each other—the Muslims and Croats, in federation against the Bosnian Serbs in late 1995, fought as recently as 1993, and mutual suspicion and distrust remain high. Some Bosnian Serbs spoke darkly of betrayal, and hinted they would refuse to accept elements of the November accord.

While many commentators faulted Clinton for waiting so long to act, they supported America's new, if belated, assertiveness. Writing in *The New Yorker*, William Finnegan dismissed as too depressing the notion that Clinton decided finally to confront the issue—in the form of air attacks on the Bosnian Serbs—because he thought a Balkan success might shore up his reelection prospects. "Let us say instead that Mr. Clinton felt he had to give other, non-military ideas for intervention a chance, that he waited to act forcefully until the strategic moment arrived," Finnegan wrote. "In any event, he has now done what is plainly right, and what he himself saw and proclaimed to be right more than three years ago, as a candidate: he has jumped in on the side of the victims and has hit the bullies hard."[12]

That said, the Bosnian peace is precarious. A disaster involving U.S. forces there—soldiers or airmen killed and wounded or taken hostage—could erase at a stroke all Clinton's claims of achievement in foreign affairs and hand his opponents a potent weapon for 1996.

Notes: Foreign Affairs Americans Shun Policeman's Lot

1. Elaine Sciolino, "Soldiering On, Without an Enemy," *The New York Times*, The Week in Review," October 29, 1995, 1.
2. Editorial, *Cedar Rapids* (Iowa) *Gazette*, June 2, 1995.
3. Todd S. Purdum, "Clinton Warns of U.S. Retreat to Isolationism," *The New York Times*, October 7, 1995, 1.
4. Ed Vulliamy, *Seasons in Hell* (New York: St. Martin's Press, 1994), 4–5.
5. Purdum, "Clinton Warns"
6. Editorial, *The Miami Herald*, June 2, 1995.
7. Elaine Sciolino, "Accord Reached to End the War in Bosnia," *The New York Times*, November 22, 1995, 1.
8. Editorial, *Los Angeles Times*, April 4, 1995.
9. David E. Sanger, "Trade Agreement Ends Long Debate, But Not Conflicts," *The New York Times*, December 4, 1994, 1.
10. James Sterngold, "Nafta Trade-Off: Some Jobs Lost, Others Gained," *The New York Times*, October 9, 1995, 1.
11. Alison Mitchell, "The Next Hurdle: Clinton Must Sell Plan to Americans," *The New York Times*, November 22, 1995, 1.
12. William Finnegan, *The New Yorker*, October 9, 1995, 5.

Notes: The Public Split on Gays in the Military

1. Eric Schmitt, "Judge Overturns Pentagon Policy on Homosexuals," *The New York Times*, March 31, 1995, 1.

10 Americans Don't Like the Media or the Message

by
Carl Rollyson

The American public is as critical of the news media as it is of the politicians the media cover. A November 1995 Gallup poll revealed that only 20 percent of respondents think highly of the honesty and ethical standards of journalists, with television reporters and commentators scoring slightly higher, at 21 percent. When figured as a separate category, newspaper reporters scored the lowest approval rating (20 percent), slightly ahead of the rating for lawyers (16 percent).

Asked if the media were out of touch with average Americans, 60 percent of April 1995 poll respondents agreed. Yet, over half also thought the media were fair to GOP House Speaker Newt Gingrich (53 percent), to President Bill Clinton (55 percent), and to the Republican Contract with America (56 percent). Concerning media bias, 17 percent believed it favored the Republicans and 25 percent the Democrats, while 48 percent thought it favored neither.

A May 1995 *Money* magazine survey revealed that Americans increasingly complain that the media get in the way of society's solving its problems. Some media critics agree, observing that reporters too often insert themselves into their stories, offer gratuitous opinion, and tailor their reports for insiders or one another.[1]

Of course, some politicians, such as Newt Gingrich, have concurred, suggesting that Americans can lead

« **Only 20 percent of respondents think highly of the honesty and ethical standards of journalists.** »

the world—if the media will let them. He advances the argument that by constantly publicizing the dark side of society, the media are endangering American society.[2] Liberal magazines such as *The Nation* counter that American anxieties are not created by the media but by social and economic problems that result when too many Americans have to scrape by on service and information-age jobs that pay barely more than the minimum wage.[3]

Gingrich's position on the media is close to that expressed in public opinion polls. As Stephen Budiansky wrote in a January 1995 article in *U.S. News & World Report*, public hostility toward the media is unprecedented. Americans feel that the national press is unnecessarily adversarial, negative, insensitive to the people it covers, irresponsible, arrogant, and elitist.[4] Writing in January 1995, Joe Saltzman observed in *USA Today* that judges and lawyers have joined in the media bashing, blaming it for tainting the impartiality of potential jurors by zealously distorting the public's perception of the accused.[5]

The Media, Race, and Crime

Approximately the same percentages of minorities (African Americans, Hispanics, Asians) said they are very or somewhat satisfied with their local daily newspapers (roughly 75 percent), with slightly higher percentages for local and national television news, according to a Gallup poll conducted in June 1994. But 45 percent of African Americans were somewhat or very dissatisfied with the way local newspapers handle race-specific issues, whereas only 23 percent of Hispanics and 25 percent of Asians expressed this level of dissatisfaction. (Local television and national television news had slightly lower percentages of dissatisfied responses on race-specific issues.) Seventy-nine percent of whites were very or somewhat satisfied with the way daily newspapers include race in regular news coverage, whereas only 56 percent of African Americans, 61 percent of Hispanics, and 60 percent of Asians expressed similar satisfaction. Again, television and ra-

« Americans feel that the national press is unnecessarily adversarial, negative, insensitive to the people it covers, irresponsible, arrogant, and elitist. »

dio received slightly higher favorable ratings than newspapers. About a quarter of whites believed that media coverage could improve relations between different ethnic and racial groups, compared with only 14 percent of African Americans who agreed, and about a third each of Hispanics and Asians. Nearly half of African Americans surveyed believed that the media worsen relations, compared with half as many Hispanics and a quarter as many Asians. Approximately half of all the groups surveyed thought the media had no effect. Almost a third of African Americans were angry at least once a week over coverage of African Americans in local newspapers, with about half that many Hispanics and Asians saying the same. Local and national television news were less likely to provoke anger among all minority groups. Twenty-four percent of African Americans, 38 percent of Hispanics, and 40 percent of Asians believed that newspapers paid attention to comments and criticism from their minority

«
Nearly half of African Americans surveyed believed that the media worsen relations.
»

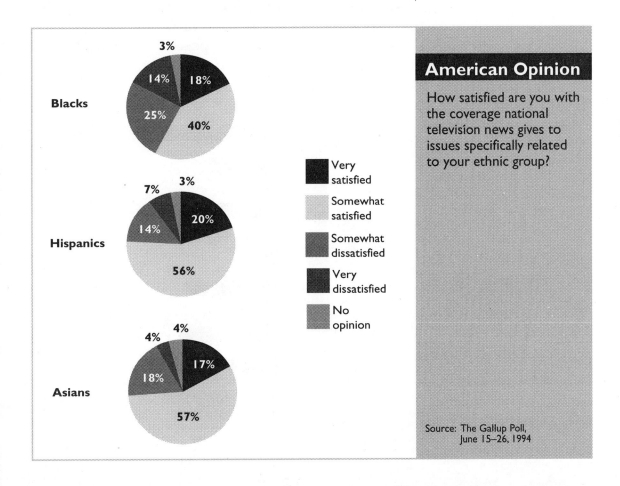

Blacks
3%
14%
18%
25%
40%

American Opinion

How satisfied are you with the coverage national television news gives to issues specifically related to your ethnic group?

Hispanics
3%
7%
14%
20%
56%

Very satisfied

Somewhat satisfied

Somewhat dissatisfied

Very dissatisfied

No opinion

Asians
4%
4%
4%
17%
18%
57%

Source: The Gallup Poll, June 15–26, 1994

readers, while 66 percent of African Americans, 45 percent of Hispanics, and 37 percent of Asians believed the opposite.

There were far fewer differences between whites and minority respondents asked about crime reporting in local newspapers. More or less a third of each group thought there was too much coverage, and between 41 percent and 53 percent of all groups thought there was just the right amount. Twenty-two percent of African Americans, 11 percent of Hispanics, 16 percent of Asians, and 10 percent of whites thought there was too little coverage. The percentages that thought local television news had too little coverage of crime rose to between 45 and 47 percent for all groups except African Americans (35 percent). Fifty-nine percent of whites, 43 percent of Asians, 51 percent of Hispanics, and 35 percent of African Americans thought national news provided too much coverage of crime.

The largest discrepancies were detected when respondents were asked about the fairness of crime reporting. Eighty-five percent of whites thought local newspapers were fair, as opposed to 38 percent of Af-

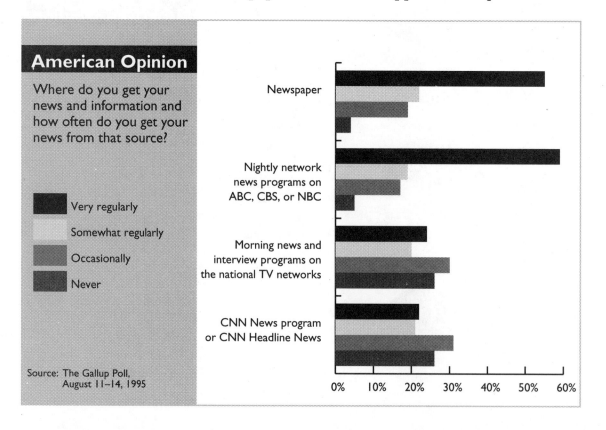

American Opinion

Where do you get your news and information and how often do you get your news from that source?

- Very regularly
- Somewhat regularly
- Occasionally
- Never

Newspaper

Nightly network news programs on ABC, CBS, or NBC

Morning news and interview programs on the national TV networks

CNN News program or CNN Headline News

0%   10%   20%   30%   40%   50%   60%

Source: The Gallup Poll,
August 11–14, 1995

American Opinion

How satisfied are you with the coverage the following media give to issues and events that interest you?

	Blacks	Hispanics	Asians	Whites
Your local daily newspaper				
Very satisfied	23%	33%	27%	25%
Somewhat satisfied	50	43	53	50
Somewhat dissatisfied	13	10	6	18
Very dissatisfied	7	4	2	4
No opinion	7	10	12	3
Local television news in your area				
Very satisfied	26%	34%	30%	30%
Somewhat satisfied	55	45	50	46
Somewhat dissatisfied	12	11	11	14
Very dissatisfied	5	9	4	5
No opinion	2	1	5	5
National television news				
Very satisfied	33%	42%	37%	25%
Somewhat satisfied	52	39	46	47
Somewhat dissatisfied	9	14	11	18
Very dissatisfied	3	3	2	7
No opinion	3	2	4	3

Source: The Gallup Poll, June 25-26, 1994

rican Americans, 61 percent of Hispanics, and 69 percent of Asians. Forty-seven percent of African Americans and 30 percent of Hispanics considered their local newspapers unfair, whereas only 10 percent of Asians and whites thought so. The percentages for local and national television news did not vary significantly, although all groups seemed to have slightly more confidence in broadcast media. Minorities felt strongly (93 to 94 percent) that local newspapers did very serious or somewhat serious harm with their unfair treatment of minorities, while only 75 percent of whites agreed with this statement. But the percentages for all groups who thought unfair crime coverage harmed minorities very seriously or somewhat seriously were in the 83-to-90-percent range for local television and the 81-to-

88-percent range for national television news. And since 1993, confidence in television news in general has dropped from 46 percent to 35 percent, according to an April 1994 Gallup poll.

Entertainment Industry Values

A June 1995 Gallup poll found that 65 percent of Americans believed that the entertainment industry is seriously out of touch with the values of the American people. Too much sex and violence in movies, television shows, and music contributed to the views of 83 percent of respondents who believed the entertainment industry should reform itself. A solid majority (63 percent) concluded that a large reduction in the amount of sex and violence in the entertainment industry would result in a significantly improved moral climate.

As troubled as people are by this issue, 63 percent declared the federal government should not become involved in restricting the amount of sex and violence in the industry—a percentage that is virtually identical to

American Opinion

Do you think the coverage of crime stories by your local newspaper treats [respondent's ethnic group/racial minorities] fairly or unfairly?

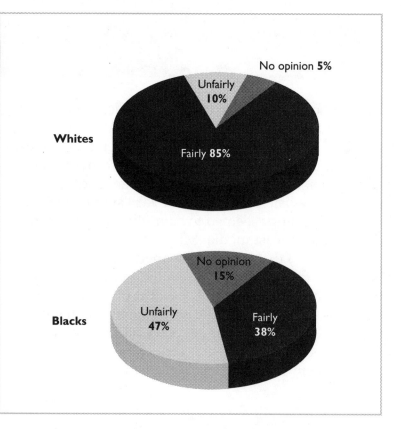

Whites
No opinion 5%
Unfairly 10%
Fairly 85%

Blacks
No opinion 15%
Unfairly 47%
Fairly 38%

Source: The Gallup Poll, June 15–26, 1994

the percentage of those expressing faith in democracy. Only 35 percent of respondents wanted government intervention. If a majority of Americans is highly critical of those who shape the nation's popular culture, most Americans also want them to remain independent and to be left alone to solve their own problems. When asked their view of politicians who criticize the entertainment industry for featuring too much sex and violence, 67 percent of those polled said the politicians were just playing politics; only 28 percent regarded the politicians as performing a valuable public service. That sex and violence are truly hot-button issues seems clear from another poll finding: by a somewhat narrower margin (51 percent to 41 percent), Americans agreed with the proposition that popular culture threatens to undermine our character as a nation.

Notes: Americans Don't Like the Media or the Message

1. Gary Belsky, "Americans Are Doing Better But Feeling Less Secure," *Money,* May 1995, 24–26.
2. Newt Gingrich, "America Can Lead the World—If the Media Will Let It," *Houston Chronicle,* January 29, 1995, C5.
3. "Age of Anxiety," *The Nation,* February 13, 1995, 187–88.
4. Stephen Budiansky, "The Media's Message: Public Hostility Toward the National Media," *U.S. News & World Report,* January 9, 1995, 45–47.
5. Joe Saltzman, "The Law vs. The Media," *USA Today,* January 1995, 65.

Faith in America's Future

by
Carl Rollyson

Americans' faith in their country's future has been at a low ebb for most of the past two decades. In a July 1995 Gallup poll, nearly two-thirds of respondents declared themselves dissatisfied with the way things were going in the United States. Throughout the Clinton administration, the percentage of those dissatisfied has hovered around 66 percent. It was even higher during the last year of the Bush administration, and similar percentages were reported dissatisfied in the first two years of the Reagan administration and the last year of the Carter administration. Indeed, except for the highwater mark registered during the Reagan administration (March 1986), when only 30 percent expressed dissatisfaction, a majority of Americans polled since 1979 has consistently expressed discontent about the state of the nation.

An April 1995 Gallup poll reported that 60 percent of Americans believe that the future will be worse than the present, with only 23 percent saying it will be better. When asked to compare the present with the past, 52 percent of Americans said they were worse off than their parents, while 35 percent said they were better off. When a June 1994 poll asked how well young adults were doing these days, 6 percent said very well, 45 percent said fairly well, 29 percent said fairly badly, and 18 percent said very badly.

«

A majority of Americans polled since 1979 has consistently expressed discontent about the state of the nation.

»

A September 1994 Gallup poll found that by a 57-to-36-percent margin, people believed the changes in values and morality that began during the 1960s had a negative effect on the country. A somewhat closer margin (51 percent to 44 percent) agreed with the statement "Usually when we try to change things in this country, they turn out worse, not better." Somewhat offsetting this negative mood was the finding that 83 percent of Americans are satisfied with their personal lives.

Outlook Mixed on Economic Prospects

Americans seem to have contradictory views on the future of the economy. Most are relatively satisfied with their own current economic status and the short-term outlook for the nation but are worried that the American economy won't be nearly as robust in the long-term as it has been in the past. Just over half (52 percent) of those polled in April 1995 indicated satisfaction with their economic status—a percentage nearly identical

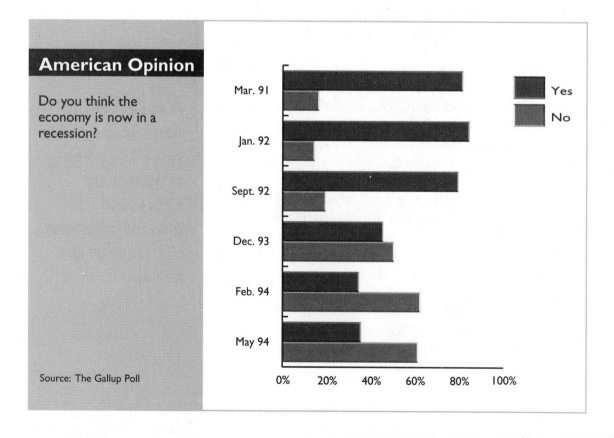

American Opinion

Do you think the economy is now in a recession?

Mar. 91
Jan. 92
Sept. 92
Dec. 93
Feb. 94
May 94

Yes
No

0% 20% 40% 60% 80% 100%

Source: The Gallup Poll

to President Clinton's approval rating at the time (51 percent). Eighty percent professed contentment with their material situation, a figure remarkably close to the 83 percent of those polled who were happy with their personal lives.

Indeed, the poll provides a picture of Americans happy in the context of their own lives: 71 percent were satisfied with their household income, 80 percent with their leisure time, 73 percent with their jobs, 75 percent with their standard of living, 77 percent with their education, 86 percent with their personal health, 90 percent with their family lives, 86 percent with their community as a place to live, 95 percent with the quality and amount of their food, 90 percent with the furniture in their home, 94 percent with their electronics and durable goods, 92 percent with their clothing, and 90 percent with their housing.

The sunny contentment the great majority of Americans profess when it comes to their own personal situation sharply contrasts with their relatively bleak outlook on the future and direction of the nation. A May 1994 Gallup poll found that 57 percent of respondents agreed that no matter how much the economy improved, good economic times would not last as long as they used to. Similarly, 54 percent agreed that even if the economy improved, it would never again be as strong as it was thirty or forty years ago. Yet, again, most Americans

« **An April 1995 Gallup poll provides a picture of Americans happy in the context of their own lives.** »

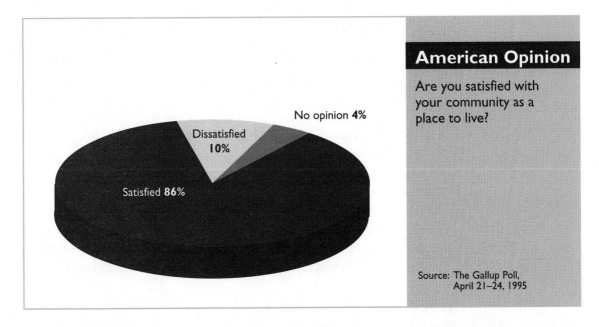

No opinion **4%**

Dissatisfied **10%**

Satisfied **86%**

American Opinion

Are you satisfied with your community as a place to live?

Source: The Gallup Poll, April 21–24, 1995

«
A June 1994 Gallup poll revealed that 48 percent believed that the next generation of Americans would enjoy less personal freedom than the current generation.
»

don't apply this pessimism to their own circumstances: 54 percent of Americans disagreed with the statement "No matter what you hear about the economy, things are not going to get better for *you* anytime soon."

A December 1994 Gallup poll found that 2 percent of respondents believed the country's economic condition was excellent, 25 percent good, 52 percent only fair, and 21 percent poor. This breakdown was the same as that of the previous two years, although the early 1990s saw Americans' confidence in the economy sink to as low as 10 percent, with nearly half of the poll respondents judging conditions poor. At the end of 1994, when Americans were asked to assess how the economy had changed over the past year, 49 percent said it was better, 34 percent said it was worse, and 15 percent said it was the same. Asked to predict the fate of the next year's economy, 56 percent said it would be better, 34 percent said it would be worse, and 10 percent said it would be about the same. About 40 percent of Americans believed they were better off than the previous year; 29 percent said they were about the same; 31 percent said they were worse off. These percentages compare favorably with surveys going back to 1976, with most years registering fewer than 40 percent who reported they were better off—except for the Reagan-Bush years of 1985–1990, when 40 percent or more felt they were better off than the previous year. In December 1994, confidence in a better economic year for individuals stood at a high of 63 percent, a percentage equaled in March 1988 and surpassed only once, in February 1990 (65 percent).

Although Reagan won both of his presidential elections by landslide majorities and enjoyed high ratings in the polls throughout his second term, only 34 percent of those responding to a November 2–6, 1994, Gallup survey said they would prefer to return to President Reagan's economic policies of the 1980s. Forty-eight percent wanted current policies continued. Respondents were more evenly divided when asked if they were more likely to vote for a congressional candidate who supported or opposed President Clinton's policies, with 41 percent declaring themselves in favor of these policies,

46 percent opposed, 8 percent expressing no preference, and 5 percent having no opinion.

Faith in Democracy

Americans fear their freedoms will be eroded in the future and that government can do little to solve the nation's problems. Idealistically, most continue to profess confidence in the country's democratic principles.

A June 1994 Gallup poll revealed that 48 percent of respondents believed that the next generation of Americans would enjoy less personal freedom than the current generation. Twenty percent said more; 30 percent said the same. The greatest threats to that freedom today were thought to be crime (83 percent), lack of economic opportunity (47 percent), government regulations (41 percent), police overreaction to crime (26 percent), and military threats from foreign countries (23 percent). Asked whether they would give up certain personal freedoms to reduce crime, 43 percent of the respondents said yes to the right to own a handgun; 25 percent said yes to the right to keep financial records private; 14 percent said yes to the right to have a lawyer when

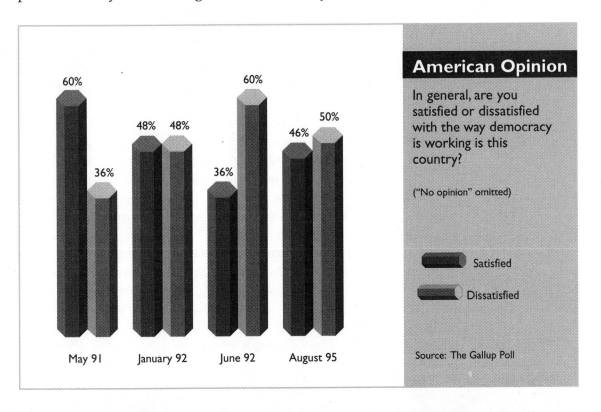

May 91   January 92   June 92   August 95

American Opinion

In general, are you satisfied or dissatisfied with the way democracy is working is this country?

("No opinion" omitted)

Satisfied

Dissatisfied

Source: The Gallup Poll

they were arrested; 20 percent said yes to the right to keep all telephone conversations private. Except in the case of handguns, the percentages of respondents opposed to relinquishing these rights were overwhelming.

Despite this fear over the future of American freedoms, a Gallup survey conducted in April 1995 found that 64 percent of respondents were satisfied with the way democracy worked. Only 11 percent of Americans said they had considered relocating to another country. This was a marked change from just nine months earlier, when an October 1994 Gallup poll reported only half of those responding were satisfied with the way democracy was working in America. In that poll, only 36 percent thought the federal government had helped make democracy better, while 54 percent thought the federal government had made the situation worse. On the other hand, a conviction that political parties made democracy better in this country was shared by 60 percent of those polled (31 percent disagreed, and 9 percent expressed no opinion). While 58 percent of respondents professed satisfaction with the choice of candidates running in their own congressional districts, 53 percent wanted to see a third party, and only 40 percent believed that two political parties were adequate. What this apparent weakening in allegiance to the two-party system holds for the future is debatable. One theory, argued by David R. Carlin in *Commonweal,* is that American democracy could be threatened by the growth of independent voters who forswear allegiance to either Democrats or Republicans. As the parties weaken, they become easier targets for fanatics and one-issue or special-interest groups. Carlin suggests that political parties, like the Catholic Church, must achieve a balance among their own average, apathetic, and fanatic members.[1]

Although term limits have been proposed as a way of reforming government and rejuvenating the two-party system by enabling more new people to be elected, only 40 percent of November 1994 poll respondents supported term limits, while 54 percent opposed them and 6 percent had no opinion.

« **Only 40 percent believed that two political parties were adequate.** »

A highly skeptical public regards government as an arm of a few big interests looking out for themselves. In a Gallup poll conducted in April 1995, there were 76 percent expressing this opinion, as opposed to 18 percent who said government was run for the benefit of all. Cynicism about special interests is currently quite high compared with the results of earlier surveys, in 1984 and 1972, when 59 percent of respondents expressed their distrust of government and big interests. A June 1994 Gallup survey reported that a sizable majority (58 percent) believed quite a few of the people running the government were a little crooked, 29 percent said not many, 6 percent said hardly any, and 5 percent said all are crooked.

According to an April 1995 Gallup poll, only 1 percent of respondents thought the federal government could be almost always trusted to do what is right; another 18 percent thought it could be trusted most of the time, while 78 percent said some of the time. By contrast, the University of Michigan National Election Study determined that between the years 1958 and 1966, 14 to 16 percent of the people polled said they could always trust government to do what is right, 48 to 62 percent said most of the time, and 23 percent said some of the time. Between 1958 and 1995, there was a dramatic shift in all categories of confidence; whereas

> **«**
> **A highly skeptical public regards government as an arm of a few big interests looking out for themselves.**
> **»**

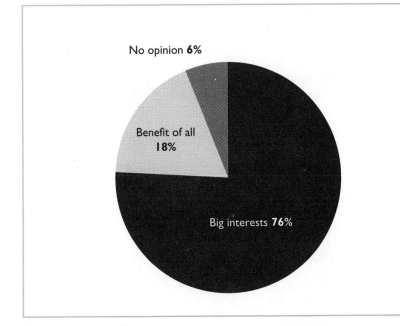

No opinion 6%

Benefit of all
18%

Big interests 76%

American Opinion

Would you say the government is pretty much run by a few big interests looking out for themselves or that it is run for the benefit of all the people?

Source: The Gallup Poll,
April 17–19, 1995

23 percent said in 1958 that government could be trusted only some of the time, 78 percent agreed with this sentiment in 1995. In the most positive category of always trusting government, percentages have not been in the double digits since 1966. Before the 1990s, the percentage of those saying they never trusted the government did not rise above 4 percent, whereas in the 1990s the number has been as high as 9 percent. In the April 1995 survey, however, this percentage dropped below 1 percent, and the category of those saying they have confidence in government only some of the time reached a peak of 78 percent.

Confidence in Government's Ability

Not only have Americans lost faith in government's intentions, they have also grown skeptical about its ability to solve the nation's problems. Indeed, many believe government makes things worse when it tries to make them better. When asked in an October 1994 Gallup poll to rate the performance of the federal government in the past twenty years, only 18 percent of respondents believed it had created more opportunities for the next generation of Americans to live better than their parents. A resounding 73 percent were dissatisfied with the federal government's role. And the percentage of those expressing faith in government's

«

Many believe government makes things worse when it tries to make them better.

»

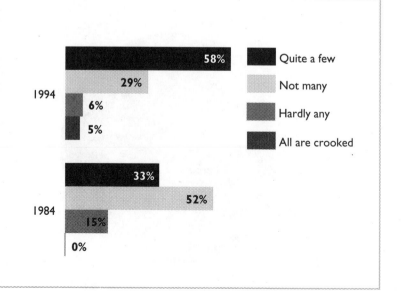

American Opinion

Do you think that quite a few of the people running the government are a little crooked, not very many are, or do you think hardly any of them are crooked at all?

1994
58% — Quite a few
29% — Not many
6% — Hardly any
5% — All are crooked

1984
33%
52%
15%
0%

Source: 1994, The Gallup Poll
1984, Michigan National
Election Study

ability to look out for everyone has fallen dramatically from the 41 percent figure recorded in 1972 and 1984. Only 38 percent of Americans surveyed in October 1994 were satisfied with the opportunities for a poor person in this country to get ahead by working hard, and 59 percent were dissatisfied. By a margin of 74 percent to 21 percent, people blamed the federal government for making the situation worse.

Skepticism about government activism can be seen in the seemingly contradictory response to specific policy issues in recent years. In a January 1994 Gallup poll, 90 percent of respondents agreed there was a welfare crisis, and 84 percent agreed there was a health care crisis. Sixty-two percent believed that both health care and welfare reform should be President Clinton's highest priority. Yet, in that same poll, Americans expressed great ambivalence about government reforms: 54 percent said government was doing too much, 39 percent said it should do more, and 7 percent expressed no opinion.

Notwithstanding the data that seem to show only low-to-moderate support for government activism, a significant segment of the population still looks to the president for leadership. At 45 percent, public confidence in the presidency as an institution ranked fourth, after the military, the police, and organized religion. Only 20 percent of those polled said they had very little or no confidence in the presidency.

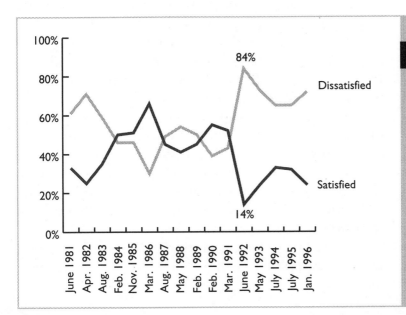

American Opinion

In general, are you satisfied or dissatisfied with the way things are going in the United States at this time?

Source: The Gallup Poll

Confidence in America's Institutions

Contributing to a low opinion of the nation's health is a pervasive lack of confidence in America's institutions, although not quite as low as it has been at some points. In fact, Gallup's April 1995 poll reported a rise in public confidence in the police (58 percent, up 4 points from the previous year), in organized religions (57 percent, up 3 points), and in the presidency (45 percent, up 7 points). The military continues to enjoy the most favorable rating, at 64 percent, unchanged from the previous year. Among the losers were television news (down 2 points) and big business (declining from 26 percent to 21 percent). Only 13 percent of respondents had a great deal of confidence in television news, 20 percent had quite a lot, and 41 percent had some, while 25 percent had very little or none (See "Americans Don't Like the Media or the Message," page 159.) Similar percentages were reported for other news media and organized labor, with Congress scoring just above big business—9 percent expressed a great deal of confidence, 12 percent quite a lot, 48 percent some, and 30 percent very little or none. Concerning Congress, 48 percent of those polled said congressional representatives consider their own welfare more important than that of their constituents, and 34 percent complained there was too much bickering in Congress. Almost all professions in the United States received higher ratings than congressmen, according to a November 1995 Gallup survey: only car salesmen edged out politicians as having the lowest ethical standards. Even lawyers, stockbrokers, and real estate agents fared better in respondents' opinions. At the top of the list were pharmacists, clergy, dentists, college teachers, engineers, medical doctors, and policemen. The 10 percent rating for congressmen was hardly bettered by senators (12 percent). Since 1976, congressmen have never exceeded a 20 percent approval rating. But the 1994 percentage was a new low, and the 1995 figures showed no improvement.

The most disturbing finding of the April 1995 poll was the low opinion of the criminal justice system: fully

> « The military continues to enjoy the most favorable rating, at 64 percent. »

42 percent of respondents said they had very little or no confidence in it. The positive ratings for banks, the medical system, and public schools were approximately half that expressed for the military.

Over the past decade, other institutions—such as the Supreme Court, the presidency, public schools, newspapers, and Congress—have suffered significant declines in public confidence, while the one institution in American life that has maintained its credibility is the military, with a positive rating never dipping below 58 percent and never rising higher than 85 percent, which it reached in March 1991, during the Gulf War.

Race Relations Evaluated

Since 1954, the Gallup organization has asked Americans if they approved of the *Brown v. Board of Education* Supreme Court decision, a landmark judgment that year, holding racial segregation in public schools to be illegal. The approval percentage since 1954 has risen from 55 percent to 87 percent. In the most recent polls, 48 percent of whites and 56 percent of African Americans surveyed agreed that race relations in this country are better now than they were forty years ago, while 20 percent of whites and 21 percent of African Americans felt they were the same, and 30 percent of whites and 17 percent of African Americans thought

«
Forty-two percent of respondents said they had very little or no confidence in the criminal justice system.
»

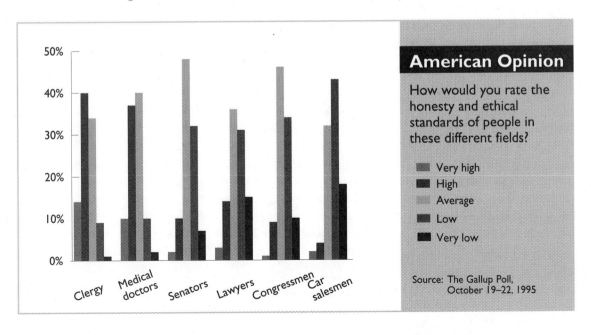

American Opinion

How would you rate the honesty and ethical standards of people in these different fields?

- Very high
- High
- Average
- Low
- Very low

Source: The Gallup Poll, October 19–22, 1995

they were worse. Nearly the same percentage of whites and African Americans (64 percent and 70 percent respectively) said integration had improved the quality of education for African-American students, and nearly the same number of whites and African Americans (29 and 25 percent, respectively) said it had not. But when asked whether integration has meant a better education for whites, only 39 percent of whites agreed, as opposed to 59 percent of African Americans, with 52 percent of whites and 33 percent of African Americans disagreeing. Sixty-two percent of whites and 75 percent of African Americans believed that integration has improved relations between the races, compared with 29 percent of whites and 18 percent of African Americans who disagreed. Many more African Americans (84 percent) than whites (52 percent) said more should be done to integrate public schools throughout the nation. Twenty-five percent of African Americans and 33 percent of whites would step up efforts to integrate; 60 percent of African Americans and 47 percent of whites

Many Worry About a Rainy Day, but Few Save for It

Americans worry about not earning enough to save for retirement, and they are burdened by concerns over financing their children's education. A Gallup poll conducted in April 1995 discovered that of those respondents with children under eighteen, 73 percent were saving for their children's education, whereas only 19 percent were saving for retirement. A May 1995 Gallup poll found that while 45 percent of respondents had personal savings, 31 percent admitted they had saved no money during the past year for retirement, and only 28 percent had saved a moderate amount. Only one-fourth of preretirement adults over thirty had managed to save $5,000 or more in the past year. According to the poll, the average amount saved by individuals the previous year was only $2,000.

Even worse, there is rampant skepticism about Social Security benefits. A December 1995 Gallup poll found that only 35 percent felt fairly sure they could count on Social Security income, whereas 66 percent were relying on their employers' pension plans and 83 percent on income from savings and investments. Only 31 percent of those polled, in May 1995 however, say they or their spouses have such plans. Only 9 percent of Americans believe they will be better off in retirement; 34 percent expect to be worse off; 56 percent expect their standard

would increase funding for schools with minority populations. Sixty-four percent of African Americans and 88 percent of whites preferred letting students attend local schools regardless of their racial makeup, compared with 33 percent of African Americans and only 9 percent of whites who preferred to transfer students to achieve integration. Only 17 percent of whites expressed a wish for more integrated communities, as opposed to 40 percent of African Americans. Similarly, 63 percent of African Americans said they would like to see the whole country more integrated, whereas only 33 percent of whites did. When asked if there is ever a circumstance in which it would be better for a black student to attend an all-black school rather than an integrated school, 38 percent of African Americans and 52 percent of whites said yes.

On issues affecting the rights of racial and ethnic minorities, the public gives the federal government credit for past accomplishments but is skeptical about its future role. In an October 1994 survey, 51 percent

> **«**
> **Only 17 percent of whites expressed a wish for more integrated communities, as opposed to 40 percent of African Americans.**
> **»**

of living to be the same. The May 1995 poll defined four categories of response to retirement planning: the happily prepared (26 percent), the cautious optimists (18 percent), the worriers (32 percent), and the woefully unprepared (24 percent). Thus well over half of those Americans polled expressed great anxiety about retirement. The woefully unprepared had an average income of just about $20,000, with fewer than half saying their employer has a retirement plan. Sixty-three percent of the woefully unprepared saved no money last year—the highest percentage among the four groups—and 100 percent say they do not have enough money to save for retirement. The worriers, however, make an average income of over $40,000 a year, second only to the happily prepared, and 94 percent of the worriers agree there always seems to be something else to spend their money on rather than saving for the future. Overall, this group is the least well informed about retirement planning. Their ignorance is remarkable when this group is compared with the cautious optimists, who have an average income of just over $30,000 a year but are well informed about their retirement options. Seventy-five percent of cautious optimists believe they do earn enough money to save for retirement, compared with just 12 percent of the worriers. Even more impressive, the cautious optimists have been able to save an average of over $5,000 in the past year—only 18 percent of the worriers have been able to save that much. Only 29 percent of cautious optimists saved nothing, compared with 40 percent of worriers.

said the federal government had made the racial and ethnic minority situation better, while 43 percent said the government had made it worse. Forty-six percent felt that they trusted the federal government in this area more than private businesses, which received only a 38 percent vote of confidence. Between May 1991 and October 1994, the percentage of those who said they were satisfied with the nation's ability to protect the rights of racial and ethnic minorities rose by 5 percentage points, from 46 to 51 percent, while the percentage of those expressing dissatisfaction decreased six points, from 50 to 44 percent.

This favorable attitude toward the federal government's role in protecting racial and ethnic minorities seems, however, a tribute to past practices that the public feels may have outworn their usefulness and should not be extended to other groups. (See "Affirmative Action: Is It Still Needed? Was It Ever?," page 47.) A Gallup poll in September 1994 reported that 58 percent of respondents opposed and 39 percent favored extending civil rights protections to homosexuals. Forty-nine percent favored and 43 percent opposed strengthening affirmative-action laws for women and for African Americans and other minorities. A March 1995 Gallup poll reported that by a margin of 56 to 40 percent, respondents opposed affirmative action for African Americans, while the margin was reversed with

« **Fifty-one percent said the federal government had made the racial and ethnic minority situation better.** »

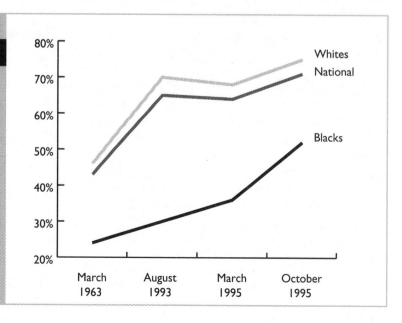

American Opinion

Do you think blacks have as good a chance as white people in your community to get any kind of job? Percentage saying: "Yes, as good a chance."

Source: The Gallup Poll

regard to affirmative action for women, with 45 percent expressing disapproval and 50 percent approving. Oddly enough, when asked if affirmative action was really needed for African Americans or women, respondents said no by virtually identical margins: 57 to 41 percent for women and 56 to 41 percent for racial minorities. Sympathy for women might be more widespread, according to the polling data, but not the perception that they actually require affirmative action to help them. This sympathy for women held steady among both men and women, and among white and nonwhite respondents.

If Americans have lessened their support for affirmative action, they have done so because they believe it has largely accomplished its purpose. Poll respondents strongly agree (80 percent to 12 percent) that when affirmative action was initiated three decades ago, it was a therapeutic measure designed to correct discrimination against women and racial minorities. Affirmative-action programs, American believe, have been successful, with 76 percent saying they have helped rather than hurt women and 70 percent believing the same is true for racial minorities. Only 9 percent believe affirmative action has had no effect on women; only 16 percent believe the same is true for racial minorities. At 55 percent, women are the stronger supporters of affirmative action, compared with 45

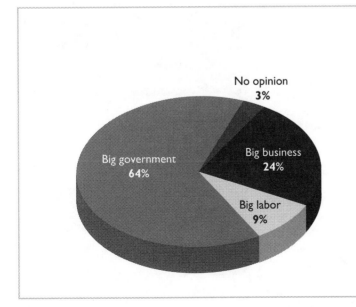

No opinion
3%

Big government
64%

Big business
24%

Big labor
9%

American Opinion

In your opinion, which of the following will be the biggest threat to the country in the future?

Source: The Gallup Poll,
August 11–14, 1995

percent of men. Forty-three percent of women support affirmative action for racial minorities, whereas only 35 percent of men do.

Americans' Greatest Fears

An April 1995 survey showed that 28 percent of Americans said their greatest fear was bad health, followed by inadequate savings for retirement (29 percent), crime (18 percent), inability to pay bills (12 percent), and job loss (8 percent). In the thirty-to-forty-nine age bracket, comprising the so-called baby-boomers, only 34 percent said they had enough time in their lives, and across all age groups 45 percent thought the time available in their daily lives was shrinking, while 29 percent said it was expanding. Forty-one percent in all categories said they put in more hours at work than their parents did, but few (only 14 percent) were willing to trade more time for less income, whereas 26 percent would actually work longer hours for more income. An even higher percentage of eighteen-to-twenty-nine-year-olds (43 percent) would take on more work and hours. Half (50 percent) of women said they did not have enough time for them-

« **Americans believe affirmative-action programs have been successful.** »

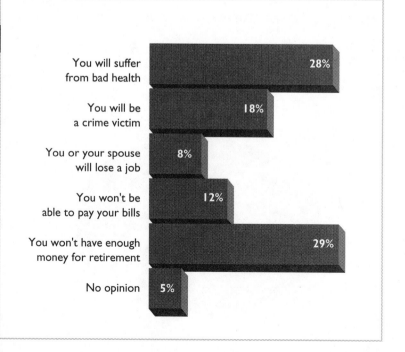

American Opinion

Which of the following do you most worry might happen to you?

You will suffer from bad health — 28%

You will be a crime victim — 18%

You or your spouse will lose a job — 8%

You won't be able to pay your bills — 12%

You won't have enough money for retirement — 29%

No opinion — 5%

Source: The Gallup Poll,
April 21–23, 1995

selves, compared with 41 percent of men who expressed the same opinion.

Americans also worry about how the changing demographics of American society will affect the character of American society. A July 1995 Gallup poll found that 62 percent of respondents agreed that the level of immigration should be decreased, with 27 percent opting for the present level. Concerns that America is being turned into a polyglot culture, and calls for the formal adoption of English as the country's official language, also reflect anxiety about the future—a fact Newt Gingrich touched on in warning Americans not to follow the example of bilingual cultures such as Canada, which may be splitting apart.

The January 30, 1995, issue of *Time* offered a mixed view of the state of the nation, observing that while Americans were disgusted with American institutions of every stripe, citizens were responding with a new resourcefulness, scrambling to find agreeable substitutes for nearly every institution, from schools to the post office to the press. *The Yankelovich Monitor*, an annual survey of 4,000 Americans, *Time* reported, showed a deep decline in faith in traditional authority but an increase in confidence in personal abilities. For better or worse, Americans' renewed sense of self-reliance is changing the way they educate their children, invest their savings, and run their communities. However grim or misguided these alternatives might seem to some commentators, they do reflect an extraordinarily energetic and daring people.[2]

«

A July 1995 Gallup poll found that 62 percent of respondents agreed that the level of immigration should be decreased.

»

Notes: Faith in America's Future

1. David R. Carlin, "Democracy's Future," *Commonweal,* April 7, 1995, 8–9.
2. "The State of the Union," *Time,* January 30, 1995, 52–57+.

12 Religion in American Life

by
Carl Rollyson

R eligion remains a powerful force in American life and politics. For over sixty years, Gallup polls have shown that a sizable majority of Americans identify religion as "very important" or "fairly important" in their lives. There has been some diminution in the "very important" percentage (from 75 percent in 1952 to 56 percent in May 1995), but well over 80 percent of Americans still consider religion a significant factor in their lives, according to Gallup poll results.[1]

In a February 1995 Gallup poll, nearly all Americans (96 percent) said they believed in God, and 88 percent affirmed the importance of religion. This attachment to religion is also reflected in church membership, which has fluctuated very little since 1937, when 73 percent of those polled said they belonged to a church or synagogue; for May 1995, the percentage was 69 percent. Since 1939, Gallup pollsters have found that approximately 40 percent of their respondents attend a church or synagogue once a week or almost every week, while another 12 percent to 15 percent attend about once a month. The number of those who seldom

> « Americans continue to testify to the significance of religion in their lives. »

or never attend has also remained steady, at about 40 percent. The polling data are remarkably consistent; they show that a majority of Americans continue to testify to the significance of religion in their lives.

Many Americans also continue to believe in the traditional core of Christianity, in a hereafter of heaven and hell, and in a world influenced by angels, devils, and miracles. Gallup polling data from December 1994 indicate that 90 percent of Americans believe in heaven, 73 percent in hell, 79 percent in miracles, 72 percent in angels, and 65 percent in the devil.

In some instances, Americans may have intensified their convictions, judging by the wide variety of current books and collectibles that feature angels. An example of "angel mania," as some dubbed the phenomenon, was reported in the *Houston Post*: twelve-year-old Miraida Martinez was quoted as saying that she had seen angels and the Virgin Mary among the flowers in her back yard, and attracted believers to her home in southeast Houston.[2] Book publishers, novelty manufacturers, and retailers have been quick to cash in on the trend. In the summer of 1995, the *St. Louis Post-Dispatch* reported the opening of the area's first angel theme shop under the name "Angel Encounters."[3] The popularity of angels is apparent in the concept of "Play with Angels," a stack of fifty-two tiny angel cards with one-word sayings and illustrations, which has reached

American Opinion

Do you happen to be a member of a church or synagogue?

Source: The Gallup Poll

more than half a million people, according to a January 1995 report in the *Chicago Tribune*.[4]

When the December 1994 Gallup survey asked about other paranormal or supernatural beliefs, 28 percent of respondents said they believed in communication with the dead, 27 percent in reincarnation, and 23 percent in astrology.

Americans have not changed their religious affiliations in significant numbers during recent decades. Polling data continue to show that approximately 60 percent call themselves Protestant and 25 percent Roman Catholic, with about 8 percent undesignated, and with 1 percent or 2 percent adhering to the Orthodox Church and 1 or 2 percent to each of the Mormon, Jewish, Muslim, and "other" religions. Among Protestant denominations, the Southern Baptists and Baptists each constitute about 9 to 10 percent, Methodists 10 to 11 percent, Presbyterians 4 to 5 percent, Episcopalians 2 percent, Lutherans 6 to 7 percent, Pentecostals 2 to 3

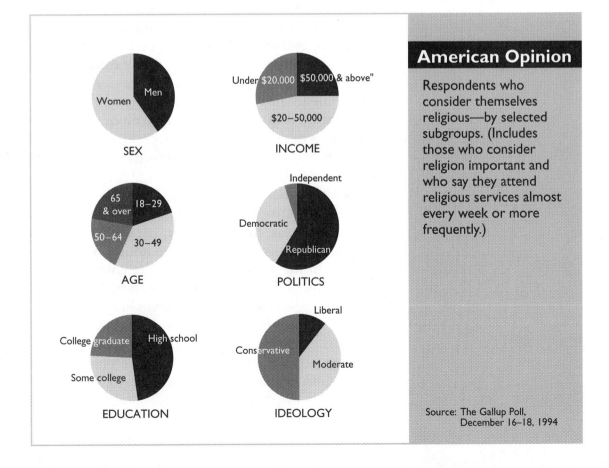

SEX

INCOME

AGE

POLITICS

EDUCATION

IDEOLOGY

American Opinion

Respondents who consider themselves religious—by selected subgroups. (Includes those who consider religion important and who say they attend religious services almost every week or more frequently.)

Source: The Gallup Poll, December 16–18, 1994

percent, members of the Church of Christ 1 to 2 percent, members of other denominations approximately 9 to 11 percent, and members of nondenominational churches 3 to 5 percent.

The Influence of Religion

«

The downward trend of confidence in religion has been attributed by many to the enormous social, political, and economic changes of the past four decades.

»

On the question of whether the influence of religion on American life as a whole is rising or falling, poll respondents have reflected changing views over the past forty years. In March of 1957, for example, 69 percent of Americans believed that the influence of religion was rising. By February 1962, only 45 percent held the same opinion, and by May 1969, the percentage had dropped to 14. Then, through the mid-1970s to the mid-1980s, confidence in religion's influence rose to as high as 48 percent (in September 1986), when Ronald Reagan as president emphasized what was positive about America and religious values, and when the economy was booming. From April 1989 to June 1994, this percentage dropped 20 points (during the last years of the Bush administration and an economic downturn), before rising again to 36 percent in May 1995 amid a flurry of activity by many different religious groups. The overall trend in confidence in religious influence has certainly been downward and has been attributed by many to the enormous social, political, and economic changes of the past four decades—changes that churches have not effectively addressed, say some critics.

In a 1994 article in the *Atlanta Journal Constitution*, writer Glenn Dowell contended that churches have let America's young people down, especially African Americans, because churches have not used their tremendous influence vigorously in the community to combat crime and violence.[5] Other writers have argued that the new generation of Americans craves spiritual renewal, but that churches must find contemporary and nontraditional appeals to young people who are alienated from established religions. One recent study of 100,000 churches, reported in the *Chicago Tribune*, revealed a steady drop in average annual donations over a twenty-five-year period.[6]

At the same time, as already noted, recent polling figures show an uptick in the American public's faith in the influence of religion (rising from 27 percent in November 1991 to 36 percent in May 1995). Several factors may account for the upward swing, including the political activism of the religious right, recent calls for social action on the part of several denominations, and evidence of a spiritual revival among younger Americans. The *Los Angeles Times* recently carried a story by John Dart reporting that religious programming, once held in relatively low esteem by the young listeners and viewers of Armed Forces Radio and Television, now dominates that network's media schedules with Christian rock music, black gospel singing, and revamped religious television shows.[7] Recent Gallup poll respondents may also be reacting to media reports of a religious revival among men. For example, under a headline reading "50,000 Men Rally for God" in a July 1995 issue of the *Denver Post*, Heidi V. Anderson described a new movement, Promise Keepers, headed by Bill McCartney, focused on helping men become more stable and more committed to their families rather than just to their work.[8]

Gallup polls have repeatedly demonstrated that whether or not Americans think that the influence of

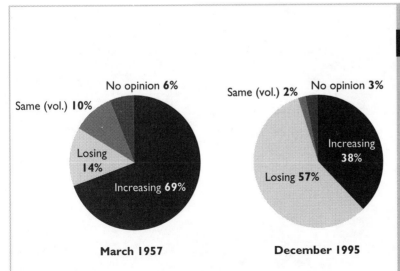

March 1957

No opinion 6%
Same (vol.) 10%
Losing 14%
Increasing 69%

December 1995

Same (vol.) 2%   No opinion 3%
Increasing 38%
Losing 57%

American Opinion

At the present time, do you think religion as a whole is increasing its influence on American life or losing its influence?

("vol." refers to a volunteered response)

Source: The Gallup Poll

American Opinion

Do you believe that religion can answer all or most of today's problems, or that religion is largely old-fashioned and out of date?

	Is a member of a church or synagogue	Attended church/ synagogue in the last 7 days	Says religion is "very important" in their life	Says religion "can answer all or most of today's problems"	Says "religion is largely old-fashioned and out of date"
Everyone	69	42	58	62	21
By Gender					
Male	62	37	50	55	24
Female	74	46	65	68	18
By Age					
Under 30 yrs. of age	61	31	44	55	31
30–49 yrs. of age	65	40	54	61	23
50–64 yrs. of age	79	53	69	70	14
65 yrs. old and older	75	50	72	63	13
By Region					
East	68	39	55	56	27
Midwest	72	45	57	63	21
South	75	47	68	74	13
West	55	34	48	49	27
By Race					
White	67	41	55	60	22
Black	82	50	82	86	7
By Education					
Attended college	70	44	53	58	22
No college	67	40	63	65	21
By Household Income					
$50,000+	70	41	48	56	22
$30,000–$49,999	72	45	56	62	22
$20,000–$29,999	65	41	56	60	25
Under $20,000	67	40	66	66	21
By Denomination					
Protestant	72	45	65	71	14
Roman Catholic	77	47	51	51	33

Source: The Public Perspective, October/November 1995

religion is waning or waxing, they believe that religion should be at the center of American values. A March 1994 Gallup survey determined that 64 percent of respondents believed religion can solve all or most of today's problems. While this confidence in religion has held more or less steady since the mid-1980s, it marks a drop from the March 1957 figure of 82 percent. (According to historic polling data, religious beliefs reached a highwater mark during the 1950s.)

School Prayer: An Ecumenical Consensus

A Gallup poll conducted in May and June of 1995 revealed that by a margin of 71 percent to 25 percent, Americans favor an amendment to the U.S. Constitution that would permit prayers to be spoken in public schools. This opinion has changed little over the past decade, with more than half of those polled saying they strongly support the proposed amendment. It is religion, however, not Christianity, that is the issue for most poll respondents. Just 13 percent said spoken prayer in the schools should be exclusively Christian, while 81 percent preferred an ecumenical approach. Perhaps because of this acknowledgment of other religions, Americans, by a margin of 70 percent to 24 percent, preferred that public schools provide a moment of silent contemplation.

So certain are Americans of the value of religion that 74 percent in the May–June 1995 Gallup poll speculated that only a "small percentage" of students' parents would object to spoken prayers in schools. A decided minority (21 percent) believed a large percentage of parents would be offended by verbal prayers. When the poll respondents were asked if spoken prayers should be allowed if a large percentage of parents objected, 55 percent said the prayers should not be allowed, while 41 percent insisted they should be. This insistence on spoken prayer was most intense among strong supporters of the constitutional amendment, who believed in the spoken-prayer requirement by a two-to-one margin (64 percent to 32 percent), whereas by a two-to-one majority (66 percent to 32 percent), moderate support-

« **In June 1995, an amendment to the U.S. Constitution that would permit prayers to be spoken in public schools was favored by 71 percent of those polled.** »

ers of the amendment would oppose spoken prayers if large numbers of parents protested them.

Religion and Politics

<blockquote>
«

Religious Americans are more likely to be Republican and politically conservative than the rest of the population.

»
</blockquote>

Spearheading the school-prayer amendment and a political agenda that stresses spiritual values is the so-called religious right. A February 1995 Gallup poll found that religious Americans are more likely to be Republican and politically conservative than the rest of the population. Only 35 percent of Americans can be classified as "religious," using a definition that requires them not only to consider religion important but also to actually attend religious services almost every week or more frequently. (The percentage of people who say they attended a religious service within the past seven days has remained remarkably steady since 1939, averaging just over 40 percent.) The people who can be classified as religious using this criterion are found in higher proportion among women and older people.

In a March 1994 Gallup survey, 45 percent of respondents identified themselves as "born-again" or evangelical Christians. Yet only 11 percent of respondents labeled themselves members of the religious right and 20 percent as conservative Christians. Only 9 percent said public issues and political candidates were discussed often in church; 43 percent said occasionally;

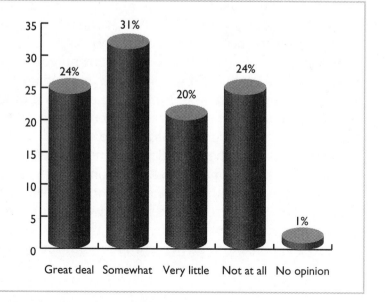

American Opinion

Do you think that the introduction of spoken prayer in the local schools would improve the behavior of the students a great deal, somewhat, very little, or not at all?

Source: The Gallup Poll,
July 20, 1995

Great deal Somewhat Very little Not at all No opinion

24% 31% 20% 24% 1%

36 percent said never. In the same survey, 17 percent said they had heard a great deal about the religious right; 30 percent said a moderate amount; 32 percent only a little; 20 percent nothing at all.

The fact that not all Americans are actively religious does not mean that they are "agnostic" on the question of whether religion and traditional values should influence public and political life. When asked in a September 1994 Gallup poll whether government should promote traditional values or not favor any particular set of values, by a 61-to-34-percent margin respondents said government should promote traditional values. Only 3 percent had no opinion.

One gauge of the current nexus between religion and politics is the Gallup survey data on the Republican and Democratic parties. In a November 1994 poll, 13 percent said the Republican party reflected their attitude about the role of religion in politics very well; 40 percent said moderately well; 24 percent said not too well; 17 percent said not well at all. Only 6 percent had no opinion. In the same poll, 12 percent said the Democratic party reflected their attitude about the role of religion in politics very well; 35 percent moderately well; 28 percent not too well; 20 percent not well at all. Only 5 percent had no opinion.

A substantial minority (41 percent) do not share the religious values of the Republican party and the reli-

> «
> **In a November 1994 poll, 13 percent said the Republican party shared their attitude about the role of religion in politics very well and 40 percent said moderately well.**
> »

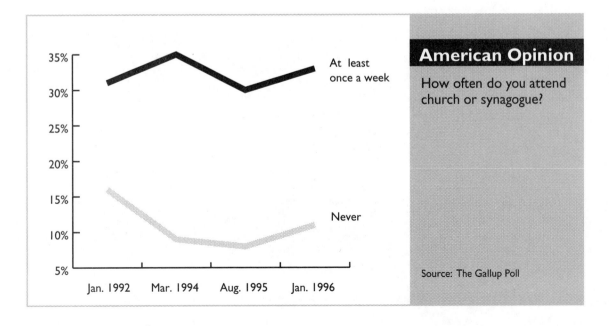

American Opinion

How often do you attend church or synagogue?

At least once a week

Never

Jan. 1992   Mar. 1994   Aug. 1995   Jan. 1996

Source: The Gallup Poll

gious right. Many leaders of the mainstream Protestant denominations have warned against an intolerant, fundamentalist orthodoxy taking over the discussion of politics and public issues. One group of Christian clerics, for example, has called for an "ideological cease-fire" in the partisan warfare on religious principles, offering what they describe as a broader-based alternative to the controversial tactics and doctrines of the

Gallup Findings About Religious Beliefs

- From 1965 to 1978, Gallup polls showed an 18-point decline (70 percent to 52 percent) in those respondents declaring religion to be "very important" in their lives. Since 1978, the percentage has varied from 53 percent to 60 percent.
- In the 1990s, the percentage of those polled who think religion as a whole is losing its influence on American life has fluctuated significantly (from 48 percent to 69 percent), with 58 percent expressing this opinion in May 1995.
- In a July 1995 Gallup poll, 70 percent of respondents said they preferred a moment of silent prayer in public schools. Over half the public (60 percent) expresses intense opinions on this issue, with 46 percent affirming they are "very"

strongly in favor of a constitutional amendment to permit school prayer. Of the 25 percent who oppose the amendment, 14 percent say they are "very strongly" against it, 11 percent are "mildly opposed," and only 4 percent are undecided. By a margin of 73 percent to 20 percent, Americans say that Jewish, Muslim, and Hindu prayers should be allowed, in addition to Christian prayers.

- Certain religious beliefs differ by region, gender, and age. A January 1995 Gallup poll found that 80 percent of Southerners believe in hell, but only 60 percent of Westerners. Eighty-six percent of women believe in miracles, compared with 71 percent of men. Seventy-eight percent of women and 65 percent of

men believe in angels. Seventy-five percent of those under age sixty-five believe in hell; above that age the figure drops sharply, to 64 percent.

- Twenty-eight percent of people now believe in communication with the dead—up 10 points from 1990, and 27 percent believe in reincarnation, up 6 points. Only astrology has lost ground, down 2 points, to 23 percent, according to the January 1995 polling data.
- The same poll showed the most skeptical group has postgraduate degrees, yet 75 percent say they are believers. Of the 13 percent who identify themselves as members of the religious right, 100 percent say they believe in heaven and hell.
- Among the 35 percent of those polled in February 1995 saying they are religious, 59 percent identified themselves as Republicans and 36 percent as Democrats.

Christian right.[9] Other writers note that the new generation of Republican representatives have formed a pro-family caucus, a vanguard of social conservatives and the religious faithful, determined to change social policy at the federal level.[10]

In the spring of 1995, conservative Christians presented GOP lawmakers with a legislative agenda, including a school-prayer amendment, an end to abortion funding, the curtailment of the campaign for gay and lesbian rights, and the abolition of the Education Department. The agenda drew quick and heavy fire from some commentators. *Detroit News & Free Press* columnist Nickie McWhirter alleged that the Christian Coalition's Contract with the American Family was a radical, religiously biased, and prejudiced political agenda, a gambit at religious domination by a presumed majority to use a revised U.S. Constitution to repress all minorities.[11] A June 8, 1995, *USA Today* editorial expressed similar sentiments, calling the congressional hearings on a constitutional amendment establishing school prayer a legal cover for inflicting the will of local majorities on those whose religious beliefs are different.

Religious conservatives have countered such attacks by creating their own legal organizations to combat what they see as a broad assault on religious liberties. More than half a dozen religious-liberty law

> **«**
> **Religious conservatives have created their own legal organizations to combat what they see as a broad assault on religious liberties.**
> **»**

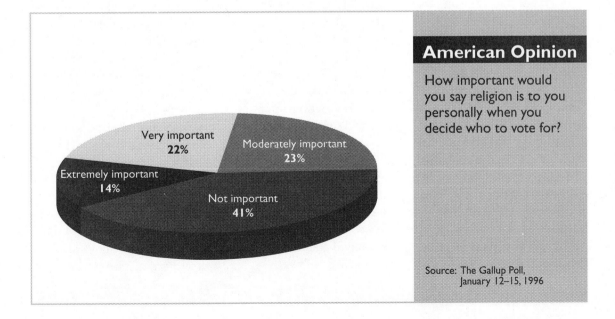

American Opinion

How important would you say religion is to you personally when you decide who to vote for?

Very important
22%

Moderately important
23%

Extremely important
14%

Not important
41%

Source: The Gallup Poll,
January 12–15, 1996

firms are waging battles in courts, schools, and city halls to establish a larger public space for religious activity and to respond to those they perceive to be attempting to curb religious expression.[13]

The volatile debate in the press, however, is somewhat belied by the Gallup survey data. While Americans have expressed a strong commitment to traditional, religious values, they have most definitely not signed on to a particular religious and social policy program. They may be sympathetic to the Republican Contract with America, but that does not mean they identify themselves with the religious right or share its views

Abortion: A Burning Issue for Some, but on the Back Burner for Most

Abortion is often perceived to be the burning moral question of the era, with activists in the "pro-life" cause claiming abortion is almost always tantamount to murder and those speaking for the "pro-choice" side insisting the right to an abortion is absolute. Yet, for all the sound and fury the topic generates, Gallup polling data suggest that it is far from a critical issue for most Americans: When a July 1995 Gallup poll asked people to list important problems facing the country today, abortion ranked eighteenth out of twenty-two problems mentioned. Here are some other key findings of Gallup polls over the years on the abortion question:

- In a July 1994 Gallup poll, 56 percent of Americans considered themselves "pro-choice" and 33% regarded themselves as "pro-life."
- Since the late 1980s, about a third of Americans say abortion should be legal under any circumstances.
- On *Roe v. Wade*, the 1973 Supreme Court decision that ruled that states cannot place restrictions on a woman's right to an abortion during the first three months of pregnancy, about a third of Americans agree it should be overturned, but nearly two-thirds disagree. These percentages have remained stable since the late 1980s.

- Since 1962, a large majority (77 percent) of Americans have believed that abortions should be legal when the mother's health is in danger.
- From 1962 to the late 1980s, about half (on the average, 54 percent) of the American public said abortion should be legal only under certain circumstances, approximately 20 percent declared it should be legal under any circumstances, and about the same percentage believed it should be illegal under any circumstances. These percentages were nearly identical for Catholics and Protestants.
- The surge of pro-life demonstrations in the early 1990s did not significantly change public opinion. An April 1993 Gallup poll determined that 54 percent of respondents agreed that anti-abortion activists are intolerant, 55 percent

on social issues. In a November 1994 Gallup poll, only 22 percent of respondents said they thought of themselves as a member of a religious-right movement; 70 percent said they did not. These percentages have not fluctuated much since the election of the Republican majority in November 1994.

Within the Gallup poll percentages, there seems to be considerable variation of approaches to religious values on the part of most Americans. They do not want to coerce others to believe as they do, yet they do insist on a fundamental core of values they deem religious. That only slightly more than a third of Americans are

agreed that anti-abortion activists were extremist, but 62 percent agreed that anti-abortion activists were very well or somewhat principled.

- An August 1994 Gallup poll reported that 42 percent of respondents agreed that if the federal government guarantees certain medical benefits for all Americans, then abortion should be included as one of those benefits; 49 percent disagreed.
- When a February 1995 Gallup poll asked, "Regardless of whether you think abortions should be legal or not, do you personally believe that having an abortion is morally wrong, or is it not morally wrong?" 51 percent of respondents thought it was morally wrong and 34

percent did not. But 80 percent felt that having performed one or more abortions should not disqualify a doctor for the post of U.S. surgeon general.

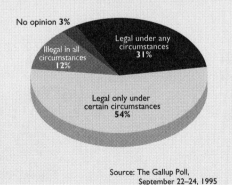

American Opinion

Do you think abortions should be legal under any circumstances, legal only under certain circumstances, or illegal in all circumstances?

No opinion 3%

Legal under any circumstances 31%

Illegal in all circumstances 12%

Legal only under certain circumstances 54%

Source: The Gallup Poll, September 22–24, 1995

- A March 1995 Gallup poll found that 70 percent of Americans would prefer a presidential candidate who

would keep the abortion laws the way they are now; 21 percent favored a candidate who would make it illegal for a woman to have an abortion under almost any circumstances.

- Gallup polls in the 1990s found that more women than men (by a narrow margin of 5 to 7 points) declared abortion should be legal under any circumstances. More whites than nonwhites (by a margin of 10 points) favored legalizing abortion under any circumstances. Over half of those with postgraduate college educations agreed that abortion should be legal under any circumstances. More Democrats (35 percent) than Republicans (26 percent) would legalize abortion under any circumstances.

regular churchgoers, while the overwhelming majority believe in the power and authenticity of religious values, suggests a firm but flexible vision of religion that could hardly be called strictly orthodox or fundamentalist, although significant minorities do hold to uncompromising stands on specific issues such as school prayer, abortion, homosexual rights, and welfare.

President Clinton's recent pronouncements on the role of religion in American life can be read as a response to the complexity of the Gallup polling data. He has consistently sought a middle ground in the religious and political debate, earning a commendatory editorial from the *Washington Post* for reassuring religious people and drawing clear lines between what is constitutional and what is not with regard to prayer in public schools.[14] Speaking to an audience of Vienna, Virginia, high school students in July 1995, Clinton declared that the First Amendment does not "convert our schools into religion-free zones." He urged Americans to encourage religious activities in public schools, including the use of Bibles in study halls and prayers at commencements, but he declined to endorse a constitutional amendment that would allow prayer in classrooms, on the ground that freedom of religious expression is already protected under the First Amendment and that a school-prayer amendment might co-

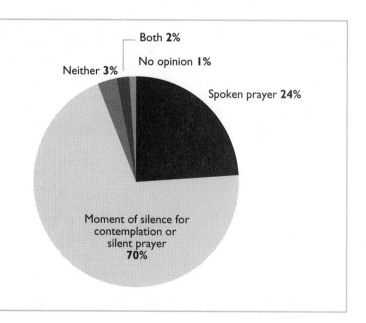

American Opinion

If you had a choice, would you prefer in the local schools, spoken prayer, a moment of silence for contemplation or silent prayer, neither, or both?

Source: The Gallup Poll,
July 20, 1995

Both **2%**

No opinion **1%**

Neither **3%**

Spoken prayer **24%**

Moment of silence for contemplation or silent prayer
70%

erce students to compromise their own religious beliefs.[15] Yet, the president also declared in July 1995 that
some school districts had gone too far in banning religious activities.[16]

President Clinton's speeches were described by
some political observers as an attempt to blunt not only
the Republican drive for a school-prayer constitutional
amendment but also the larger Republican agenda,
which has had the solid backing of conservative religious groups. Gallup polling data suggest, however,
that Clinton is also speaking to the current diversity of
American opinion on the role of religion in public life
and politics. When respondents to Gallup surveys moderate their support of the constitutional amendment
that others find offensive, or opt for a form of silent
prayer, or stress that religious observance must be ecumenical, they are expressing a tolerant, even pliant view
somewhat similar to President Clinton's modulated
position.

To recognize the diversity of opinion on values in
America, President Clinton invited leaders from religious and public service groups, entertainment,
academia, sports, the media, and business for a day-
long discussion of U.S. problems on July 21, 1995.[17] His
effort echoed the recommendations of several interfaith
leaders, such as the Reverend Dr. Joan Brown Campbell,
general secretary of the National Council of Churches,
who has remarked that Americans of all faiths should
work for the good of all, especially children, at a time
when some programs to help the poor are under attack.[18] Similarly, a coalition of religious and civil liberties groups have put their differences aside and
unveiled guidelines on religion in public schools, em-
phasizing that schools are not "religion-free zones," in
an echo of President Clinton. The guidelines were
drafted by thirty-five groups representing Christian,
Jewish, Muslim, and Eastern religions, as well as the
American Civil Liberties Union and other public
policy groups.[19]

Such unprecedented cooperation, as well as the
fierce debate between religious and political groups,
reflects the extraordinary level of discussion of religion

> « **President Clinton is speaking to the current diversity of American opinion on the role of religion in public life and politics.** »

«

Gallup polling data demonstrate a commitment to religion that cuts across sex, age, region, community, race, education, politics, and income.

»

and values in contemporary America. Although the religious right has captured the headlines, and the Republican party seems to have benefited most from its support, causing a fundamental shift in political power in this country, the Gallup polling data demonstrate continuity in religious affiliation and belief. Large numbers of Americans may desire radical change in religion's role in society, or they may be anxious, at different times, about the extent to which religion can solve problems or have an impact on society, but these fluctuations in mood are buttressed by long-term loyalties to religious institutions and to the family.

The idea of religion itself is what abides in the minds of most Americans, who cherish tradition and their faith. In the December 1994 Gallup survey, 96 percent of respondents said they celebrate Christmas. Only 8 percent do not believe in heaven, while 24 percent of an apparently optimistic people do not believe in hell. Only 12 percent do not believe in miracles, while another 9 percent are not sure. Only 11 percent said religion is not very important in their lives, and 20 percent (in a March 1994 poll) found aspects of religion old-fashioned. Since 1939, the lowest percentage of people saying they had attended a religious service was 37 percent, and that was a response to a Gallup poll in 1940. Regular church attendance peaked at 49 percent in 1955, but it has been as high as 43 percent as recently as 1991. The numbers are never the whole story, but the Gallup polling data does seem to demonstrate a commitment to religion that cuts across sex, age, region, community (urban, suburban, and rural), race, education, politics, and income. To be sure, within these categories there are measurable distinctions to be made, but an aggregate view of the data presents a remarkably unified picture of the nation's commitment to religious values.

Notes: Religion in American Life

1. George Gallup, Jr., "Religion in America. Will the Vitality of Churches Be the Surprise of the Next Century?" *The Public Perspective,* October/November 1995, 1-8.
2. Salatheia Bryant, "Girl's Visions of Angels Attract Faithful," *Houston Post,* April 17, 1995, A13.
3. Patricia Corrigan, "On the Side of the Angels," *St. Louis Post-Dispatch,* July 8, 1995, D3.
4. Richard Knight, Jr., "Stacking the Deck for a Change," *Chicago Tribune,* January 15, 1995, 5.
5. Glen Dowell, "African-American Churches Have Failed Youths in Trouble," *Atlanta Journal Constitution,* April 24, 1994, G4.
6. Larry Hartstein, "Americans Giving Less at Church, Study Says," *Chicago Tribune,* December 9, 1994, C10.
7. John Dart, "Armed Forces Turn to Contemporary Religious Programs," *Los Angeles Times,* March 12, 1994, B5.
8. Heidi V. Anderson, "50,000 Men Rally for God," *Denver Post,* July 31, 1995, B5.
9. Robert Shogan, "Another Christian Voice Sounds on Politics," *Los Angeles Times,* May 24, 1995, A13.
10. David Grann, "As Congress Takes Up Social Issues, Whose Values Will Prevail?" *Washington Post,* May 7, 1995, C3.
11. Nickie McWhirter, "Coalition Seeks Religious Domination," *Detroit News & Free Press,* May 27, 1995, C3.
12. Tony Mauro, "Church-State Debate Begins Anew Today," *USA TODAY,* June 8, 1995, A6.
13. Gustav Niebuhr, "Conservatives' New Frontier: Religious Liberty Law Firms, *New York Times,* July 8, 1995, A1.
14. "Church and School," *Washington Post,* July 14, 1995, A20.
15. Bill Nichols, "Clinton: Prayer Protected," *USA TODAY,* July 13, 1995, A6.
16. Doyle McManus, "Clinton to Issue Guidelines on School Religion Rights," *Los Angeles Times,* July 13, 1995, A1.
17. "Clinton to Meet with Diverse Set of Leaders," *Washington Post,* May 17, 1995, A6.
18. Patricia Rice, "Interfaith Leader Warns of Growing Intolerance," *St. Louis Post-Dispatch,* May 31, 1995, B5.
19. Shannon Johnson, "Groups Issue Guidelines on Religion in Schools," *Atlanta Journal Constitution,* April 14, 1995, A7.